BLACKSTONE AND HIS *COMMENTARIES*

Among the most celebrated works in the Anglo-American legal tradition, William Blackstone's *Commentaries on the Laws of England* (1765–9) is currently attracting renewed scholarly interest. While the *Commentaries* no longer dominate legal education, they continue to be regularly cited in superior courts throughout the common law world, besides providing a remarkably comprehensive account of public and private law in England on the cusp of the Industrial Revolution.

The life and character of Blackstone himself, the nature and sources of his jurisprudence and the impact of his great book are the main themes of this collection. Individual essays discuss Blackstone's early architectural treatises and their relationship to the *Commentaries*; his idiosyncratic bibliophilia; his views on the judiciary, statutory interpretation, the law of marriage, natural law, property law and the legalities of colonisation. Together with the dissemination and reception of the *Commentaries*, Blackstone's bibliography and iconography also receive attention. Combining the work of both eminent and emerging scholars, this interdisciplinary venture sheds welcome new light on a legal classic and its continued influence.

Blackstone and his *Commentaries*

Biography, Law, History

Edited by
Wilfrid Prest

HART PUBLISHING

OXFORD AND PORTLAND, OREGON
2014

Published in North America (US and Canada) by
Hart Publishing
c/o International Specialized Book Services
920 NE 58th Avenue, Suite 300
Portland, OR 97213–3786
USA
Tel: +1 503 287 3093 or toll-free: (1) 800 944 6190
Fax: +1 503 280 8832
E-mail: orders@isbs.com
Website: http://www.isbs.com

First published in 2009. Reprinted in paperback 2014.

Hart Publishing is an Imprint of Bloomsbury Publishing plc.

Hart Publishing Ltd, 16C Worcester Place, Oxford, OX1 2JW
Telephone: +44 (0)1865 517530 Fax: +44 (0)1865 510710
E-mail: mail@hartpub.co.uk
Website: http://www.hartpub.co.uk

British Library Cataloguing in Publication Data
Data Available

ISBN: 978-1-84113-796-4 (Hardback)
978-1-84946-642-4 (Paperback)

Typeset by Columns Design Ltd, Reading
Printed and bound in Great Britain by
CPI Antony Rowe Ltd, Chippenham, Wiltshire

Preface

One of the most celebrated works in the Anglo-American legal tradition, William Blackstone's *Commentaries on the Laws of England* (1765–69), is currently attracting renewed attention. Of course the *Commentaries* no longer dominate legal education and studies as once they did, espcially in North America during the century after their first publication. But Blackstone continues to be regularly cited in courts on both sides of the Atlantic, and elsewhere throughout the common law world. His *Commentaries* provide constitutional, cultural, intellectual and legal historians with a remarkably comprehensive account of the roles of law, lawyers and the courts in the imperial superpower that was England on the cusp of the industrial revolution. But they also retain some contemporary relevance, and not only for their literary qualities; indeed the sustained impact of Blackstone's work, long after its first publication, is a further reason why the author and his book can still repay further study.

This volume had its origins in a symposium on 'William Blackstone: Life, Thought, Influence' held over two hot Adelaide days in December 2007. That Antipodean setting was in one respect highly ironic, since the metropolitan capital of South Australia is the outcome of a nineteenth-century venture in systematic colonisation specifically endorsed by Jeremy Bentham, Blackstone's former student and life-long critic. Yet the diversity and quality of the papers presented, and the liveliness of discussion, could leave no doubt that both the *Commentaries on the Laws of England* and their author continue to hold the attention of scholars from many parts of the world.

Most of the following essays were presented in draft on that occasion, and subsequently revised for publication. Ian Doolittle, John Emerson and myself were participants, but wrote our contributions after the event, while those by John Baker and Mary Sokol were kindly prepared in response to specific editorial requests. The four parts into which this book is divided (not very rigorously or exclusively) broadly follow the plan of the symposium, with the addition of the final coda on sources. Needless to say, the aim has not been to provide an encyclopaedic coverage, but rather to touch upon some main themes: the life and character of Blackstone himself, the nature and sources of his jurisprudence as expounded in the *Commentaries*, and the influence of his great book, both within and beyond his native shores.

It is a pleasure to acknowledge subventions from research funds provided by the University of Adelaide's Faculty of the Humanities and Social Sciences and the Faculty of the Professions, which made it possible to hold the Blackstone symposium and also assisted in the protracted process of converting conference papers into book chapters. Numerous friends and colleagues generously supported the enterprise in various ways; I am especially grateful for the expert advice of all those who acted as anonymous referees. In the final stages of putting the book together, Cecile Storey played a crucial role as copyeditor. The office staff of the School of History and Politics and the Law School gave invaluable support throughout. While a particular debt of gratitude is owed to Mary Sokol and John Baker for their willingness to contribute at relatively short notice, I should like to thank all my fellow-contributors, as well as the superbly efficient production team from Hart Publishing, for their generally patient and prompt responses to editorial demands and importunities.

Wilfrid Prest

Contents

Contributors

Thalia Anthony teaches law at the University of Technology, Sydney.

Norma Aubertin-Potter is Librarian-in-Charge of the Codrington Library, All Souls College, Oxford.

Sir John Baker is Downing Professor Emeritus in the Faculty of Law, University of Cambridge.

The late **Morris Cohen**, Professor Emeritus and Professorial Lecturer in Law, is the former Librarian of Yale Law School.

Horst Dippel is Professor Emeritus of British and American Studies at the University of Kassel.

Ian Doolittle, formerly a Junior Research Fellow at Christ Church, Oxford, is a partner in the law firm Trowers & Hamlins LLP in London.

John Emerson holds a Visiting Research Fellowship in the Law School, University of Adelaide.

Nicole Graham is Senior Lecturer in the Faculty of Law, University of Technology, Sydney.

Michael Hoeflich is John H and John M Kane Distinguished Professor in the Law School, University of Kansas.

John Langbein is Sterling Professor of Law and Legal History at Yale Law School.

Carol Matthews holds an administrative position at the University of Bedfordshire.

John V Orth holds the William Rand Kenan Jr Chair of Law at the University of North Carolina, Chapel Hill.

Wilfrid Prest is Professor Emeritus and Visiting Research Fellow in the Law School and School of History and Politics, University of Adelaide.

Mary Sokol holds an Honorary Research Fellowship in the Bentham Project at University College London.

Tim Stretton teaches history at St Mary's University, Halifax, Nova Scotia.

Abbreviations

Bentham, *Correspondence*	*The Correspondence of Jeremy Bentham*, ed TL Sprigge and others (London, 1968–2006).
Clitherow, 'Memoirs'	J. Clitherow, 'Preface, Containing Memoirs of his Life', from [W. Blackstone], *Reports of Cases Determined in the Several Courts of Westminster-Hall, from 1746 to 1779*, ed J Clitherow (London, 1781) volume I pp i–xxi
Commentaries	W Blackstone, *Commentaries on the Laws of England* (Oxford, 1765–69; facsimile edition Chicago IL, 1979)
Doolittle, *Blackstone*	I Doolittle, *William Blackstone A Biography* (Haslemere, 2001)
Eller	CS Eller, *The William Blackstone Collection in the Yale Law Library: A Bibliographical Catalogue* (New Haven CT, 1938)
ER	English Reports
HEL	WS Holdsworth, *History of English Law* (London, 1922–66)
HUO	*The History of the University of Oxford*, ed T Aston. Volume V: *The Eighteenth Century*, ed LS Sutherland and LG Mitchell (Oxford, 1986)
Letters	*The Letters of Sir William Blackstone 1744–1780*, ed W Prest (London, 2006)
ODNB	*Oxford Dictionary of National Biography*, ed HCG Matthew and B Harrison (Oxford, 2004)
Prest, *Blackstone*	W Prest, *William Blackstone: Law and Letters in the Eighteenth Century* (Oxford, 2008)
Reports	W Blackstone, *Reports of Cases Determined in the Several Courts of Westminster-Hall, from 1746 to 1779*, ed J Clitherow (London, 1781)
TNA	The National Archives, London (incorporating the Public Record Office)
UCL	Bentham manuscripts, University College London (cited by box and folio number)

Illustrations

I Life

THE MAIN FACTS of Blackstone's life are soon summarised. Born in London in 1723, the posthumous younger son of a near-bankrupt City shopkeeper, William Blackstone was educated at the Charterhouse School under the care of his mother (who also died when he was 12) and a maternal uncle. Winning a scholarship to Pembroke College, Oxford, he was elected a fellow of All Souls College in his 21st year. After graduating BCL in 1745 he began to study the common law in London, being called to the bar at the Middle Temple shortly thereafter, while still maintaining numerous commitments in and around Oxford. Having failed for political reasons to win a professorship in civil (or Roman) law, in 1753 he abandoned Westminster Hall, and launched a private lecture course in Oxford on England's common law and constitution. A leading and increasingly divisive figure in university politics, as well as a scholar and man of letters, he was elected (not without controversy) to the newly endowed Vinerian Chair in English Law in 1758, returning to the London bar shortly afterwards. His marriage in 1761 voided his fellowship, but he maintained a presence in Oxford for the next five years with the sinecure headship of New Inn Hall and his professorial lectures. He also served as a busy back-bench MP, pursued an expanding legal practice and angled for professional promotion, while fathering a growing family. In 1765 he published the first volume of his Oxford lectures, with the remaining three volumes of *Commentaries on the Laws of England* appearing over the next four years. After a change of ministry early in 1770 he was at last promoted to the judicial bench and knighted. A capable and conscientious judge, albeit increasingly obese and testy, Sir William Blackstone died in February 1780 at the relatively early age of 56.

The four following essays supplement this bare outline with further context and additional perspectives. My own looks at previous attempts to write Blackstone's life and the problems they have encountered, points to ways in which readings of his *Commentaries* may be influenced by the view taken of that life, and suggests further reasons why Blackstone's career may interest a broad range of scholars. Carol Matthews then reveals some important links between Blackstone's architectural activities and writings, of which she has made a special study, and the form and content of the *Commentaries*. In her contribution, Norma Potter traces the lineaments of Blackstone's close friendship with his older All Souls colleague Benjamin Buckler, thereby increasing our appreciation of a decidedly non-legal dimension to his life. Finally, Ian Doolittle augments his own pioneering biographical investigations with a finely detailed essay exploring the intellectual and psychological motivations behind Blackstone's remarkably extensive collection of the printed works of William Prynne, the seventeenth-century Puritan lawyer, polemicist and antiquary. Our subject's life story was indeed more complex and multi-layered than at first glance might appear.

1

Blackstone and Biography

WILFRID PREST

TOWARDS THE END of the last century a group of historians and literary scholars fortunate enough to be spending an academic year at the National Humanities Center in North Carolina met for informal lunch hour discussions of the biographer's art and craft. My own contribution reflected the experience of working over the previous few months on a memoir of Sir William Blackstone, commissioned for and eventually published in what became the *Oxford Dictionary of National Biography*. After the usual throat-clearing preliminaries, I pronounced Blackstone anything but an ideal biographical subject. Not only was there a serious lack of source material, in the form of personal, professional or family papers, but the very nature of Dr Blackstone's life 'seems at first—or even second—glance, neither particularly colourful nor eventful'.[1]

Heedless of my own caveat, I now find myself responsible for a free-standing life of the author of the *Commentaries on the Laws of England*.[2] If nothing else, such recklessness may qualify me to attempt a brief overview of previous attempts to write Blackstone's life, to look at how understandings of that life may affect readings of the book which was its greatest achievement, and finally to consider Blackstone's other claims to the attention of posterity.

1 BIOGRAPHICAL PERSPECTIVES ON BLACKSTONE

In 1999 it was still the case that 'the only published book-length studies of Blackstone's life are somewhat unsophisticated labours of love by two American lawyers, D. A. Lockmiller and L. C. Warden'.[3] The inadequacies

[1] W Prest, 'The Great Commentator: Sir William Blackstone and the Laws of England' (unpublished ts, 21 January 1999) 1.

[2] Prest, *Blackstone*.

[3] Prest, 'The Great Commentator' (n 1) 1. DA Lockmiller, *Sir William Blackstone* (Chapel Hill NC, 1938); L Warden, *The Life of Blackstone* (Charlottesville VA, 1938).

of both these works had been succinctly arraigned by the English medievalist Theodore Plucknett shortly after their near-simultaneous appearance in 1938. Plucknett's astringent review went on to assert that

> the only way to make [Blackstone's] life vivid and significant would be to treat it as part of the eighteenth-century scene and to make Blackstone intelligible as a man by tracing with lavish detail his penetration into those two very select microcosms, the legal profession and the academic world of eighteenth-century England. Blackstone would then appear to us as he did to his contemporaries, with his position fixed by his birth, his learning, his friends, his politics, and finally by his offices and his fortune.[4]

Yet 40 years would pass before Plucknett's prescription began to be acted upon, and then by a scholar who disclaimed any intention of contributing to legal knowledge. In the early 1970s Professor Dame Lucy Sutherland, the eminent Australian-born and South African-educated historian of Hanoverian Britain, began her last major scholarly project, as editor of the eighteenth-century volume for a new official history of the University of Oxford. It is scarcely surprising that Sutherland became interested in Blackstone, given his status as Oxford's 'most powerful and enterprising individual' (to quote her own words), during the middle years of that century.[5] From this perspective at least, Blackstone's life story was anything but run-of-the-mill, and far from lacking in action or drama.

Sutherland managed to write only a brief, if penetrating, essay, which clarified the circumstances surrounding Blackstone's failure to gain election to the Regius Chair of Civil Law in 1753, followed by a chapter on his successful challenge to the binding force of the university's seventeenth-century Laudian statutes. This latter was published posthumously in the volume of *The History of the University of Oxford* which became her memorial. Blackstone also featured prominently in the other three chapters contributed by Sutherland to the same work, and his Oxford years were explored in a Bodleian Library temporary exhibition to mark the bicentenary of his death for which she helped prepare catalogue notes.[6] Under her guidance, and assisted by her findings, a postdoctoral research fellow was also encouraged to embark upon 'a project . . . to write a full-length biography of Blackstone'. The first-fruits appeared as three articles shortly after Sutherland's death, but Ian Doolittle then left Oxford for London, where he became a practising solicitor. Not until 2001 did his biography

[4] TFT Plucknett in (1939) 52 *Harvard Law Review* 721.

[5] LS Sutherland, 'William Blackstone and the Legal Chairs at Oxford' in R Welleck and A Ribiero (ed), *Evidence in Literary Scholarship: Essays in Memory of James Marshall Osborn* (Oxford, 1979) 229–40, 230.

[6] *Ibid*; LS Sutherland, 'The Laudian Statutes in the Eighteenth Century', in *HUO* 191–203. *Blackstone and Oxford: An Exhibition held at the Bodleian Library, Oxford* (Oxford, 1980).

appear in print.[7] Although relatively brief and focused on Blackstone's public career, this self-published monograph would provide an indispensable starting point for all subsequent investigation of Blackstone's life, not least my own.

In explaining why 'Blackstone has received less than his due attention from biographers', Sutherland herself first cited the failure to provide 'an adequate memoir' by way of a foreword to the edition of his *Reports* published posthumously in 1781. Due to the illness and death of his old Oxford friend Benjamin Buckler, that responsibility fell to James Clitherow. This much younger man, a former All Souls colleague whose sister had married Blackstone, became in succession his brother-in-law's trustee, executor and editor, but proved, as Sutherland put it, 'a singularly unenterprising biographer'.[8] Clitherow certainly professed great reluctance, claiming that only the absence of Buckler's 'abler pen' had forced his hand: 'rather than Injustice should be done to a Character he so much esteemed, by an incorrect or injurious Narrative, He has ventured, though totally unused to writing for the public Eye, to undertake the Task himself'. Notwithstanding this show of (possibly quite genuine) modesty, Clitherow was in no doubt that he possessed 'ample Materials for the Purpose', thanks to an 'intimate Acquaintance' with his subject over more than three decades, the input of friends who had known him even longer, and 'a short Abstract of every Circumstance of Consequence in his Life, written by himself with his accustomed Accuracy'.[9] While corroborative evidence is lacking, there seems no reason to doubt that Blackstone did indeed compose an autobiographical memoir, which now survives only as incorporated in Clitherow's text.

Given the circumstances and timing of its publication, the nature of Clitherow's sources and his personal loyalties, the tone and content of that introductory 'Memoirs of [Blackstone's] Life' could hardly have been anything but sympathetic, not to say eulogistic. Despite his emphatic declaration of intention to provide a 'faithful and impartial Account', as distinct from a 'professed Panegyric', Clitherow saw no conflict between the claims of truth-telling and the 'Tribute due to the Memory of so respectable a Person'.[10] The lack of any other substantial contemporary life, as also of a Blackstone archive from which alternative perspectives might have been derived, therefore makes it unsurprising that, in the words

[7] I Doolittle, 'William Blackstone and the Radcliffe Camera, 1753' (1982) 11 *Bodleian Library Record* 47–50; 'Jeremy Bentham and Blackstone's Lectures' (1982) 6 *Bentham Newsletter*, 23–5; 'Sir William Blackstone and His *Commentaries on the Laws of England* (1765–69): A Biographical Approach' (1983) 3 *Oxford Journal of Legal Studies* 99–112; Doolittle, *Blackstone*.

[8] Sutherland, 'William Blackstone' (n 5) 229.

[9] Clitherow, 'Memoirs' i–ii.

[10] *Ibid* xix, xx, xxiv.

of the assiduous Victorian judicial biographer Edward Foss, Clitherow's version 'detailing all the incidents of his career . . . from its fairness and impartiality has formed the groundwork of every future memoir'.[11]

Foss's judgement was doubtless too kind, in that Clitherow certainly presented a selective perspective on his subject. This is apparent throughout his text, especially in his final summing up of Blackstone's 'Character' (despite his proclaimed intention 'to do Justice to the Merit of such a Character, without incurring the Imputation of Flattery'), but also in his persistent playing down of the extent and significance of Blackstone's lifelong literary (as opposed to legal) interests. But while scarcely unbiased or wholly objective, Clitherow did not attempt to exclude from his account all material which might lend support to other less favourable points of view. This is apparent from an earlier and notably more ambiguous testament to the authority of his 'Memoirs'. Published in the year after Blackstone's *Reports* with Clitherow's introductory biographical sketch first appeared in print, *The Biographical History of Sir William Blackstone* is essentially a scissors-and-paste compilation of extracts from Clitherow, with an excessively diffuse and rambling editorial commentary. Professedly the work of an anonymous and quite possibly fictitious 'Gentleman of Lincoln's Inn', this speculative literary venture was issued under the imprint of a bookseller-printer who specialised in 'popular and ephemeral literature'.[12] Yet although largely derivative in content, *The Biographical History* provided substantial hints of an alternative and markedly less sympathetic view of its subject, by way of anecdotal glosses to Clitherow's somewhat defensive insistence on Blackstone's fundamental benevolence, notwithstanding his intimidating physical presence, bad temper, and 'rigid Sense of Obligation'. Clitherow was probably seeking to counter the suggestion made in Jeremy Bentham's anonymously published *Fragment on Government* (1776), that the logical confusion and moral complacency which he detected in Blackstone's *Commentaries* were directly linked to their author's failings of character and intellect.[13] Bentham and his followers never provided a full-scale biographical riposte to Clitherow's portrayal of his brother-in-law. However, the muddled reactionary at whom they sneered can scarcely have seemed a more interesting biographical subject than the conscientious, hard-working worthy whose various achievements had been memorialised at some length by Clitherow.

Moving beyond or behind these essentially flat and stylised two-dimensional portraits, whether of virtuous public figure or obscurantist conservative, would require the mobilisation of more and different kinds of

[11] E Foss, *The Judges of England* (London, 1848–64) vol 8, p 250.

[12] HR Plomer et al, *A Dictionary of Printers and Booksellers . . . from 1726 to 1775* (Oxford, 1932) 25.

[13] J Bentham, *A Fragment on Government*, ed R Harrison (Cambridge, 1988) 3–4.

evidence than either Blackstone's eulogists or his detractors deployed during the 150 years after his death. Since there existed no readily accessible inventory of primary source material from which Blackstone's character and life story might be reconstructed in a more nuanced fashion, a willingness to seek out and exploit such evidence was also necessary. For while the lack of a Blackstone archive was plainly one major reason for the dearth of new biographical insights until very recent times, earlier biographers were also handicapped by a lack of interest in discovering additional sources, or indeed in more closely scrutinising those they already had. Thus despite their occasional references to unpublished manuscript evidence, even the more substantial biographies by Lockmiller and Warden are dominated by and essentially derived from a limited range of printed material. While a notably more critical and enterprising attitude was shown by the Cambridge legal scholar Gareth Jones in his lively introduction to a selection of extracts from the *Commentaries* published at about the time Sutherland was beginning her Oxford volume, Jones unfortunately never took this promising work any further.[14]

But from the late 1940s onwards both the quantity and quality of primary sources available to students of post-mediaeval British history had expanded by leaps and bounds, as country house owners increasingly availed themselves of opportunities to deposit their family papers in newly established county record offices staffed by trained archivists and funded by local government. Thus an extensive run of letters between Blackstone and his friend Sir Roger Newdigate, the Warwickshire squire and long-serving MP for the University of Oxford, came to Sutherland's attention in the Warwickshire County Record Office, together with the long-running sequence of diaries in which Newdigate briefly noted his daily engagements and social activities. The accounts of James Clitherow as Blackstone's executor were similarly incorporated in the Clitherow family papers deposited in the Greater London Record Office, now the London Metropolitan Archives, after their discovery in the attic and stables of a Yorkshire country house in 1975.[15] Transcripts of another important collection of Blackstone letters and related manuscripts, assembled by an American lawyer-collector and deposited at the Free Library of Philadelphia, were published in 1957.[16] More letters came to light among the Shelburne papers at Bowood Park before these manuscripts were widely dispersed among private collectors in Britain and the United States. Oxford University's Bodleian Library acquired at different dates between 1925 and 1971 and from various sources (including 'salvage') a large collection of

[14] G Jones (ed), *The Sovereignty of the Law* (London, 1973).

[15] Wiltshire County Record Office, ACC CR 136; London Metropolitan Archives, ACC 1360/580–1, 587, 715.

[16] HJ Heaney, 'The Letters of Sir William Blackstone in the Hampton L Carson Collection of the Free Library of Philadelphia' (1957) 1 *American Journal of Legal History* 363–78.

estate papers and other documents relating to the estates of the Bertie family, earls of Abingdon, Blackstone's most important clients during the 1760s.[17] These various assemblages of manuscript material supplemented two small collections of Blackstone's own papers relating to his role in the reform of the university's printing house and other controverted academic issues, acquired by the Bodleian's Department of Western Manuscripts and the University's Archives Office during the nineteenth century. The muniments of All Souls College, where Blackstone spent some eighteen active and productive years as a fellow and college officer, had been catalogued as far back as the 1870s,[18] and became still more accessible to scholars when they were largely transferred to the Bodleian Library on long-term loan after the Second World War.

So by the time that Sutherland and Doolittle turned their attention to Blackstone, original non-published sources that offered substantial opportunities to refine and supplement Clitherow's account had become available on an hitherto unprecedented scale. More recently the advent of digital technology and the Internet have made it increasingly possible for researchers based anywhere in the world to track down otherwise elusive archival and manuscript sources.[19] The same technology also permits us to search and retrieve nuggets of information and opinion from otherwise forbiddingly bulky and unindexed runs of contemporary newspapers and journals. Thus despite the apparent disappearance of most of Blackstone's own personal, family and professional papers, the richly detailed contextualisation of his life that Plucknett had called for is now far more feasible than it was or could have been in Plucknett's day. Access to this material makes it easier to recognise that, quite apart from the *Commentaries*, Blackstone did indeed have a life, and one by no means entirely devoid of colour and excitement.

II TEXT AND BIOGRAPHICAL CONTEXT

Because human beings are not all alike, each biographical subject presents particular opportunities and problems. The most challenging (if potentially rewarding) task facing Blackstone's biographers is to uncover and elucidate the connection between their subject and his exceptionally influential *Commentaries*, thereby negotiating the complicated interaction of what

[17] AJ Arrowsmith, M Clappinson & R Dunhill, 'Catalogue of the Papers of the Bertie Family, Earls of Abingdon', ts (Oxford, 1982), 'Introduction'.

[18] CT Martin, *Catalogue of the Archives in the Muniments Room of All Souls' College* (London, 1877).

[19] See W Prest, 'Reconstructing the Blackstone Archive: Or, Blundering after Blackstone' (2006) 31 *Archives* 108–18.

Laura Kalman has termed 'private self and public life'.[20] Of course this is easier said than done, since both sides of the equation present huge epistemological problems. Biography may well appear an 'impossible art'; how can we realistically hope to comprehend any human being, more especially someone whom we have never met and who lived several centuries ago?[21] By the same token, it hardly needed Michel Foucault to point out that, once launched into the world, books assume identities and meanings of their own, largely independent of their author's conscious intent. But these salutary warnings against interpretative dogmatism scarcely invalidate the interpretative process itself. For in everyday life we are constantly engaged in judging the character and personality of other people, always on the basis of incomplete evidence, while our reading of texts in all genres, especially non-fiction, cannot but be influenced by what we may know, or think we know, about their authors.

In relation to Blackstone and his *Commentaries*, Ian Doolittle has demonstrated the crucial importance of the fact that the *Commentaries* are 'essentially a work of the early 1750s, not the mid 1760s'.[22] Because their basic form and structure follows that of his lecture course, first offered at the University of Oxford in the academic year 1753–54, Blackstone could not do full justice to the significant reshaping of commercial and other branches of law achieved by Lord Mansfield as chief justice of King's Bench from 1756, since 'Blackstone's Oxford lectures had already taken shape before these reforms began'.[23] Here then is one explanation for what is often seen as a major inadequacy of the *Commentaries* as a statement of English law at the beginning of George III's reign. Yet Doolittle has also pointed out that Blackstone did manage to contrive various minor adjustments to the text of his lectures as reproduced in books II and III of the *Commentaries*, so as to take some account of Mansfield's jurisprudence. This redrafting was entirely characteristic of his authorial practice, for Blackstone was the sort of writer who found it very difficult to refrain from tinkering with his text. Hence the process of amendment, correction and updating did not cease once the manuscript lectures had been metamorphosed into print, but rather continued to affect all eight editions of the *Commentaries* published during Blackstone's lifetime, as well as the first posthumous edition of 1783, which purports to include his final manuscript revisions. To that extent at least, the *Commentaries* was a work-in-progress, whose composition extended over more than a quarter

[20] L Kalman, 'The Power of Biography' (1998) 23 *Law and Social Inquiry* 491.

[21] *Cf* I Clendinnen, 'Biography—The Impossible Art?' (State Library of Victoria, National Biography Award Lecture 2007): www.slv.vic.gov.au/programs/events/2007_nat_bio-lecture.html.

[22] Doolittle, 'Sir William Blackstone . . . A Biographical Approach' (n 7) 111.

[23] *Ibid.*

of a century. Yet the successive changes made by Blackstone to his original text have never been systematically examined, partly because the only variorum edition of the *Commentaries*, produced by W. G. Hammond towards the end of the nineteenth century, is neither widely available, nor very user friendly (with numbered footnotes indicating changes to successive editions, rather than grouping all such material in a separate appendix), while doubts persist about the accuracy of the collations, undertaken as they were by Hammond's students.

Once seen in this light, as a teaching book 'not originally compiled with any view of submitting it to public inspection',[24] and subject to continued piecemeal revision by its author, Blackstone's *Commentaries* lose something of the stable, monumental quality which they have subsequently acquired, not least as the target of numerous critical attacks. Among those critics the most committed, ferocious, and influential was Jeremy Bentham, who never wavered from his famous initial condemnation of the *Commentaries* as fundamentally flawed by an 'antipathy to reformation', of which (as he claimed) their author was 'a determined and persevering enemy'.[25] The anathema Bentham pronounced on Blackstone and his book in the professed interests of 'true science' and 'liberal improvement' retains some force even today. Yet Bentham's 'everything-as-it-should-be Blackstone', purblind defender of the unreformed common law, is little more than a straw man, impossible to reconcile with either the actual content of the *Commentaries*, or its author's real-life record as an energetic innovator and tireless 'improver'. Its persistence, in the face of various iterations of the numerous specific points on which the *Commentaries* combined exposition of the laws of England with criticism of their shortcomings, stems in part from failure to appreciate the full range and variety of Blackstone's reformist endeavours.

His major activities and achievements in this capacity occurred during the Oxford years—notably the struggle to restrict the role of birth rather than academic merit in elections to All Souls College fellowships, the rescue and rehabilitation of the university's near-moribund printing and publishing arm, and the pioneering lectures on the common law, from which sprang a new academic discipline, as well as the *Commentaries* themselves. But Blackstone also continued to pursue 'improvement', or as we would say reform, to the very end of his life. Indeed it is symptomatic of Bentham's blinkered animus that he never acknowledged his former teacher's instrumental role in drafting and promoting the legislative initiatives which culminated in the Penitentiary Act of 1779 (the first attempt to

[24] Blackstone to G Stuart, 16 March 1778: *Letters* 195.

[25] Bentham, *A Fragment on Government* (n 13) 4.

establish rehabilitative confinement in purpose-built prisons or 'penitentiaries' as a humane penal alternative to execution, flogging or transportation), despite having hailed the Hard Labour Bill, its immediate precursor, as a 'capital improvement'—before he became aware of Blackstone's prime responsibility for that draft.[26]

Knowing something of Blackstone's impressive credentials as a real-life reformer should at least help to sensitise us to the criticisms and suggestions for improvement of current institutions and practices which recur throughout the *Commentaries*. A better informed appreciation of his literary talents can contribute to the same end. Only minimal acquaintance with what the old *Dictionary of National Biography* termed the 'strained and stilted mannerisms of the period' is required to discount Blackstone's literary skills, and to conclude with the same source that 'nothing has been lost to English literature by Blackstone's seeking in poetry only a relaxation'.[27] Yet his first published work, a poetical essay entitled *The Pantheon* (1747), appeared under the imprint of London's Robert Dodsley, whose status as a publisher of poetry in mid-Georgian England was roughly equivalent to that of the house of Faber today.[28] According to his friend and fellow poet Richard Graves, 'being on a serious subject, and coming out at precisely the same time as some of Gray's Odes', *The Pantheon* was 'less noticed than it deserved'. Blackstone's poetical skills help explain the careful choice of words and construction of his prose sentences, albeit always within the polite linguistic conventions of the age. So when he refers to the acquisition of the British colonies in North America 'by right of conquest and driving out the natives (with what natural justice I shall not at present enquire)' his disapproval of that transaction, while implicit, is impossible to doubt. Similarly the condemnation in the first chapter of Book IV of the proliferation of capital offences is no less effective for being prefaced by 'an apology for some of the ensuing remarks' and the avowal that he is obliged 'to hint . . . with decency, to those whose abilities and stations enable them to apply the remedy' of the existence of such 'outrageous penalties'. That by now Blackstone was himself in his second term as a conscientious working member of the House of Commons doubtless added further contemporary credibility to his protest that such serious measures 'ought not to be left as a matter of indifference to the passions or interest of a few, who upon temporary motives may prefer or support such a bill'.[29]

[26] *Cf* Prest, *Blackstone* 296–9.

[27] GP Macdonell, 'Blackstone, Sir William (1723–1780)' in S Lee (ed), *Dictionary of National Biography* (London, 1885) vol 5, p 133.

[28] I am grateful to Prof Michael Suarez for this illuminating comparison.

[29] *Commentaries* vol 4, pp 4–5.

One final example of how Blackstone's life history can inform our reading of the *Commentaries* (and vice-versa) concerns his discussion of marriage. As Mary Sokol and Tim Stretton point out in their respective chapters below, Blackstone's account of the relationship of husband and wife downplayed the traditional emphasis upon the husband's superior physical strength, and was indeed generally characterised by a broadly idealistic and optimistic view of marriage..[30] It is hard to imagine that Blackstone's personal marital experience, in the words of his brother-in-law 'near nineteen Years in the Enjoyment of the purest domestic and conjugal Felicity . . . which, he used often to declare, was the happiest part of his Life' had absolutely no connection with, or relevance to, his book's treatment of marriage as a legal institution (even granting the latter's origins in lectures written while the author was still a bachelor Oxford don).[31]

III BLACKSTONE IN HISTORY

Some historians are sceptical about biography, believing that any focus upon a single individual must inevitably foster a distorted and incomplete view of the times through which that person lived. Besides the problem of the extent to which one person may be taken as representative or typical of the population at large, there is the broader difficulty of encompassing all the complexities of past events and structures within the parameters of a single life. Yet every form of historical enquiry is open to comparable objections. Historians can at best hope to present only partial segments of the past, and cannot possibly embrace the whole diverse and massive sweep of lived human experience. On the other hand, historical biography has an unrivalled potential to awaken interest and even imaginative identification with people in past times, thereby providing what Barbara Tuchman nicely termed 'a prism of history', one that 'encompasses the universal in the particular'.[32]

In the remarkable drive and energy with which he pursued his various projects, the righteous indignation with which he detailed the shortcomings of Oxford's university press while castigating the university's rulers for their lack of concern to redress these and other abuses, and the touches of wry humour which flavour his accounts of other people, and himself, Blackstone's character is neither wholly remote nor entirely unsympathetic. Yet as his younger admirer William 'Oriental' Jones noted, Blackstone was emphatically a 'guarded man'.[33] Even if we knew a good deal more than

[30] See below, pp 91–127.
[31] Clitherow, 'Memoirs' xvi.
[32] BW Tuchman, *Practising History* (New York NY, 1981) 81.
[33] G Cannon (ed), *The Letters of Sir William Jones* (Oxford, 1970) vol 1, p 609.

we do at present or are ever likely to know about his conjugal, domestic and private lives, an awkward mixture of self-deprecating shyness, prickly sensitivity, aloofness and perhaps a touch of priggish self-righteousness would resist attempts to establish an empathetic relationship with such a person across the intervening centuries. But then human beings hardly need be likeable to attract and retain our attention. It is perfectly possible to place oneself imaginatively in somebody else's shoes without either approving or endorsing their style and fit.

The origins of that 'natural Reserve and Diffidence' which (according to Clitherow) affected Blackstone 'from his earliest Youth' are likely to remain elusive.[34] As with various other aspects of his complex and driven personality—obsessive punctuality, a powerful sense of duty and a marked sensitivity to personal slights—this trait invites speculation about elements of deprivation and insecurity in the orphaned William's infancy and childhood. The concern for order, method and system evidently manifest in the meticulous keeping of his (now lost) personal and professional accounts, as well as in the content of the *Commentaries* and other writings, may possibly represent a reaction to the financial chaos in which the father whom he never knew left the silk drapery business on which his family depended when he died five months before his third son was born. Unfortunately we know nothing of William's relations with his mother, although it is surely significant that the uncles who supervised his early education came from her side of the family, while he appears to have had no recorded dealings whatever with his paternal relations.

Yet aside from these intriguing personal issues, of particular interest to historians of childhood and the family, not to mention any surviving psychohistorians, Blackstone's life story would be well worth attention even if the *Commentaries* had never been published. His very mixed family background (London middling sort on his father's side, parochial Wiltshire gentry on his mother's) and sponsored upbringing as a scholarship boy following the early deaths of both parents, the brilliant academic career at the Charterhouse and Oxford, and the somewhat strained relations which he enjoyed with various aristocratic patrons, all yield significant insights on the interactions and tensions between landed and urban elites in mid-Hanoverian England. His cultural tastes as an erudite bibliophile and collector, and his own literary productions—from poetic juvenilia to political pamphlets and squibs, from works of historical scholarship to the extensive critical notes contributed to Edmond Malone's two-volume *Supplement to the Edition of Shakespeare's Plays* (1780)—provide revealing case studies in the fast-expanding worlds of the eighteenth-century

[34] Clitherow, 'Memoirs' xxvii.

book trade and print media generally. In this context his canny management of the production and marketing of his largely self-published legal and historical writings is of particular interest. Other themes in contemporary historical scholarship on which Blackstone's life story casts significant light include the dynamics and texture of religious belief and practice among the educated laity, as well as the nature of relations between the Church of England and Dissent in the second half of the eighteenth century; academic politics and educational reform in the 1750s and '60s; and the operation of the criminal justice system. The same goes for his political activities, first at Oxford as Sir Roger Newdigate's electoral manager for the Tory 'Old Interest' during the 1750s, and then on his own account as a parliamentary back-bencher during the turbulent first decade of George III's reign, likewise the occasional tantalising hints about some decisive interventions by that monarch in the shaping of Blackstone's career.

Sir William Blackstone will always, and rightly, be best known as the author of the *Commentaries on the Laws of England*. Yet understanding how that exceptionally influential book came to be written in the way it was requires us to attend to many aspects of its author's life, some of which might seem not immediately relevant to the composition of the *Commentaries*, as well as to dislodge oversimplified images which have too long substituted for a multi-dimensional portrait of an intriguingly complex and talented personality. If my own work has contributed to those ends, there are still many gaps and silences, even despite the additional insights provided by other contributors to this volume. For example, further evidence of the nature of Blackstone's legal practice at the Westminster bar, especially the regional and social characteristics of the clients who retained him, may yet be uncovered in the unwieldy and voluminous surviving records of the central courts. More also remains to be learnt about the relative leniency or otherwise of his sentencing practices as a judge. Blackstone's European contacts and correspondents would certainly repay further investigation. A detailed examination of student notebooks, in order to map the changing content of the Oxford lectures and their evolution into what became the *Commentaries* is another obvious need. In short, the scope for further writing of William Blackstone's life is far from exhausted.

2

A 'Model of the Old House'

Architecture in Blackstone's Life and *Commentaries**

CAROL MATTHEWS*

SIR WILLIAM BLACKSTONE'S celebrated *Commentaries on the Laws of England* (1765–69), was one of the most influential books of the English eighteenth century. Yet Blackstone also composed a long poem on an architectural theme, wrote two versions of a treatise on classical architecture and was involved in a string of building projects. These architectural interests have received surprisingly little attention. The oversight is curious, given historians' recent interest in the eighteenth-century culture of politeness, where knowledge of classical architecture played an important role.[1] Nor have legal scholars asked whether Blackstone's early study of classical architecture, with its emphasis upon rules and precedents, might have influenced the development of his jurisprudence.

This essay has three main objectives. The first is to provide a brief survey of Blackstone's architectural activities and then to identify the sources upon which he based his treatise, in order to attempt an explanation of his

* Carol Matthews's chapter is based upon research conducted for her thesis 'Architecture and Polite Culture in Eighteenth-Century England: Blackstone's Architectural Manuscripts' (PhD, University of Adelaide, 2007) with the support of an Australian Research Council postgraduate scholarship. Funding to support research in the Codrington Library was provided by the University of Adelaide, while the J Paul Getty Trust subsidised her work at the Getty Research Library, Los Angeles.

[1] For a contemporary view of the role architecture played in polite culture, see [Anonymous], *The Polite Arts, or, a Dissertation on Poetry, Painting, Musick, Architecture, and Eloquence* (London, 1749). See also A Tinniswood, *The Polite Tourist: A History of Country House Visiting* (London, 1989); P Ayres, *Classical Culture and the Idea of Rome in Eighteenth-Century England* (New York NY, 1997) 115–32; J Black, *A Subject for Taste: Culture in Eighteenth-Century England* (London, 2005) 44–82; L Klein, 'Politeness and the Interpretation of the British Eighteenth Century ' (2002) 45 *Historical Journal* 869–89.

architectural motivations. The second is to demonstrate that his interest in architecture throws new light upon his personal life and religious views. Lastly, and most importantly, I want to propose that Blackstone's characteristically meticulous study of classical architecture influenced the methodology, structure and anti-feudalism of his great legal text.

While not closely examined, Blackstone's interest in architecture has at least been long acknowledged. Until very recently James Clitherow's memoir was regarded as the authoritative account of Blackstone's life. That memoir's declared aim, however, is to portray its subject as

> a bright Example of a Man, who, without Fortune, Family Interest, or Connexions, raised himself by a diligent Attention to his Studies, even from his earliest Youth, and the strictest Sense of every moral and religious Duty, to a very eminent and honourable Office in his Profession.[2]

Consequently, Clitherow emphasises Blackstone's academic and legal careers and downplays such aspects of his personal life as his interest in architecture. The unnamed author of an 1829 article agreed with Clitherow that Blackstone's study of classical architecture was merely 'the recreation of his leisure hours'.[3] GP Macdonell's *DNB* entry looked no further than Clitherow with regard to architecture, and two insipid biographies published in 1938 did little more to enhance our appreciation of Blackstone's enduring interest in this subject.[4] With the dawn of the twenty-first century, however, Ian Doolittle's brief but welcome biographical account drew upon new sources in order to delve more insightfully into Blackstone's private life and expand a little upon his property dealings and architectural activities.[5] Not until 2003, though, when Prest highlighted Blackstone's use of architectural metaphor in the *Commentaries* and suggested that it might offer a new perspective on the text, did Blackstone's involvement with architecture attract more than a passing interest.[6] In short, scholars have tended to follow Clitherow's lead and approached Blackstone through, rather than because of, his great legal text. As a result, the significance of architecture in the life and thought of the *Commentaries*' author has been largely overlooked.

In fact Blackstone's architectural activities span some 30 years: from the 1740s to the 1770s. It is unclear when the seed of his enthusiasm was actually planted, but it first bore fruit in 1743 (the year he turned 20).

[2] Clitherow, 'Memoirs' i, ii.

[3] [Anonymous], 'Life and Writings of Sir William Blackstone' (1829) 1 *American Jurist and Law Magazine* 118.

[4] GP Macdonell, 'Blackstone, Sir William' in S Lee (ed) *Dictionary of National Biography* (London, 1886) vol 5, pp 133–40; D Lockmiller, *Sir William Blackstone* (Chapel Hill NC, 1938); L Warden, *Life of Blackstone* (Charlottesville VA, 1938).

[5] Doolittle, *Blackstone*.

[6] W Prest, 'Blackstone as Architect: Constructing the *Commentaries*' (2003) 15 *Yale Journal of Law & the Humanities* 107–8.

Towards the end of that year he penned *The Pantheon: A Vision*, a poem of some 500 lines which became the first of his published works.[7] *The Pantheon* employs an architectural metaphor with which to represent 'the several Religions that have prevailed in the world'.[8] Blackstone undoubtedly drew upon the knowledge of architecture he had gained earlier that year during the compilation of a manuscript he entitled 'An Abridgement of Architecture'.[9] The 'Abridgement' aims to establish the fundamental rules of classical architecture and, as its title may hint, so closely follows the content and organisation of Sir Henry Wotton's influential *Elements of Architecture* (1624) as to be a virtual redaction.[10] Blackstone makes, however, two original additions: a diagrammatic 'Analysis of this Abridgement' (see Figure 1) and an index of some 700 architectural terms. The lines of text, closely. spaced over 51 pages, are in Blackstone's typically neat hand (see Figure 2). The manuscript itself is in good condition though stubs indicate the removal of 14 pages which seem likely to have been illustrations.

In 1746 and 1747 Blackstone returned to his 'Abridgement', revising and expanding the manuscript into a fully fledged treatise entitled 'Elements of Architecture' (1746–47).[11] Indeed, the pages of the 'Abridgement' bear considerable evidence of this painstaking revision process. Sections ranging from sentences to entire paragraphs are struck through[12] and frequent marginalia indicate meticulous attention to emendations and insertions.[13] That marginalia appear in both black and brown inks as well as in pencil suggests that Blackstone reviewed his text on more than one occasion. The most obvious revisions are to Chapters II (Of the Situation), IX (Of the Pedestal, Column, and Entablature), XVI (Of the Intercolumnation), XVIII (Of Pilasters), XXVI (Of Staircases and Stairs), and XXX (Of the Several Sorts of Rooms). Page numbers in the index have been struck through and new numbers noted alongside, in Blackstone's hand, which correspond to the pagination of the 'Elements'. An expanded Index now lists 'about nine hundred Terms' though the increase does not necessarily

[7] [W Blackstone], *The Pantheon: A Vision* (London, 1747). The preceding advertisement states that it was composed 'towards the close of the year 1743'; see also W Prest 'The Religion of a Lawyer? William Blackstone's Anglicanism' (2004) 21 ns *Parergon* 159.

[8] Blackstone, *The Pantheon* (n 7) ii.

[9] 'An Abridgement of Architecture' (1743): Research Library, The Getty Research Institute, Los Angeles, CA (MS 890227) 51. Blackstone's own notation on its final page confirms that he completed the 'Abridgement' on 22 July 1743.

[10] H Wotton, *The Elements of Architecture, Collected by Henry Wotton Knight, from the Best Authors and Examples* (London, 1624).

[11] W Blackstone, 'Elements of Architecture' (1746–47), Codrington Library, All Souls College, Oxford (MS 333).

[12] Blackstone, 'An Abridgement of Architecture' (n 9) 12, 13, 24, 26, 28, 29, 30, 31, 33, 40, 44.

[13] *Ibid* 3, 4, 5, 6, 8, 9,10, 11, 12, 20, 28, 29, 30, 32, 34, 35,37, 38, 39, 41, 42, 43, 44, 45, 46, 47, 49, 50.

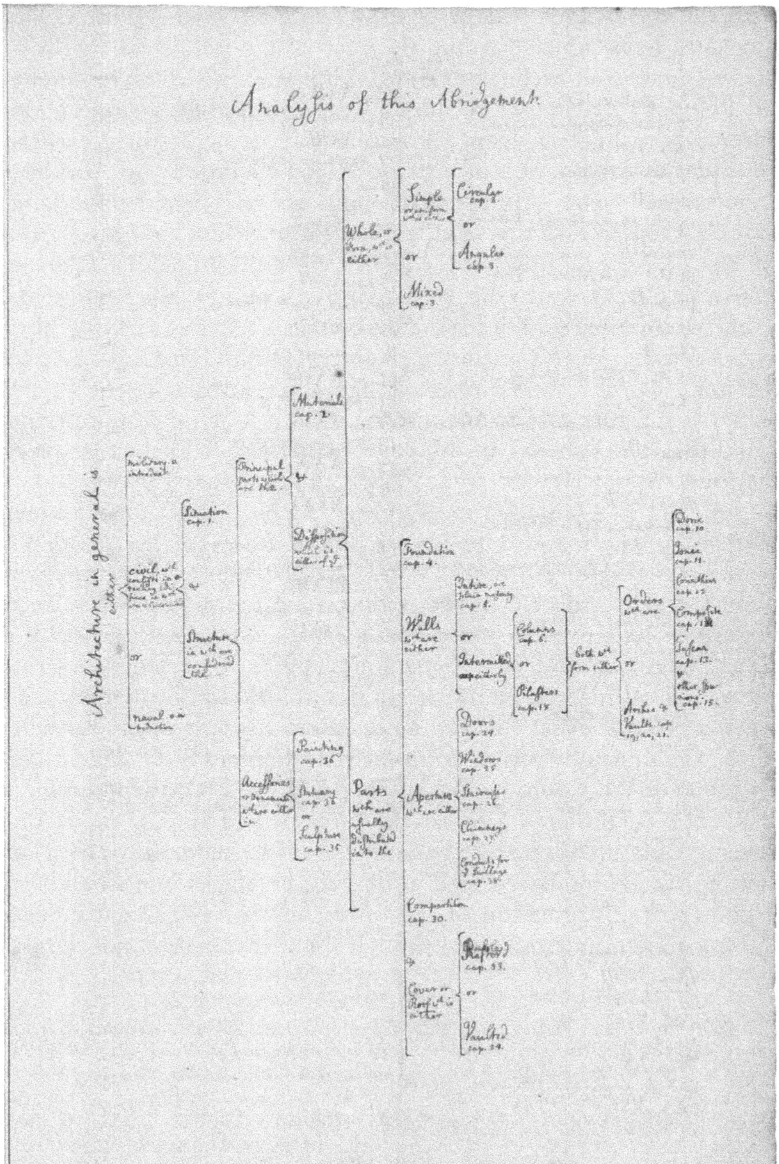

Figure 1. Blackstone's 'Analysis of this Abridgement' (1743)
Research Library, The Getty Research Institute, Los Angeles, California (890227)

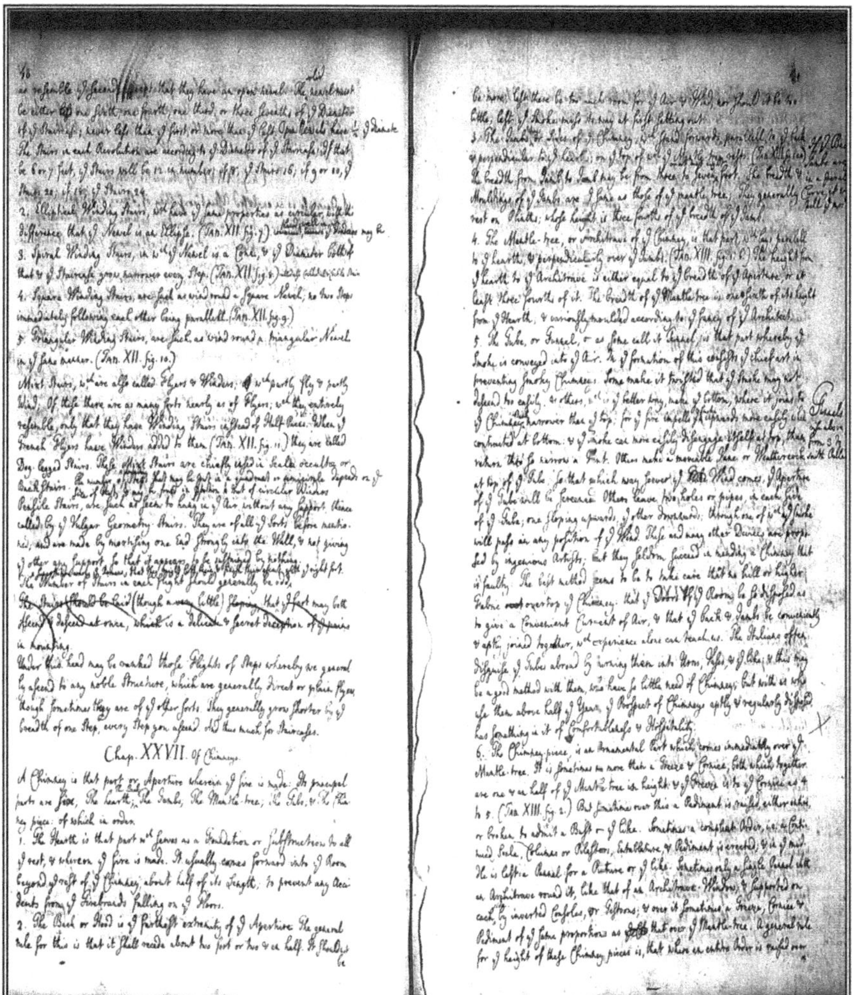

Figure 2. 'An Abridgement of Architecture' (1743) 40–41
Research Library, The Getty Research Institute, Los Angeles, California (890227)

imply a greater range of architectural terminology because the 'Elements' lists several variations of many terms. The fillet, for example, is also listed under Cimbia, Cincta, Cincture, Diadema, List, Listell, Orle, Orlet and Orlo.[14] The 'Elements' contains 29 rather than 32 chapters (as in the 'Abridgement') but over 137 rather than 51 pages. The text is more widely spaced in the 'Elements' and appears within neatly ruled borders and with double-ruled lines to delineate the chapters (Figure 3). Twenty-three neat pen-and-ink drawings, featuring grey wash to indicate shading, illustrate the text (Figure 4). Thus the 'Elements' emerged from an extensive revision process as a significantly more complex work than its predecessor.

The 'Elements' has been held since 1892 by the Codrington Library of All Souls College, Oxford. Not only a more attractive document than the 'Abridgement', the 'Elements' is also more intellectually engaging. Its text incorporates a wider range of sources, representing a selection of architectural theory both ancient and modern. Blackstone acknowledged the authorities upon which he drew, declaring that:

> [t]he Method made use of, and many of the Observations, are borrowed from Sir Henry Wotton's Elements. The rest are, in great part, taken from Monsr. Fréart's Parallel, and Mr. Evelyn's Account of Architects and Architecture annexed to it; from Monsr. Perrault's Admirable Translation and Comment on Vitruvius, and his Abridgement of the same Author; and from Palladio's elegant Designs, as they are now illustrated by the Notes of Inigo Jones. A few mechanical Precepts, for the more commodious drawing of the several Parts of Architecture, are borrowed from Mr. Gibbs's Rules; and as to the several Definitions, and synonymous Terms of the Members, they have been chiefly furnished from Mr. Chambers's Cyclopaedia.[15]

It is unclear where or when he accessed all but three of these sources. According to the catalogue of an 1845 sale of the Blackstone library, paintings and plate, Blackstone had owned an unidentified edition of John James' English translation of what the catalogue lists as 'Perrault's Architecture, by James'.[16] He also owned a 1733 edition of John Evelyn's English translation of Roland Fréart's *Parallel of the Ancient Architecture with the Modern*.[17] Evelyn's handy compendium comprised the *Parallel* with both Wotton's *Elements of Architecture* and his own *Account of*

[14] Blackstone describes the fillet as 'a little flat member, generally used as a sort of Crown over a greater Moulding': Blackstone, 'Elements' (n 11) 21.

[15] Blackstone, 'Elements' (n 11) i.

[16] *Bibliotheca Blackstoneiana . . . A Catalogue of a Library of 4,500 Volumes* (London, 1845), 18 (lot 237). This assumes that editions dated prior to his death in 1780 may tentatively be identified as Blackstone's; those published after that date clearly cannot.

[17] *Ibid*. R Fréart [Sieur de Chambray], *A Parallel of the Ancient Architecture With the Modern, to which is added an Account of Architects and Architecture, in an Historical and Etymological Explanation of Certain Terms Particularly Affected by Architects. With Leon Baptista Alberti's Treatise of Statues*, tr J Evelyn (London, 1733).

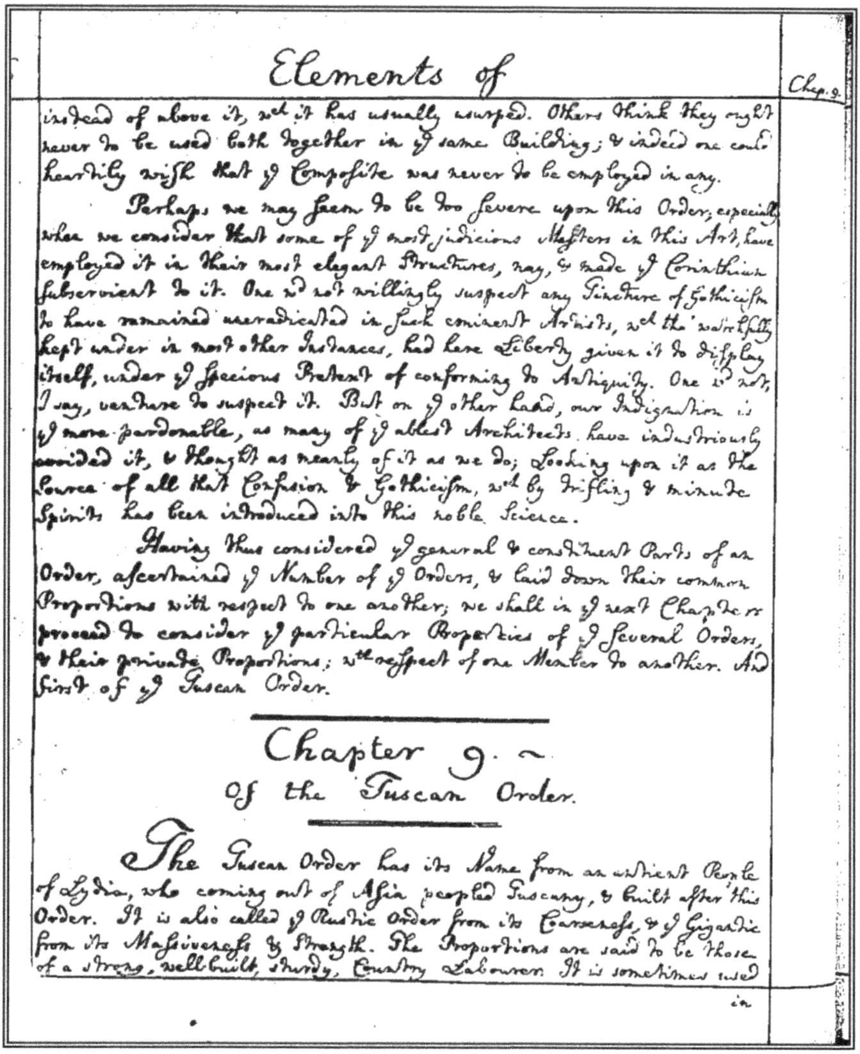

Elements of

Chap. 9.

instead of above it, wch it has usually usurped. Others think they ought never to be used both together in ye same Building; & indeed one could heartily wish that ye Composite was never to be employed in any.

Perhaps we may seem to be too severe upon this Order, especially when we consider that some of ye most judicious Masters in this Art, have employed it in their most elegant Structures, nay, & made ye Corinthian subservient to it. One wd not willingly suspect any Tincture of Gothicism to have remained uneradicated in such eminent Artists, wch tho' carefully kept under in most other Instances, had here Liberty given it to display itself, under ye specious Pretext of conforming to Antiquity. One wd not, I say, venture to suspect it. But on ye other hand, our Indignation is ye more pardonable, as many of ye ablest Architects have industriously avoided it, & thought as meanly of it as we do; looking upon it as the Source of all that Confusion & Gothicism, wch by trifling & minute Spirits has been introduced into this noble Science.

Having thus considered ye general & constituent Parts of an Order, ascertained ye Number of ye Orders, & laid down their common Proportions with respect to one another; we shall in ye next Chapter proceed to consider ye particular Properties of ye several Orders, & their private Proportions; wth respect of one Member to another. And first of ye Tuscan Order.

Chapter 9.

Of the Tuscan Order.

The Tuscan Order has its Name from an antient People of Lydia, who coming out of Asia peopled Tuscany, & built after this Order. It is also called ye Rustic Order from its Coarseness, & ye Gigantic from its Massiveness & Strength. The Proportions are said to be those of a strong, well-built, sturdy, Country Labourer. It is sometimes used

in

Figure 3. 'Elements of Architecture' 36
Reproduced with the kind permission of the Warden and Fellows of All Souls College, Oxford.

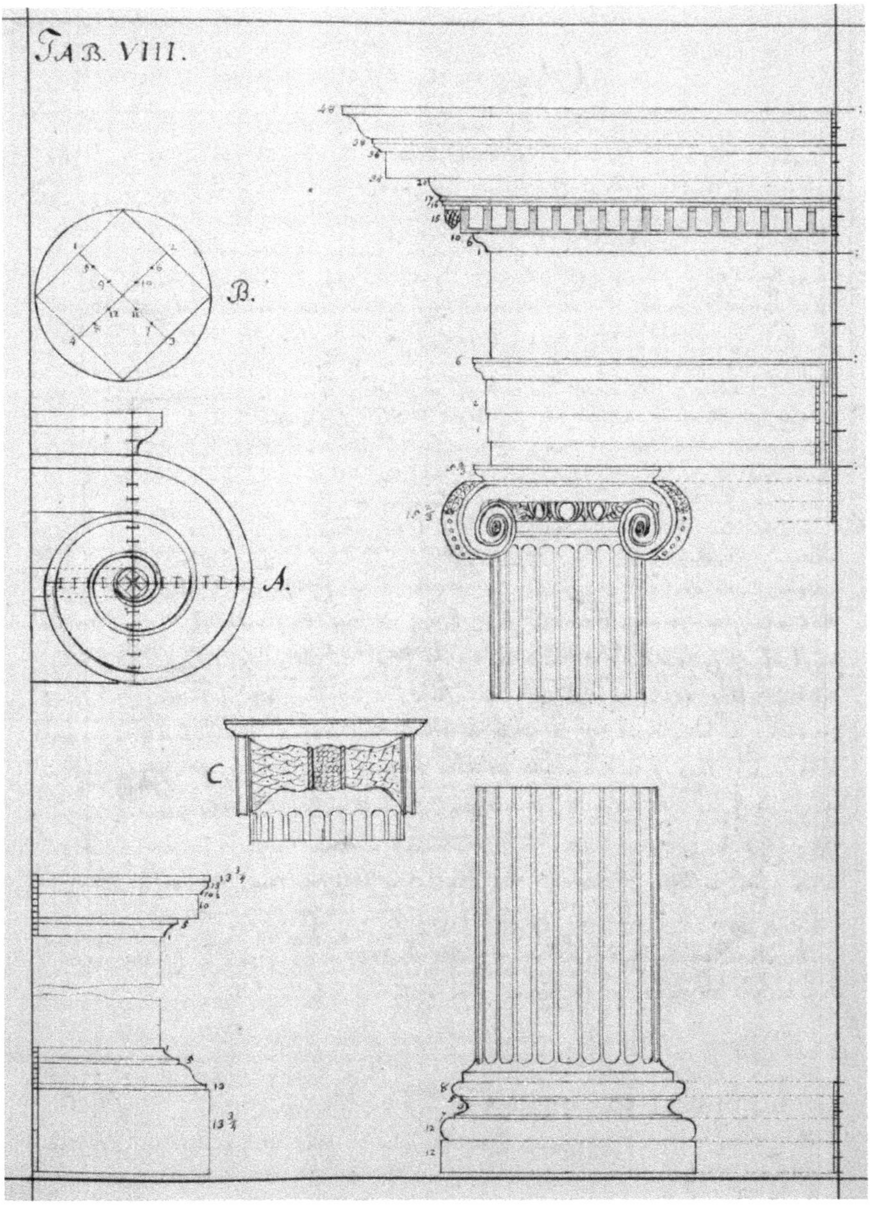

Figure 4. 'Elements of Architecture', The Ionic Column and Entablature
Reproduced with the kind permission of the Warden and Fellows of All Souls College, Oxford

Architects and Architecture.[18] (The latter is a collection of architectural terms gleaned during Evelyn's travels in Italy during what has been called 'one of the great seventeenth-century examples of the grand tour' between 1641 and 1647).[19] The other work Blackstone apparently owned was the impressive, two-volume fourth edition (1741) of Ephraim Chambers' *Cyclopaedia: or, An Universal Dictionary of the Arts and Sciences*; a copy bearing Blackstone's bookplate is now held by the library of Balliol College, Oxford.[20]

This list of authorities raises an important point. One of the difficulties associated with an analysis of Blackstone's 'Elements' is that it is possible to read the treatise on two levels. It could be argued that the 'Elements' is no more than a conglomeration of various readily available authorities: its principles borrowed from one source or another as they appealed to the young Blackstone. The problem with this reading is that such a casual approach would not only be uncharacteristic of Blackstone's meticulous nature but also underestimates his intellectual capacity. Nowhere does Blackstone explain his choice of these particular sources but several possibilities exist from which some tentative conclusions, of varying significance, can be drawn.

Firstly, these publications span much of the accumulated theoretical knowledge available to him in the 1740s—a perfectly good reason for his having selected this combination. One might also conclude that Blackstone simply chose those which were most accessible, perhaps among friends and extended family, or at the university. On the other hand, it may be that he deliberately selected these works as representing a thoughtful blend of philosophy and practicality. In Wotton he finds the humanist concern with harmonic proportion, in Perrault and Fréart the neo-Platonist idealisation of beauty, and in Chambers the rational, pragmatic, Newtonian approach of the early Enlightenment.

A further possibility is that these sources represent a cross-section of those more genteel available works, which highlighted a distinction between the learned architect and the mere mechanic builder. Evelyn endorsed this distinction in his *Account*, advising his readers that 'as the great Plato has somewhere designed him … Architect is not to be taken for the commonly illiterate *Mechanick* … but for the person who *Superintends* and *Presides* over him'.[21] In this light, the fact that Blackstone did not include any of the popular but 'vulgar' works aimed at the surveyor and builder, such as William Halfpenny's *Art of Sound Building* (1725) gains

[18] Listed as 'Freart's Architecture, by Evelyn, *plates*, 1733': *Bibliotheca Blackstoneiana* (n 16) 18 (lot 237).

[19] *ODNB*, 'John Evelyn (1620–1706)'.

[20] Shelf mark 1555.h.1 (I owe this information to Wilfrid Prest).

[21] Fréart (tr Evelyn), *A Parallel of the Ancient Architecture* (n 17) 3.

significance when we consider an observation made by Prest.[22] By 1746 Blackstone was a Fellow of All Souls, a

> college dominated … by 'Persons of great Fortunes and high birth' [so] a city-born and bred scholarship boy elected to a fellowship on his second application from one of Oxford's least grand societies [Pembroke College] might well have felt the need to cultivate some … mark of gentility.[23]

If that were Blackstone's aim, the study of architecture would certainly have been helpful because, as Gloag reminds us, 'throughout the Georgian period anybody with any pretensions to taste, anybody in fact who considered themselves to be educated, was naturally familiar with the orders of architecture and the system of design to which they supplied the key'.[24] That classical 'system of design' (or, in the language of architecture, design grammar) was an expression of the elegance, grace, reason and sense of proportion, the sociability, harmony, civility and urbanity, which together characterised polite culture.

Architecture's sheer intellectual stimulation may well also have appealed to a young man as bright and industrious as the 20-year-old William Blackstone. In fact, Evelyn's *Account* provides a tantalising hint that it may have motivated the 'Elements', at least in part. Evelyn protests the current state of English architecture and calls for

> some more entire Treatise of the whole Art than is yet extant among us; and to be delivered by some industrious Person, who shall oblige the *Nation* with a thorough Examination of what has already been written by *Vitruvius* 1.2.c.3 and 9. *Palladio* 1.c2. *Leon Alberti* 1.2.c.45.46. *Dan Barbaro* 1.II. Sir H. Wotton in his concise and useful *Theorems* … and in what shall be found most beneficial for our *Climate*. It were I say, becoming our great Needs that some ingenious Person did take this in Hand, and advance upon the *Principles* already established, and not to acquiesce in them as if there were a *Non Ultra* Engraven upon our *Columns* like those of *Hercules*, after which there remained no more to be discovered ….[25]

This is substantially what Blackstone has done. The material from Book One of Vitruvius to which Evelyn refers comprises the 'Fundamental Principles of Architecture' (ie definitions of 'Order', 'Arrangement', 'Eurhythmy', 'Propriety' and 'Economy') and his three-way division of

[22] W Halfpenny, *The Art of Sound Building: Demonstrated in Geometrical Problems: Showing Geometrical Lines… Wherin Are Laid Down (Suited to Every Capacity) Easy Practical Methods for Carpenters, Joiners, Masons, or Bricklayers, to Work by* (London, 1725).

[23] Prest, ' Blackstone as Architect' (n 6) 123.

[24] J Gloag, *Georgian Grace: A Social History of Design from 1660–1830* (London, 1956) 17.

[25] Fréart (tr Evelyn) (n 17) 5 ('Account of Architects & Architecture'). See also L Le Faivre and A Tzonis, *The Emergence of Modern Architecture* (London, 2004) 129; Evelyn is referring to Barbaro's Italian translation of Vitruvius' *Ten Books* (Vinegia, 1556).

architecture (into 'the art of building, the making of time-pieces, and the construction of machinery').[26] Blackstone incorporates the first of these but ignores much of the rest, presumably because its astrological content was outdated and because his own discussion is limited to domestic architecture. However, he does include the material from Palladio which outlines the use of various building materials from foundations to roof, and Palladio's general 'Rules for all Edifices'.[27] Blackstone did not refer directly to either Alberti or Barbaro, but Wotton's *Elements* is based upon their works as well as his own firsthand knowledge. Wotton's 'useful *Theorems*' however Blackstone incorporates into the 'Elements' as chapter eighteen 'Of Arches and Vaults'. In addition, he takes every opportunity to identify sensible adaptations of antique designs to the English climate. In chapter twenty-three, for example, he mentions the need for chimneys.[28]

According to Clitherow the young Blackstone became interested in architecture as a diversion, motivated by a need to enliven the 'dry study' of mathematics.[29] Prior to the computer age, skills in both geometry and proportion were fundamental to the design and appreciation of classical architecture. In fact Evelyn went so far as to proclaim classical architecture 'the flower and crown of all the sciences mathematical'.[30] The statement was certainly justified, because the beauty of a classical building resides precisely in the harmony achieved when each room and architectural element conforms to a standard set of mathematical proportions. Thus Clitherow's explanation sounds feasible. On closer examination, however, it does not suffice. Blackstone himself wrote that by observing the 'principal Rules ... in this most excellent Art',

> a Man may easily acquire a Taste for the Beauties, and perhaps make some Proficiency in the Practice of Architecture; a Science which for its Use, Nobility and Delight has not its equal in the Universe, having had the honour of employing the Divine Majesty itself; in the Temple erected by God's Direction at Jerusalem.[31]

Thus although mathematics may well have helped arouse Blackstone's interest in studying architecture, a wider range of motivations must be considered. As the passage just quoted makes clear, he considered knowledge of architectural principles important for social and cultural reasons: besides its practical utility, the study of classical architecture was perceived

[26] M Vitruvius, *The Ten Books of Architecture* (tr) HM Morris (New York NY, 1960) Book 1, pp 2, 3, 13–17.

[27] G Leoni, *The Architecture of A. Palladio* (ed and tr) I Jones (London, 1742) vii.

[28] Blackstone, 'Elements' (n 11) 97 ('Of Chimneys and the Conducts for the Suillage').

[29] Clitherow, 'Memoirs' v.

[30] See H Colvin and J Newman, *Of Building: Roger North's Writings on Architecture* (Oxford, 1981) xiii.

[31] Blackstone, 'An Abridgement of Architecture' (n 9) 51.

as ennobling, assisting in the development of a polite deportment which would enhance his claims to gentility.

Whatever his original motivations, it was not long before the knowledge and taste acquired during the composition of the 'Abridgement' and 'Elements' proved invaluable. Blackstone's duties as Dean and then Bursar of Laws at All Souls College involved him in the completion of the Codrington Library building as early as 1746, the year in which he also commenced the 'Elements'. By 1757 he was occupied with another architectural project, this time converting what Clitherow calls a 'confused Heap of Ruins' at Queen's College into 'that handsome Pile of Building towards the *High Street*'.[32] He also attempted, in vain, to persuade the University of Oxford to accept a plan to use the Radcliffe Library as a dedicated manuscript library.[33] Acting in a private advisory capacity to Lord Abingdon during the following decade he supervised the rebuilding of the Botley causeway on Oxford's western approaches.[34] The design of a stone toll-bridge bridge erected at Swynford as part of a related project hints that he may well have commissioned the fashionable architect Robert Taylor.[35]

Blackstone married in 1761 and soon undertook renovations to his new family home in the nearby town of Wallingford, Berkshire.[36] An attractive house, boasting a Jacobean wing, Castle Priory (formerly Priory Place) still nestles on the banks of the Thames near St Peter's church and the graceful Wallingford Bridge. Its lawns sweep from the house to the river: the epitome of the ideal polite eighteenth-century situation as described in the 'Elements'.[37] Blackstone referred affectionately to the home as his 'Cabin in Thames Street'[38] and though he also maintained lodgings in New Inn Hall and kept a London residence in Lincoln's Inn Fields towards the end of his life, Castle Priory was his family home from 1761 until his death in February 1780.[39] The town of Wallingford itself benefited from his renovations to the neighbouring church of St Peter's. He commissioned

[32] Clitherow, 'Memoirs' xiii. For a more detailed account of Blackstone's building projects see Prest (n 6) 116–18.

[33] I Doolittle, 'William Blackstone and the Radcliffe Camera' (1982) 11 *Bodleian Library Record* 47–50.

[34] See Doolittle, *Blackstone* 108.

[35] On these projects, see Prest (n 6) 116–18; also now Prest, *Blackstone* 223–4.

[36] Doolittle, *Blackstone* 101. For Taylor's involvement see HM Colvin, *Biographical Dictionary of British Architects* (London, 1978) 816.

[37] For two residences situated in just this manner, the Countess of Suffolk's house (James Mason after Augustin Heckell, 1749) and Alexander Pope's villa (after Augustin Heckell, *c*1750), see J Bryant, 'Villa Views and the Uninvited Audience' in *The Georgian Villa*, ed D Arnold (Stroud, 1996) 14–15.

[38] *Letters* 133.

[39] Doolittle, *Blackstone* 103. Blackstone maintained 55 Lincoln's Inn Fields as his town residence between 1768 and 1780: EB Chancellor, *The Romance of Lincoln's Inn Fields and its Neighbourhood* (London, 1932) 63.

Robert Taylor for an extensive refurbishment of the church's interior and again in the early 1770s for a neo-gothic spire—which appears less incongruous from across the river than from the street. He also provided funds for a clock face on the church tower's southern facade.[40] Thus it is clear that, whether from personal interest or when acting in a professional capacity, Blackstone's involvement in architectural projects occupied his attention over a period of some 30 years.

Indeed, on occasion his knowledge of architecture brought together the public and private sides of his life, as during his long and close friendship with Sir Roger Newdigate, MP for the university, whose architectural interests have received more scholarly attention than Blackstone's.[41] Newdigate's papers include a sketch of the floor plan of 'the Chapel of Nuneaton surveyed by Willm. Blackstone'. It bears the date '24 Aug. 1752' and is in Newdigate's handwriting. It appears to be a rough sketch of the dimensions of the parish church of St Nicholas, according to measurements kindly 'Made out by the very extraordinary Genius of Wm Blackstone Dr. of Laws'.[42] In 1758 Newdigate presented Blackstone with a copy of Isaac Ware's *Complete Body of Architecture*.[43] Newdigate also earlier involved Blackstone in negotiations over the donation by his kinswoman Lady Pomfret of a large collection of classical statuary to Oxford University.[44] This gift prompted a flurry of letters between Blackstone and Sir Roger between February and October 1753. Blackstone proposed a plan to move the marbles into a suitable temporary location until 'the Magnificence of a Greek or Roman Temple to display them to proper Advantage' could be provided. He proposed that the schools of Logic and Philosophy be moved to create a 'large, public Room, well lighted, &c, what is a main Article, on the ground Floor' and enclosed a sketch of the area.[45] Their correspondence reveals his enthusiasm and confidence that the university would cheerfully bear 'the Expense of Removing & Fitting up the Marbles with proper Pedestals & Inscriptions'. His confidence, however, proved unjustified, and Blackstone wrote again to say that he was 'sorry to hear Frugality so much talked of upon this occasion'. Indeed the collection's temporary

[40] Clitherow, 'Memoirs' xvii; Prest, *Blackstone* 281–3.

[41] See eg A Wood, 'The Diaries of Sir Roger Newdigate, 1751–1806' (1960) 78 *Birmingham Archaeological Society Transactions* 40–54; M McCarthy, 'Sir Roger Newdigate: Drawings for Copt Hall, Essex, and Arbury Hall, Warwickshire' (1973) 16 *Architectural History* 25–36, 77–88.

[42] Warwickshire Record Office, CR136/B 2587 .

[43] Newdigate's diary entry for 15 April 1758 records his intention to 'buy Ware a present to Blackstone': Warwickshire Record Office, CR136/A589. The intended gift seems to have been a copy of I Ware, *A Complete Body of Architecture Adorned with Plans and Designs* (London, 1756).

[44] The Pomfret marbles were originally part of the famous Arundel Collection: HEL Hayes, *The Arundel Marbles* (Oxford, 1975).

[45] The sketch is reproduced in *Letters* 33.

home was more likely to be either a 'Room under the Museum, a common Throughfare & of no size; [or] in the Anatomy School, up one pair of Stairs; a Lumber Room for dry bones & stuft Alligators'. Such 'frugality' he attributed to 'a coldness of Constitution natural to those advanced in Years . . . better qualified perhaps for adorning the University by their Learning, than their Taste in the politer Arts'.[46]

Apart from anything else this episode reveals about Blackstone's opinions (or the 'frugality' of universities), it demonstrates his freedom of expression with Newdigate, his appreciation of classical architecture as part of a polite comportment and his architectural endeavours on the university's behalf. Indeed Blackstone's architectural activities confirm and enrich much of Clitherow's account. He is revealed as a deeply practical man, actively involved in his collegiate and municipal communities. In illuminating one of his most significant friendships Clitherow's assurances that Blackstone's aloofness was something of a public mask is also confirmed.

Blackstone's architectural writings also provide previously overlooked evidence of his religious views. Thus he traced the origins of architecture to the Old Testament rather than classical mythology. Not only do the closing lines of the 'Abridgement' assert the divine origin of the design of Solomon's Temple, but a footnote in *The Pantheon* comments that 'Villalpandus has undertaken to prove, that the Ornaments and Proportions of the *Grecian* Architecture were borrowed from *Solomon's* Temple at *Jerusalem*.'[47] Blackstone mentioned the theory again three years later in chapter twelve of the 'Elements', where he describes the Corinthian as:

> the most delicate of all the Orders, the very Perfection, and *Ne plus ultra* of regular Architecture. It is said to have been invented by the famous Callimachus of Corinth, the Reason and Manner of which Invention is minutely related by Vitruvius. Yet on the other hand Villalpandus would persuade us (and plausably enough) that is only an Imitation of an Order erected in Solomon's Temple, the Capital of which was of Palm Branches, and the whole Composition, as he designed it, exceeding glorious.[48]

The 'Advertisement' preceding the *Pantheon* states that it takes a '*Poetical* View of the several Religions, that have prevailed in the World, which are represented by different *Genii* residing in their different Temples, with the proper Symbols of their respective Faiths'.[49]

[46] *Letters* 35.

[47] *Letters* 248. Juan Bautista Villalpando was co-author of a commentary on Ezekiel: In Ezechielem Explanationes et Apparatus Urbis, ac Templi Hierosolymitani Commentariis et imaginibus illustratus (Rome, 1596–1604).

[48] Blackstone, 'Elements' (n 11) 51.

[49] Blackstone, *Pantheon* (n 7) ii.

The poem relates a dream in which non-Christian religions are depicted as buildings occupying the four points of the compass. Thus Paganism appears as 'A lofty Temple . . . of cubic form but rising from the midst an ample dome', with (to the north) a 'pointed arch . . . delicate | With gothic pride and lavish ornament', to the east a wall encrusted with jewels, and to the south 'pointed obelisks'.[50] Westward stands 'an arch, on Dorian columns rais'd', which 'Supports the fabled Gods of ancient Greece, and Rome's proud tow'rs'.[51] Blackstone subsequently subdivides Christianity into '*Popery, Sectarism,* and *true Religion*', by which he means the Church of England 'the most pure and Apostolical upon Earth'. These divisions he represents as three distinct architectural styles: 'Popery' is associated with 'a lordly pile' in 'gay Corinthian mode, | Rich with luxurient art and wanton pride'.[52] Protestant 'Sectarism' he describes as being 'Of clumsy Tuscan dress, unhewn and rude'.[53] The Church of England, however, is envisioned as a 'beauteous dome, whose marble portal, [is] deck'd | With chaste Ionic ornaments' and indeed 'our sacred structure'.[54]

This depiction of religious beliefs and movements in architectural terms was carried over into Blackstone's legal writings. In an early letter of 1746 to his uncle Seymour Richmond he mused:

> I have sometimes thought that the Common Law, as it stood in Littleton's Days, resembled a regular Edifice: where the Apartments were properly disposed, leading one into another without Confusion; where every part was subservient to the whole, all uniting in one beautiful Symmetry: & every Room had its distinct Office allotted to it. But as it is now, swol'n, shrunk, curtailed, enlarged, altered & mangled by various & contradictory Statutes &c; it resembles the same Edifice, with many of its most useful Parts pulled down, with preposterous Additions in other Places, of different Materials & coarse Workmanship according to the Whim, or Prejudice, or private Convenience of the Builders. By which means the Communication of the Parts is destroyed, & their Harmony quite annihilated; & now it remains a huge, irregular Pile, with many noble Apartments, though awkwardly put together, & some of them of no visible Use at present. But if one desires to know why they were built, to what End or Use, how they communicated with the rest & the like; he must necessarily carry in his Head the Model of the old House, which will be the only Clue to guide him through this new Labyrinth.[55]

An adapted version occurs more than ten years later in his inaugural lecture as Vinerian Professor of English Law in October 1758. The 'common law of England', he then declared,

[50] *Ibid* 9–13.
[51] Blackstone, *Pantheon* (n 7) 14.
[52] *Ibid* 22–3.
[53] *Ibid* 24.
[54] *Ibid* 27, 30.
[55] *Letters* 4.

> has fared like other venerable edifices of antiquity, which rash and unexperienced workmen have ventured to new-dress and refine, with all the rage of modern improvement. Hence frequently its symmetry has been destroyed, its proportions distorted, and its majestic simplicity exchanged for specious embellishments and fantastic novelties.[56]

The fully developed, polished metaphor graces his concluding remarks in the final volume of the *Commentaries* in 1769. 'It hath been the endeavour of these commentaries', he writes,

> however the execution may have succeeded, to examine [the common law's] solid foundations, to mark out its extensive plan, to explain the use and distribution of its parts, and from the harmonious concurrence of those several parts to demonstrate the elegant proportion of the whole. We have taken occasion to admire at every turn the noble monuments of ancient simplicity, and the more curious refinements of modern art. Nor have its faults been concealed from view; for faults it has, lest we should be tempted to think it of more than human structure: defects, chiefly arising from the decays of time, or the rage of unskilful improvements in later ages. To sustain, to repair, to beautify this noble pile, is a charge entrusted principally to the nobility, and such gentlemen of the kingdom, as are delegated by their country to parliament. The protection of THE LIBERTY OF BRITAIN is a duty which they owe to themselves, who enjoy it; to their ancestors, who transmitted it down; and to their posterity, who will claim at their hands, this the best birthright, and noblest inheritance of mankind.[57]

Over some two decades, then, Blackstone extended and refined the image which he appears to have first conceived in 1746. By 1769 it no longer simply represents the law as an edifice but equates that edifice with liberty itself, charging his readers with the maintenance and restoration of the same structure as part of their birthright.

There are indications that the compilation of the 'Abridgement', and especially, of the 'Elements' influenced the methodology, structure and anti-feudalism of the *Commentaries*. In his *Analysis of the Laws of England*, first published in 1756, Blackstone had explained that before Henry VIII's reign, Glanville, Bracton, Britton and 'the author of Fleta' were too concerned with 'ancient' learning to integrate their works into a modern systemisation.[58] He rejected the alphabetical arrangements of Fitzherbert, and Brook as the least acceptable 'of any to convey the Rudiments of a Science'. He regretted the 'narrowness' of Bacon's methodology which consists of 'dis-joined Aphorisms' and declared Coke's *Institutes* (1628) 'unfortunately as deficient in Method as they are rich in

[56] *Commentaries* vol 1, p 10 ('Introduction'): first published as *A Discourse on the Study of the Law* (Oxford, 1758).

[57] *Commentaries* vol 4, p 436.

[58] W Blackstone, *An Analysis of the Laws of England* (Oxford, 1756) v.

Matter'. Wood's *Institute* (1713) had been so modernised as to leave the reader mystified as to the origins and purpose of some laws.[59] Blackstone preferred Sir Henry Finch's method, but found the end result badly written and obsolete. His own method he declares to be based upon Sir Matthew Hale's *Analysis of the Law* (1713), the 'most natural and scientifical of any, as well as the most comprehensive'.[60] Twenty years before Blackstone had selected Wotton's *Elements* as a methodological model for his 'Abridgement'. He integrated new sources into the 'Elements' but its preface still declares that 'the Method made use of, and many of the Observations, are borrowed from Sir Henry Wotton's *Elements*'. The process of evaluating and then selecting a previous study upon which to base his methodology is strikingly reminiscent of that followed in his earlier architectural writings.

Legal scholars have long pondered and debated the structure of the *Commentaries*.[61] Watson notes that the common law is made by judges in the light of precedent: strictly speaking, it has no structure. It is rather, as Blackstone says in the *Analysis*, an 'antient collection of unwritten maxims and customs', and as the *Commentaries* would have it, 'not committed to writing but only handed down by tradition, use, and experience'.[62] In this regard, knowledge of the common law was unlike that of architecture. Thus if Blackstone were to render it comprehensible to beginners and laymen as he intended, he had of necessity to draw a structure from an external source.[63] The *telos* of any treatise is to communicate knowledge. It does this best when information is presented in a structured, systematic way.[64] Perhaps, therefore, the most important thing about the structure of the *Commentaries* is that it actually has one. To render the previously formless common law comprehensible Blackstone not only needed a method, a structure, but he needed an analogy. He had already found it in architecture.

Just as significant for an understanding of the *Commentaries* is the relationship in Blackstone's attitudes to both gothic architecture and feudal law. The 'Elements' contained several disparaging remarks about gothic architecture. The most indicative example is found in chapter fourteen, 'Of Irregular and Spurious Orders', which informs us that the gothic style 'was certainly the Work of great Labour and Industry'. Yet he sees

> something oddly artificial in it. Huge ponderous Roofs being raised on slender Pillars, or rather Groups of Staves; great Masses of Stone, like Rocks, hanging in

[59] *Ibid* vi.

[60] *Ibid* vii.

[61] See eg A Watson, 'The Structure of Blackstone's *Commentaries*' (1988) 97 *Yale Law Journal* 795–815; A Alschuler, 'Rediscovering Blackstone' (1996) 145 *University of Pennsylvania Law Review* 1–55.

[62] Blackstone, *An Analysis* (n 58) xxxviii; *Commentaries* vol 1, p 17.

[63] Watson, 'The Structure' (n 61) 796.

[64] *Ibid*.

> the Air without any visibly sufficient Support, and threatening every instant to fall. Every thing is crammed with Roses, Lace, Crosses, Monkeys, and other Quaintnesses, which glut the eye instead of filling it, by means of such a profusion of silly Ornaments. Whereas in the Greek Architecture there is not a single Member or Ornament but has its Propriety as well as Beauty. Add to this, that unreasonable Thickness of Gothic Walls, their clumsy Buttresses, Pinacles, and Turrets, their sharp-pointed Arches and narrow Doors give it a heavy Look among all its trite and incongruous Embellishments.[65]

To be sure, Blackstone's antipathy to gothic architecture was based upon conventional prejudice, but also and significantly upon its divergence from the fundamental logic of classical design. He has two main criticisms. First, gothic buildings offend the eye because they appear unnecessarily 'heavy' and 'clumsy'. Secondly, they offend the mind because they are 'unreasonable'. The slender gothic pillars appear unable to support the 'great Masses of stone … threatening every instant to fall'. To put it another way, the point of the gothic buttresses and other contrivances to which Blackstone objects is to conceal and support the building's structure. Thus he concedes that gothic architecture involves some ingenious engineering but maintains that it is nevertheless not only ugly but illogical. The point of the classical orders on the other hand is to reveal the building's structure: to bear and be seen to bear the weight of the entablature and roof.

Furthermore, Blackstone makes an important distinction which illuminates the disdain for gothic, or feudal, law apparent in the *Commentaries*. He describes the final chapter of the *Commentaries*, 'Of the Rise, Progress, and Gradual Improvements, of the Laws of England', as an 'historical review … of the state of our laws'.[66] It is also is a succinct exposition of his view of feudal law. In summary, Blackstone sees the Anglo-Saxon King Alfred as the architect of an unwritten constitution and legal system designed to protect traditional English liberties. In this system the king functions as 'supreme magistrate' in whose person 'all the executive authority of the law was lodged, and from whom justice was dispersed to every part of the nation by distinct, yet communicating ducts and channels'.[67] His very phraseology here resonates with the image of the law as a building. He lists nine distinguishing features of Saxon laws and justice, including 'the constitution of parliament, or rather, general assemblies', elected magistrates, an hereditary monarchy, rarity of capital punishment for first offences, the requirement of military service in proportion to land ownership and the descent of land to all males equally. Serious cases were settled in the courts of justice, by the king in person, or a panel of civil and

65 Blackstone, 'Elements' (n 11) 58.
66 *Commentaries* vol 4, p 400.
67 *Ibid*, p 404.

ecclesiastical representatives, or by juries.[68] Saxon law was thus the 'law of liberty'.[69] Blackstone indeed perceived a fundamental logic in the Saxon legal system, just as he did in the beautiful simplicity of classical architecture.

The Normans were responsible for five deleterious changes to a generally more benevolent Saxon constitution. The first was the separation of ecclesiastical from civil courts. Second, new forestry laws not only depopulated large areas, but made game and its hunting a royal monopoly. Third, Norman judges were imposed upon, and the native language banned from, English courts, so transforming law from 'a plain rule of action' to 'a science of the greatest intricacy'.[70] Fourth was the introduction of trial by combat rather than by jury, and fifth the imposition of feudal land tenure, with an 'oppressive train of servile fruits and appendages'. The result was 'so complete and well concerted a scheme of servility' that 'it has been the work of generations … to redeem themselves and their posterity'. Hence in his own day courts were

> frequently obliged to have recourse to unaccountable fictions and circuities, in order to recover that equitable and substantial justice, which for a long time was buried under the narrow rules and fanciful niceties of metaphysical and Norman jurisprudence.[71]

The imposition of a foreign ecclesiastical and legal system in the wake of the Norman Conquest meant that his readers had inherited not a monument of ancient simplicity but, as he famously expressed it in Book III of the *Commentaries*,

> an old Gothic castle, erected in the days of chivalry, but fitted up for a modern inhabitant. The moated ramparts, the embattled towers, and the trophied halls, are magnificent and venerable, but useless. The inferior apartments, now converted into rooms of convenience, are chearful and commodious, though their approaches are winding and difficult.[72]

The specific mention of 'Gothic' is significant. In today's world architectural styles can seem, 'removed from the beliefs and public ceremonies which gave them their content', mere artistic convention .[73] But one of the consequences of discounting Blackstone's background when reading the *Commentaries* is that we fail to appreciate the power of his architectural

[68] *Commentaries* vol 4, pp 409, 405–7.
[69] *Ibid*, p 406.
[70] *Ibid*, p 409–10.
[71] *Ibid*, pp 413, 411.
[72] *Commentaries* vol 3, p 268.
[73] EB Smith, *Architectural Symbolism of Imperial Rome and the Middle Ages* (New York, 1978) 5.

symbolism. It would not have been lost on his contemporaries. One of Blackstone's most important authorities, Chambers' *Cyclopaedia*, states of gothic architecture:

> the ravages of the *Visigoths*, in the fifth century, destroyed all the most beautiful monuments of antiquity; and *Architecture* thence forwards, became so coarse and artless, that their professed architects understood nothing at all of just designing, wherein its whole beauty consists: hence a new manner of building took its rise, called the *Gothic*.[74]

Blackstone and many of his contemporaries understood gothic architecture very much in this light. Blackstone's gothic castle is symbolic of a labyrinthine degradation of the original edifice. It represents a 'hodgepodge' structure which generations of jurists had been forced to add to and modify in order to apply the law in a manner consistent with its original purpose. On another level, it could be seen as symbolic of the rule of a foreign and oppressive power: of political and cultural dominance. Whether he writes of the gothic cathedral in the 1740s, or of the law as a gothic castle in the 1760s, the edifice is not merely illogical and badly ornamented: it is also the architecture of oppression.

To conclude, his study of architecture may not have been entirely responsible for Blackstone's ability to systematise the large and complex body of knowledge that was the common law. However it does appear to have played an important role in developing his ability to visualise the common law as a coherent system, very much like the original plan of that old house to which he refers in 1746. Indeed, juxtaposing several versions of this metaphor suggests that Blackstone consciously developed it in order that the *Commentaries* should serve his reader quite literally, as 'the model of [an] old House' now in need of repair and restoration. This essay has merely sketched the breadth, depth and intellectual ramifications of Blackstone's architectural activities, to suggest that they throw new light upon his life, religious views and jurisprudence. Many questions remain. Above all, it seems that Blackstone was studying architecture and the law simultaneously. Therefore, if we are to understand both Blackstone the man and his *Commentaries* we must understand more deeply a consequent, and apparently fundamental, relationship in his thought between history, Christianity, architecture and the law.

[74] E Chambers, *Cyclopaedia: or, An Universal Dictionary of Arts and Sciences* (London, 1741) sv 'Architecture'.

3

'A Mighty Consumption of Ale'

Blackstone, Buckler and All Souls College, Oxford

NORMA AUBERTIN-POTTER*

AMONG THE MANY portraits that line the walls of the dining hall of All Souls College, Oxford, are those of two eighteenth-century fellows who played a vital role in the physical and financial restoration of the college. Ironically, the smaller is of the more famous man: William Blackstone, a fellow from 1744 until his marriage in 1761.[1] The larger portrait depicts Benjamin Buckler (1717–80), fellow from 1739 until his death in 1780.[2] The story of their close working relationship, as outlined in the following pages, underlines the point that Blackstone's life was anything but wholly devoted to legal theory or practice.

Blackstone had initially sought a fellowship in 1742 at the age of 19; although this first attempt was unsuccessful, he was elected the following year. By contrast Buckler was elected at his first attempt in 1739, having then already reached the more advanced age of 22 years. Only four years after his election young Blackstone was rapidly elevated to a college post, becoming bursar of laws in 1747. Although much his senior, Buckler's first college position, that of sub-warden, was not achieved until 1750. In discussing Blackstone's and Buckler's friendship, Dame Lucy Sutherland referred to the former as 'a past master in the art of presenting his own views through the mouths of others under his influence'. Buckler – 'a man of much wit and miscellaneous learning and absolutely no personal

* Norma Aubertin-Potter would like to thank Julie Blyth, Nigel Heard, Ian Maclean, Gaye Morgan, Sally Thompson and Judith Winchester.

[1] This is a copy of the 1774 Gainsborough portrait, now in Tate Britain, London; see below, p 235.

[2] The artist is unknown, the portrait itself was purchased by the college in 1956. Buckler and Blackstone both sat for Gainsborough in 1774: E Waterhouse, *Gainsborough* (London, 1966) 56.

ambition' was one such mouthpiece.[3] While there is a good deal in print on Blackstone and All Souls,[4] Buckler's activities in the College have been largely ignored. The four main areas in which both men played an important and mutually supportive role were the constitution and administration of the Codrington Library, the problem of founder's kin, the administration of the college estates, and – perhaps most important in the eyes of some of their colleagues – the establishment of the college's wine cellar.

Very little has been written about Buckler. Indeed a recent memoir by Leonard W. Cowie appears to be the only relatively detailed account of his life.[5] Briefly, Buckler was the youngest of three children born to Thomas and Mary Buckler of Boreham, a tiny hamlet just outside Warminster on Wiltshire's Salisbury Plain. Two branches of the Buckler family were then living in the area, one of Dissenters or Protestant non-conformists trading as maltsters, the other the gentry family of Benjamin's parents. Benjamin's eldest brother William, later to be known as Mr Counsellor Buckler, had, it seems, non-conformist leanings in common with those of his local relations.[6] Benjamin matriculated from Oriel College, Oxford, in February 1733;[7] he went on to receive his BA in 1736, was elected to a Robinson exhibition at Oriel in 1737, and graduated MA in 1739. Ordained a deacon in 1741, he became a priest in 1748. But it was not until 1755 that Buckler acquired his first ecclesiastical benefice as the vicar of Cumnor, a village on the outskirts of the city of Oxford, then in Berkshire, now part of Oxfordshire. Next year Buckler was appointed to the Berkshire living of Frilsham, while in 1769 he gained that of Kingston Pitney, Somerset. Both Cumnor and Frilsham were under the patronage of the then nearly bankrupt Bertie family and at the time Blackstone was heavily involved in trying to restore their finances. While this fact may explain the appointment of Buckler to these two Berkshire livings, there is no clue as to the reason for his appointment to the living of Kingston Pitney, unless perhaps some connection with his mother's family, as she originated from Horsington, Somerset.

[3] *HUO* 140.

[4] See most recently P Neill, 'Blackstone, Oxford, and the Law' in SJD Green and P Horden (ed), *All Souls under the Ancien Régime: Politics, Learning, and the Arts, c. 1600–1850* (Oxford, 2007) 268–98.

[5] CA Buckler, *Bucleriana: notices of the Family Buckler* (London, 1886); LW Cowie, 'Buckler, Benjamin (1716/17–1780), antiquary': *ODNB*.

[6] HM Gunn, *The History of Nonconformity in Warminster* (Warminster, 1853) 28.

[7] J Foster, *Alumni Oxonienses, 1715–1886* (London, 1887–88) vol 1, p 184

In many ways Buckler was Blackstone's perfect college counterpart to Blackstone. From its first foundation the fellows of All Souls were divided between 'lawyers' and 'artists'; in the college academic structure Blackstone was on the law side and Buckler on that of the artists.[8] In the eighteenth century the college's governing body included both a bursar of laws and one of arts. These positions were held for a year, with appointments or elections made by the warden, sub-warden, two deans and six other fellows. Buckler was bursar of arts twice, in 1753 and again in 1771; Blackstone served as bursar of laws in 1747 and 1751. Buckler was dean of arts on nine occasions, the last being in 1780. Blackstone held the corresponding position of dean of laws in 1746, 1748 and 1750. So it is apparent that after a late start in gaining, or perhaps desiring, admittance to the higher levels of the governing body, Buckler regularly held office at All Souls. His belated rise to the higher collegiate hierarchy may well have owed something to the encouragement and support of his friend Blackstone.

At the time of Buckler's and indeed Blackstone's entrance into the fellowship, All Souls College must have resembled a building site. From 1703 until his death in 1736, Dr George Clarke,[9] with his chosen architect Nicholas Hawksmoor, oversaw the new building work in the Great Quadrangle. This undertaking included the magnificent Codrington Library begun in 1716, the Common Room and South Tower (also commenced that year), and work on the Wharton Room range and the North Tower begun in 1720. When Clarke and Hawksmoor both died in 1736 the buildings were in various stages of completion. By the time of Buckler's election in 1739, work on the new Library had been halted because of lack of funds to complete the grand scheme.[10] The exterior was complete but there was uncertainty as to Hawksmoor's intentions for the interior, except that it should include a two-tiered gallery. In April 1740 James Gibbs, then engaged in building the adjacent Radcliffe Camera, recommended a reduction to only one gallery. By 1743 the interior woodwork of the building had proceeded to such an extent that a number of fellows were issued with library keys, Buckler having key 25, and Blackstone starting off with key 9, although later switching to number 37.[11] From the beginning Blackstone to have been drawn to the new

[8] In 1438 Archbishop Chichele had divided the fellowship into 24 'Artists', who were to study philosophy or theology, and 16 'Jurists', who studied canon and civil law.

[9] *ODNB;* fellow 1680–1736. By the time of his death in 1736 Clarke had fallen out with his All Souls' colleagues, and consequently left his estate and collection of architectural drawings to Worcester College, Oxford.

[10] H Colvin and JSG Simmons, *All Souls: An Oxford College and its Buildings* (Oxford, 1989).

[11] All Souls College, Warden's MS 42. It is interesting that not all of the then current fellowship received keys.

Library building.[12] In 1747 he signed a minute authorising Jeremiah Franklin to complete the woodwork in the new Library.[13] One year later, a John Franklin was dismissed for not completing this task. The relationship of Jeremiah and John has not been traced, but Blackstone seems to have been unaware that the former had died in 1748—a possible indication that Blackstone was heavy-handed in his dealings with staff. A college minute of 26 August 1748 announced a revised plan of the new building on show in the bursary. Was this Blackstone's handiwork? His brother-in-law James Clitherow thought so: in his biographical preface to Blackstone's *Law Reports* he tells us that his subject 'rectified several Mistakes in the Architecture'.[14]

With building work nearing completion, thoughts turned to furnishing the new Library. Blackstone was commissioned to order vases and busts to line the top of the gallery, and to talk to the sculptor Roubiliac[15] about a bust of Henry Chichele for the Library ante-room, where it is still to be found today. In July 1751 while Bursar, Blackstone was authorised to purchase five mahogany desks on castors and two large tables to stand at either end of the Library. These desks and tables are still in daily use.

The new Library was now ready to receive the books and manuscripts shelved in the college's original medieval library, as also ten thousand volumes bequeathed by Christopher Codrington. Henceforth Buckler was an almost permanent member of the Library committee, and can be seen to play a vital role in the development and running of the Codrington Library. The original Library regulations, possibly drafted by Blackstone, were signed by the college fellowship on 8 November 1751.[16] The signatures of Blackstone and Buckler follow immediately after those of the warden and sub-warden. Blackstone's signature on Library resolutions appears nine times between 1754 and December 1761, whereas Buckler's hand recurs regularly from 1751 to 1775. On 5 December 1751, Buckler was among the signatories of a resolution ordering a catalogue of the collection. From the outset care of the fabric was a major priority. Buckler signed a Library

[12] For his 'Elements of Architecture' (1747), now All Souls MS 333, see ch 2 above, pp 17–23 and passim.

[13] Codrington Library, Acta in Capitulis, 1707–1753, 21 August 1747. On 23 December 1730 Jeremiah Franklin had been contracted to complete the Library. CT Martin, *Catalogue of the Archives . . . of All Souls' College* (London, 1877) 295. Jeremiah had married on 2 July 1699, Catherine the daughter of William Townsend, the mason engaged on the stonework of the new buildings: Oxfordshire Family History Society, *Oxfordshire Marriage Index, 1538–1837*. HM Colvin, 'The Townsends of Oxford: A Firm of Georgian Master-Masons and Its Accounts' (2000) 10 *Georgian Group Journal* 43–60.

[14] Clitherow, 'Memoirs' viii.

[15] Louis François Roubiliac (c.1705–1762). An assistant to Sir Henry Cheere, Roubiliac was paid fifty guineas for the work: R Gunnis, *Dictionary of British sculptors, 1660–1851* (London, 1968) 331; see also below, pp 238–9.

[16] All Souls College, Codrington Library Minute Book (8 November 1751–8 December 1945).

minute in January 1753 authorising payment of thirty shillings to reimburse Isabel Haskins for her purchase of mops and brooms, and allowing her three pounds a year to wash and sweep the building.[17] Blackstone and Buckler both signed an entry later that year whereby Howell Harris, a clerk, was to be paid twelve guineas for pasting bookplates bearing the college's arms into all Library books.

Most entries in the Library committee's minutes concerned books to be purchased, or indeed duplicates to be sold. Both men signed the minute of 9 May 1755 for the purchase of Samuel Johnson's newly published *Dictionary of the English Language*. While on several occasions Blackstone was authorised to purchase law books, Buckler signed on 13 July 1758 a resolution authorising purchase of Peter Whalley's proposed edition of John Bridges's *Northamptonshire*. Buckler himself had originally been commissioned to undertake the completion of Bridges's text for the sum of £600, but then declined the task 'as too complicated'[18] in favour of Whalley, a fellow of St. John's College, Oxford.[19] On 16 December 1762 it was decided to purchase Guthrie's Peerage,[20] a work Buckler evidently found 'useless', and so annotated the minute book entry. This judgement may possibly reflect his experience of that work gained in examining the pedigrees of prospective fellows claiming precedence as 'founder's kin'. Buckler was also a signatory to the purchase of Diderot's *Encyclopédie* on 21 June 1764.[21]

The archives of the College also demanded attention from Blackstone and Buckler. On 7 September 1767 Buckler signed an entry ordering shelves to be provided in the 'Record Room' for rolls and papers, doubtless in consequence of the re-arrangement of the College muniments previously undertaken by Blackstone. While there is no direct evidence to substantiate the suggestion, it seems likely Buckler had assisted with this task.[22] Buckler certainly re-numbered and re-arranged into three volumes the greater part of the college's collection of the drawings of Christopher Wren (a former fellow) acquired in 1751. At that time Blackstone was bursar of laws, and Buckler sub-warden; it was Blackstone who had organised the purchase of

[17] Isabel Haskins also cleaned the Chapel; payments to her appear regularly in the Titling Books at this time: Bodleian Library, MSS D.D. All Souls e 267–9.

[18] J Nichols, *Literary Anecdotes of the Eighteenth Century* (London, 1812) vol 2, p 107.

[19] CRJ Currie and CP Lewis, *A Guide to English County Histories* (Stroud, 1997) 293–4.

[20] W Guthrie *A Complete History of the English Peerage* (London, 1763). First published in monthly parts, this title is no longer in the Codrington Library.

[21] D Diderot, *Encyclopédie*. Not all vols had yet been printed; this entry possibly relates to vols 1–4, then in print. The Library does have the complete set although it is not mentioned again in the minutes. Prof Ian Maclean, Fellow Librarian of All Souls College, has pointed out that in some entries Buckler's French spelling is incorrect, suggesting that he was not a French speaker or scholar.

[22] As University Archivist from 1777–80, Buckler compiled an index which is still in use: RL Poole, *A Lecture on the History of the University Archives* (Oxford, 1912) 26.

429 drawings for the sum of £21 from the estate of Dr Thomas Slack. For some reason Buckler did not complete his task, arranging only 324 of the drawings purchased.

By the late 1760s the Codrington Library's ceiling was showing signs of wear and tear. The problem was found to be the weight of the lead roof bearing down heavily on the beams, and on 7 February 1770 Buckler signed the order for the roof to be covered in Westmorland slate. The resulting thirty to forty tons of lead were put on display in the cloisters to be sold by 'Holloway' presumably at auction.[23] Buckler last wrote an entry in the Library Minute Book on 13 July 1780; suffering from arthritis, his signature was shaky. The previous entry, on 18 January 1780, again signed by Buckler, provided for the acquisition of three significant contemporary works on printing and typography: 'Bowyer's 2 Tracts on Printing, More's on Founders, Caslon's Fell's & Oxford Types'.[24] Buckler shared Blackstone's keen interest in the art, history and science of printing. Having been Blackstone's willing aide in the reform of the Oxford University Press,[25] in 1759 Buckler presented to the Library what is now one of its greatest treasures, William Caxton's '1493' printing of John Gower's *Confessio Amantis*.

In 1750 while dean of laws Blackstone turned his attention to the cellars under the Codrington Library and the east range of the Great Quadrangle. Hawksmoor had insisted that vaulted cellars should be constructed under the whole single-storeyed library building, 'other wayes the books will suffer much'.[26] But no other use seems to have been suggested for this large space. Richard Graves tells us that Blackstone's intention was that

> the sober part of the College might drink a pint, or even half a pint of good wine, and return to their studies, without going to the tavern across the street; where the jovial part went after dinner, to drink bad wine; and where they were often tempted, I fear, to loiter a good part of the afternoon.[27]

Blackstone himself notoriously 'composed his *Commentaries* with a bottle of port before him; and found his mind invigorated and supported in the fatigue of his great work, by a temperate use of it'.[28] From 1750 to 1759 the College Wine Book is largely in Blackstone's handwriting. An entry of 23 March 1750 sets out his justification for overhauling the previous

[23] *Jackson's Oxford Journal*, 17 February 1773.

[24] ie C Middleton, *The Origin of Printing in Two Essays* (London, 1776); ER Mores, *A Dissertation upon English Typographical Founders and Founderies* (London, 1778); W Caslon, *A Specimen of Printing Types* (London,1766).

[25] IG Philip, *William Blackstone and the Reform of the Oxford University Press in the Eighteenth Century* (Oxford, 1955).

[26] Colvin and Simmons (n 10) 86–90.

[27] R Graves, *The Triflers* (London, 1806) 56.

[28] J Boswell, *Life of Johnson*, ed RW Chapman (Oxford, 1960) 1135–6.

system; accounts 'being much confused & mistaken, through the inaccuracy of servants' it was necessary 'to restate the whole'. A list in the manuscript shows the allocation of the bins in the Library cellar to Fellows; Blackstone himself had Bin 2 and Buckler Bin 4. Twelve Fellows were allocated their own bin; the remaining bins held wine purchased by the college, for instance Bin 6 was full of rum and white wine. The cellars were replenished in spring and autumn. Fellows were to provide their own bottles if requiring wine 'from the pipe' (that is, in bulk), when the cost was 5s. 6d. a gallon. Blackstone and Buckler both purchased port and other wine on a regular basis. Thus on 14 November 1757 Blackstone bought twenty bottles of port for £6 and Buckler eighteen bottles of port for £5 8s 0d Buckler also had a liking for Madeira, paying £3 3s 0d for eighteen bottles on 19 December 1766.[29]

While Blackstone was arranging the cellars, Buckler published (anonymously) his *Oinos Krithinos: Dissertation concerning the Origin and Antiquity of Barley Wine*.[30] This brief parody of biblical and classical scholarship, complete with a table of 66 'Authors quoted in the foregoing Treatise', purports to trace the historical development of 'strong Liquors' as the means by which, after the Fall, mankind could 'raise a gaiety and briskness of spirit'. In mock apology, by way of conclusion, the author protested that 'if in treating of so many useful particulars, I have been too tedious, I have only to ask pardon, and to promise that I will never give myself further trouble about Ale or Beer, unless for my own drinking'.[31] Judging by the rosy cheeks in his portrait, we may safely assume that he kept that promise!

Blackstone also dealt with the college estates. On 20 May 1749 he was appointed by Warden Niblett Steward of Edgware manor 'and elsewhere', a position he was to hold until 1759.[32] Almost immediately he began a book of leases and rents that was to be kept in the bursary.[33] In 1753 he compiled a notebook of a 'rental of the Manor of Edgware and Kingsbury with its Members in the County of Middlesex'.[34] The position of Steward of Edgware provided financial benefits, in that the holder of the post was entitled to all the fees arising from business relating to the estate.[35] Buckler also maintained an interest in the management of the College's landed property; as early as 1741 his colleague Peregrine Palmer (fellow 1724–42)

[29] Bodleian Library, MS D.D. All Souls e 332.

[30] B Buckler, *Oinos Krithinos: Dissertation concerning the Origin and Antiquity of Barley Wine* (Oxford, 1750) sig A2.

[31] *Oinos Krithinos* (n 80) 38.

[32] Bodleian Library, MS D.D. All Souls c 266.

[33] All Souls College, Warden's MS 42.

[34] Bodleian Library, MS D.D. All Souls c 245.

[35] All Souls College, Warden's MS 22, vol. 3, fo 22.

gave him a notebook containing an account of the College estates in 1682.[36] Buckler added entries to this document when he was sub-warden in 1750 and 1751.

In 1753 Buckler was elected bursar for the first time and seemingly asked his friend Blackstone to advise him how best to discharge this responsibility. The result was a 'Dissertation on the Accounts of All Souls College', in which Blackstone provided a detailed description of how each office and department of the college estates worked, and how to keep the account books in order.[37] He wrote that 'The method of keeping our Accounts is a very particular & exact one; & is, of consequence, rather more minute & tedious in some instances than could be wished'.[38] One way to stay in credit was to make sure that the baker delivered to the college not 13 (a baker's dozen) but 14 loaves, and that the fellows paid one penny for each loaf, making a profit for the bursar of two pence on every dozen. It was also essential to ensure that the fellows paid a high price for any beer consumed. One can only hope that Buckler understood the niceties of totalling the figures:

> if A's Battels and Debetur are equal to A's Allocates & B's Allocates & Debet are equal to B's Battels, it of course follows that A's Battels and Debetur, joined with B's Battels, will be equal to B's Allocates & Debet, joined with A's Allocates: For if two equal Sums be respectively be added to two equal sums, the Totals will be also respectively equal.[39]

One further service that both Blackstone and Buckler performed for the college was to address the thorny question of founder's kin, whereby an individual could be preferentially elected to the fellowship on proving his descent from one of Henry Chichele's two brothers, Robert and William. A detailed genealogical pedigree must be submitted to and accepted by the warden and college officers before an election was made. In the early eighteenth century the college had started to look at such claims more closely, refusing them not only on the grounds of remoteness of relationship and inadequate proof of descent, but also for lack of learning and moral defects on the part of the candidate. In 1749 Blackstone acted as counsel for the college in the case of one Henry Bennet, whose pedigree had been rejected on the grounds that he was too distantly related to

[36] All Souls College, Warden's MS 80.

[37] For many years it was believed that MS 300, housed in the Codrington Library, was the only copy of the 'Dissertation'. But Derrick Arkley, the college accountant, recently found in the bursary a second contemporary copy with additions by subsequent bursars. On brief examination the two mss appear to be identical; my page references are to the 1898 Roxburghe Club edition by Sir William Anson.

[38] 'Dissertation on the Accounts' 4.

[39] *Ibid* 8.

Chichele.[40] The College lost the case and was ordered to pay costs. Next year Blackstone published his *Essay upon Collateral Consanguinity*,[41] which argued that descent from Chichele could no longer be satisfactorily proven. In this connection Blackstone and Buckler had both consulted the Bodleian Library's MS Tanner 340 on a number of occasions. While that volume includes letters and reports on many subjects, its main interest for Blackstone and Buckler lay in some late seventeenth-century papers relating to an earlier investigation into the election of fellows during the wardenship of Thomas Jeames.[42] Faced again with the successful appeal of Richard Harvey 'having proved his pedigree'[43] on being refused a fellowship in the elections of November 1750, Blackstone drafted a letter on behalf of the warden to the college's visitor, Archbishop Thomas Herring, seeking 'Resolution of certain Doubts which had arisen upon our Founder's Statute with regard to the Election of Fellows'.[44]

Blackstone's *Essay* found favour with most of the fellowship. On 18 December 1758 the college was asked whether 'any had objections' to a proposal that Blackstone 'be at liberty to publish some Collections made from the Pedigrees in the College and other books and Papers, of the several familys related to the Founder'. This was agreed 'without a division, provided he publisht meerly as private person', without claiming any 'sanction or authority of the college'.[45] The eventual result was *Stemmata Chicheleana* (1765), edited by Buckler on Blackstone's behalf,[46] a work setting out 284 individual pedigrees for families whose pedigrees had been proved between 1457 and 1763. In 1775 a supplement was printed, the edition to be paid for by the college and reimbursed from the sale of the volumes.[47] In this supplement, again edited by Buckler, a further 243 pedigrees were added, together with revised information on some of the pedigrees in the earlier edition. That Buckler was given John Honywood's[48] pedigree to examine in September 1767, before the latter's

[40] GD Squibb, *Founders' Kin: Privilege and Pedigree* (Oxford, 1972), 63–4; Prest, *Blackstone* 86–8. See also J Davis, 'Founder's Kin' in SJD Green and P Horden, *All Souls Under the Ancien Regime* (n 4) 233–67.

[41] *An Essay upon Collateral Consanguinity, Its Limits, Extent, and Duration* (London and Oxford, 1750).

[42] Blackstone called up this manuscript in the Bodleian Library on 23 January. 1746, 3 March 1748, 17 October 1750 and 4 April. 1752, while Buckler saw it on 16 and 20 April 1752: Bodleian Library Records, MS e 555, e 556, e 558.

[43] Martin (n 13) 369 (no 587).

[44] *Ibid* (no 582).

[45] Codrington Library, Warden's MS 36.

[46] *Stemmata Chicheleana or, a genealogical account of some of the families derived from Thomas Chichele, of Higham Ferrers in the County of Northampton* (Oxford, 1765).

[47] Codrington Library, Acta in Capitulis, 28 April 1775. *A Supplement to the Stemmata Chicheleana, containing corrections & very large additions to the tables of descents from Thomas Chichele* (Oxford, 1775).

[48] John Honywood, fellow 1767–81.

election as fellow, suggests that the college by then looked upon him as the semi-official chronicler and gatekeeper of founder's kin. It has been suggested that Buckler deliberately excluded from these published pedigrees any non-gentry or noble families, in order to ensure that the college retained its social exclusivity for the 'charmed circle of county families', although this cannot be proved from the surviving documents.[49]

Buckler was elected sub-warden in 1750 and 1751; this was a post Blackstone never held, for despite his work on behalf of the college, he was not universally popular. In April 1759, Blackstone and Radcliffe Howord[50] were candidates for the office of sub-warden; Howord was elected because certain members of the fellowship felt Blackstone could not legally remain a fellow while holding the Vinerian Professorship in English Law.[51] Buckler had been one of the committee members (or Delegates) charged with administering the estate which Charles Viner had bequeathed to establish a chair in the common law at Oxford. Opposition to Blackstone was led by John White,[52] who called on Warden Niblett on 20 April 1759 to request an enquiry into Blackstone's status by the officers of the college.[53] The resultant meeting on 27 April 1759 had to consider not only White's claim but the counter-claim of Blackstone—that White himself could not hold a fellowship, as he was also a salaried curate. After deliberation it was agreed unanimously that 'the said Professorship is not anyway under the statute of the College'[54] and therefore Blackstone could retain his fellowship while holding the Vinerian Chair.

Blackstone wrote to the Warden on 7 May 1761 telling him of his marriage to Sarah, the eldest sister of James Clitherow,[55] and on 6 November 1761 his fellowship was declared void.[56] By now Buckler was established as a reliable member of college and continued to be elected to internal posts. Yet only one historian of the college, Montagu Burrows, has recognised Buckler's contribution as 'one of the most useful of its members.'[57] On 10 June 1766 Buckler officiated at the funeral service of Warden Stephen Niblett, who was buried in the chapel near to his wife who had died in February 1765.[58] In 1776 Buckler purchased a new Register of Admissions for the College.[59] One of his last acts, in May 1778,

[49] Squibb, *Founders' Kin* 48.

[50] Fellow 1737–68.

[51] Codrington Library, Warden's MS 36; Prest, *Blackstone* 159–60.

[52] Fellow 1740–64.

[53] Codrington Library,Warden's MS 36.

[54] *Ibid.*

[55] Fellow 1750–53.

[56] Codrington Library, Warden's MS 36.

[57] *Worthies of All Souls: Four Centuries of English History* (London, 1874) 419.

[58] *Jackson's Oxford Journal*, 1 June 1766. Niblett had been a fellow 1720–26 and warden 1726–66.

[59] Codrington Library, Acta in Capitulis, 11 November 1776.

was to have his servant, Thomas White, matriculated into Oxford University. This is not so unusual as it sounds, since many local tradesmen who served the University and its colleges enjoyed the privileged status conferred by matriculation.

This is not the place to discuss in detail Blackstone's and Buckler's substantial involvement with the local politics and administration of the city of Oxford itself: but it is worth mentioning that both were to the fore in the ill-tempered 1754 Oxfordshire county election.[60] They also served as administrators of the bequest to Queen's College, Oxford of John Michel, a bequest which maintained eight fellows and four scholars. On 8 July 1780, five months before his death, Buckler as the senior surviving administrator appointed Dr Thomas Wenman[61] of All Souls to take the place of the deceased Blackstone.[62]

It was perhaps appropriate that these two close friends should both die within the same year, Blackstone on 14 February 1780, and Buckler from a stroke on Christmas Eve 1780.[63] Buckler, 'One of Mr Justice Blackstone's oldest and most intimate Friends' had previously declined an invitation to write a biographical memoir as a preface to his published law reports.[64] Blackstone's will, composed on 4 October 1778,[65] left Buckler and three other 'worthy friends' each a ring to the value of 20 shillings. Written somewhat earlier, in November 1774, Buckler's will[66] appointed his brother William as executor and expressed the wish that the fellows of All Souls should not feel compelled to attend his funeral. To Warden Tracy he left all his books, manuscripts and papers relating to the college, its administration and estates. He also bequeathed £200 for the use of the college's clerks and choristers. Blackstone and Warden Tracy were also entrusted with the investment of £100, the interest of which was to be used to provide Bibles and prayer books for the parish church at Cumnor, and to receive for their trouble 5 guineas to buy a silver tumbler, on which they were to have his name engraved.

In December 1780 the fellows of All Souls College decided to erect a statue to Blackstone. Buckler immediately added a codicil to his will leaving £50 towards the cost, in 'Memory of my dear Friend Sir William Blackstone'. Buckler's signature on this document was witnessed by Warden Tracy and two others to prove that the signature was Buckler's; by

[60] R J Robson, *The Oxfordshire Election of 1754: A Study in the Interplay of City, County and University Politics* (Oxford, 1949).

[61] Fellow 1765–96.

[62] Oxfordshire Record Office. Thame II/ii/13.

[63] *Jackson's Oxford Journal*, 24 December 1780. JJ Daniell, *The History of Warminster* (Warminster, 1879) 230.

[64] Clitherow, 'Memoirs' ii.

[65] TNA, PROB 11/1061.

[66] TNA, PROB 11/1073.

now his arthritis had become so severe he could hardly hold a pen. The codicil poses a problem for the historian, because while both *Jackson's Oxford Journal* and the memorial in Cumnor Church say that Buckler died on 24 December, the codicil is dated 26 December.

John Bacon's statue of Blackstone now stands in the Codrington Library, appropriately above part of his wine cellar. There is no college memorial to Buckler, other than two portraits, one hanging in hall, the other (depicting a much younger man) in the Warden's Lodgings. However a fulsome memorial tablet is to be found in Cumnor Church, where Buckler was buried as he wished in the churchyard on 27 December 1780. The *Gentleman's Magazine* of 1792 tells us that Blackstone himself had composed the inscription, which speaks of Buckler's devotion to his college and university, his 'sound mind' and 'good conscience': a 'mean action was his contempt'.[67]

The surviving manuscript evidence makes it apparent that Blackstone and Buckler worked closely to bring some order to the daily running of All Souls College. Much of the administrative structure which they established for the estates, the bursarship, the wine cellar, and the Codrington Library still exists today. But Buckler and Blackstone seem not to have shared an interest in matters legal. Perhaps that explains why they remained such close friends. They worked together on college affairs, but Buckler did not encroach upon his friend's legal activities, and so did not threaten what became Blackstone's chief raison d'etre.[68]

[67] *Gentleman's Magazine* (1792) 224–5. Buckler signed the Library Minute of 26 April 1770 authorising purchase of the 'complete collection of the Gentleman's & London Magazines'. Of course it is not impossible that Blackstone wrote this eulogy for his friend some time before his own death.

[68] Buckler's *A Proper Explanation of the Oxford Almanack for this Present Year MDCCLV* (London, 1755) claims that he had been informed about 'a Maxim in the Canon Law', without stating from whom or where this information came (13); we might reasonably suppose that Blackstone was the source.

4

William Blackstone and William Prynne

An Unlikely Association?

IAN DOOLITTLE

AT FIRST SIGHT there seems little to connect William Blackstone and William Prynne.[1] The former is renowned as the author of the *Commentaries on the Laws of England* whose elegant defence of the British constitution earned him Bentham's sobriquet 'everything-as-it should-be Blackstone'. The latter is most widely remembered as the scourge of Archbishop Laud, whose ears were cropped not once but twice. Blackstone's success with his pen led to Parliament, the Bench and extensive Thames-side property. Prynne's ferocious pamphleteering produced no wealth, only more controversy. Blackstone had nine children; Prynne was a bachelor. The smooth, rationalising prose of the *Commentaries* was far distant from Prynne's argumentative, angular compilations. Blackstone's references were occasional, gentle reminders at the foot of the page; Prynne's were constant, thudding challenges at the side of the text: hence *his* sobriquet, Marginal Prynne. Blackstone was painted by Thomas Gainsborough and sculpted by John Bacon. His pride in his judicial stature and his great work, not to mention his comfortable stoutness, are all too evident. The best Prynne could manage was a Wenceslaus Hollar etching. He scowls at us, his gaunt face framed by long hair which performs a service very different from Blackstone's wig.

It is true that recent scholarship has blurred some of these snapshots. On the one hand, Blackstone has been rescued from Bentham's self-serving vitriol. We can now see clearly how Blackstone was simply a dialectical

[1] For details of Blackstone's life see Doolittle, *Blackstone* and Prest, *Blackstone* (which appeared after this essay had been completed). For Prynne the definitive biography is W Lamont, *Marginal Prynne* (1963). Lamont also wrote the *ODNB* entry.

convenience in Bentham's campaign for law reform.[2] He was fully aware of those aspects of the legal system which required amendment, at least to alleviate arbitrary criminal 'justice'.[3] And he never entirely lost an Oxford Tory's suspicion of Westminster power and pride in an Englishman's freedoms.[4] Likewise Prynne is now taken much more seriously. His angry, jolting journey from anti-Laudian polemicist in the 1630s, through Presbyterian (initially anti-Independent) pamphleteer in the 1640s and ancient constitutionalist in the 1650s to monarchist-historian in the 1660s, has been described, convincingly, as underpinned by principles which, if not entirely consistent, were certainly deep-seated.[5] Nevertheless, despite this revisionism, Blackstone and Prynne remain far apart. The snapshots may have lost their focus but they remain portraits, not caricatures.

I BLACKSTONE'S COLLECTION

It is therefore surprising to discover Blackstone's close interest in the works of William Prynne. When he died in 1780 Blackstone bequeathed to his (main) Oxford college, All Souls, a collection of no fewer than 129 works by, attributed to or otherwise connected with Prynne.[6] Even allowing for the few spurious or third-party works, the collection bears comparison with that used to compile the best bibliography of Prynne's work, ie at the Huntington Library (which has 181 originals) and with that at Prynne's Oxford College, Oriel (which has 140).[7] Blackstone's collection clearly deserves the epithet 'remarkable' conferred by its former custodian at the

[2] A host of texts could be cited on Bentham/Blackstone. See, for example, JH Burns, 'Bentham and Blackstone: a lifetime's dialectic' in GJ Schochet, PE Tatspaugh and C Brobeck (ed), *Empire and Revolutions* (Washington DC, 1993) 261–78 and R Cross, 'Blackstone v. Bentham' (1976) 92 *Law Quarterly Review* 516. See also my 'Jeremy Bentham and Blackstone's Lectures' (1982) 6 *Bentham Newsletter* 23

[3] Sir William Holdsworth was probably the first to draw proper attention to this: 'Some Aspects of Blackstone and his Commentaries' (1932) 4 *Cambridge Law Journals* 261, 273.

[4] Doolittle, *Blackstone*, ch 3. I have also described Blackstone's politics in 'Sir William Blackstone and his *Commentaries on the Laws of England* (1765–9): A Biographical Approach' (1982) 3 *Oxford Journal of Legal Studies* 99 at 104. I use 'Tory' with reservations: it is a convenient shorthand and certainly has merit up to (say) 1754; but I can understand Professor Thomas's exasperation with Professor Colley's conflation of the terms Tory and Country Gentleman throughout the 1715–60 period : PDG Thomas, 'Sir Roger Newdigate's Essays on Party, c1760' (1987) 102 *English Historical Review* 394. For an example, involving Blackstone himself, see L Colley, *In Defiance of Oligarchy* (Cambridge, 1982) 284 and fn 54 (359).

[5] See Lamont's concluding remarks in his *ÓDNB* article.

[6] Blackstone's will is in TNA, PROB 11/1061/61. The Codrington reference is SR 54 d. 1–18 (or 19). For the provenance of the volumes and other bibliographical issues, see the Appendix to this chapter. The total given in the text is mine. The figures are taken from the indexes at the front of each volume, prepared by Blackstone and others.

[7] MI Fry and G Davies, 'William Prynne in the Huntington Library' (1956) 20 *Huntington Library Quarterly* 53. I have made my own totals from the items listed in the

Codrington Library, the late John Simmons.[8] Its quality was recognised by contemporaries. Jeremy Bentham, no less, learnt about it from Lord Shelburne's agent.[9] The core of the collection was clearly purchased in 1773, after the death of James West.[10] Certainly many (possibly 11) of the 18 volumes betray signs of West's ownership.[11] But Blackstone did more than simply acquire even these volumes. He supplied or supplemented the indexes where necessary and his catalogue of Prynne's works (in both alphabetical and chronological form) was prepared afresh, based on careful use of contemporary catalogues. In so doing he superseded West's own lists of his collection, even if the new lists produced totals which, with 125 items in chronological form and 137 in alphabetical form, differed disconcertingly from the volume-by-volume indexes (which included some prepared by Blackstone himself).[12] And Blackstone made considerable efforts to add to West's collection. His literary friends were obviously under instructions to hunt down missing tracts.[13] This searching continued up to his death. On 9 January 1780, when he was a sick, possibly dying, man and in his last known letter, Blackstone thanked George Steevens for 'a valuable piece of Mr. Prynne's towards completing my collection'.[14] The bequest included any works acquired after his will was made. So it is clear that the Prynne collection mattered to Blackstone. He invested significant effort—including emotional effort—in it. The question is, why? Why did Justice Blackstone interest himself in Marginal Prynne?

II BIBLIOPHILIA

There was undoubtedly some straightforward bibliophilia. Blackstone loved and collected books throughout his life. He started with student texts and more general works. He was a poor boy, dependent on the generous support of the Bigg family and other relatives; and his first library, much of which found its way via his son James to New Inn Hall and thence Balliol

article. Like Blackstone's (and West's) collection, the Huntington and Oriel ones include some extraneous works. The criteria seem similar enough to permit the comparison of overall totals given in the text.

[8] *Blackstone and Oxford: An exhibition held at the Bodleian Library, Oxford* (Oxford, 1980) 10. John Simmons gave 125 as the total number of tracts.

[9] Bentham, *Correspondence* vol 3, pp 16–17.

[10] *Bibliotheca Westiana. A Catalogue of the Curious and Truly Valuable Library of the Late James West esq* (London, 1773) 111 (item 1839). I have used the remounted, annotated copy in the British Library, reference 821 ee 25 (5).

[11] See Appendix below.

[12] There are a few duplicates but they do not account for the differences.

[13] See Doolittle, *Blackstone*, 107 fn.

[14] *Letters* 189. Here and elsewhere I have modernised spelling and punctuation.

College, was to a significant degree second- or third-hand.[15] As he got older and wealthier Blackstone made substantial acquisitions himself. It seems fair to assume that most of the pre-1780 volumes in the catalogue of his grandson's sale in 1845 were William's.[16] And there are no doubt many others in a still more impressive catalogue of 1803; but frustratingly this was a joint sale and there is no way of distinguishing Blackstone's books from Philip Stanhope's.[17] In addition to these collections, Blackstone seized opportunities to obtain rare and old texts. Alongside Prynne's tracts, he left to All Souls

> my old manuscript Registrum Brevium, two ancient manuscript reports of cases in the Star Chamber, and another ancient manuscript treatise concerning ecclesiastical courts; together with my old and curious edition of Littleton's Tenures, printed by Lettou and Machlina, and the old abridgement of the statutes bound up therewith; another edition of Littleton, printed by Tailleur at Rouen; my old edition of the Book of Entries; all my editions of the statutes, in whatever size or language, printed previous to the year 1660 . . .[18]

Some of these can clearly be identified in the Codrington today;[19] and there are other items too which show signs of Blackstone's ownership.[20] It is interesting to note that at least one of the bequests was acquired considerably before the Prynne purchase in 1773.[21] Even in less comfortable days Blackstone was looking for rare books.

It will come as no surprise that Blackstone involved himself in library affairs. There may be no sign of any formal role in the university's library, the Bodleian (at least not in relation to its book collections), but he played a very significant part in the development of his college library, the Codrington. His most striking contribution was to sort out the bequest which gave the library its name; but there were many other services in the 1740s and '50s (often performed in conjunction with his friend Benjamin

[15] The collection is housed under reference 1550 at Balliol College. The religious works have been analysed by WR Prest in 'The Religion of a Lawyer? William Blackstone's Anglicanism' (2004) ns 21 *Parergon* 153–68.

[16] *Bibliotheca Blackstoneiana . . . A Catalogue of a Library of 4,500 Volumes* (London, 1845).

[17] *A Catalogue of the Law Library of Philip Stanhope … to which is added the reserved part of the library of the late Justice Blackstone* (London, 1803).

[18] TNA PROB 11/1061/61. Blackstone wrote (it was a holograph will) 'Machlinia' rather than Machlina and 'Roan' not Rouen.

[19] The Registrum Brevium is at LR 2 b12 (MS 65); the Star Chamber cases at LR 1 h22 (MS 177); the Ecclesiastical Courts treatise at LR 1 h21 (MS 175); and Littleton's Tenures at l 9.1.

[20] eg, *Le liver des assizes* (l 9.9); *The Boke of Magna Carta* (l 14.8); *Magna Carta cum aliis statutis* (l14.5); *Reports temp. Hen. VI* (l 9. 11–12); *Nova Statuta* (l infra 2.3). (This last may be 'the old abridgment . . .').

[21] See the reference to the Lettou and Machlinia [sic] printing of the statutes in the first edition (1765) of the *Commentaries* at vol 1, p 229. See also W Blackstone, *The Great Charter and Charter of the Forest* (Oxford, 1759) lxvii.

Buckler).[22] Needless to say, Blackstone was a diligent reader at both the Bodleian and All Souls.[23] Much of his reading has been traced in the borrowing records of both libraries and it reveals a wide range of often recondite books, especially when required by his historical enquiries (on his own account and for his college).[24]

The production as well as the possession and study of books fascinated Blackstone. He was chiefly responsible for the thorough-going reform of the Oxford University Press in the 1750s.[25] In so doing he made himself an expert in all aspects of publication, from printing to copyright. His determined work has been analysed in Ian Philip's volume for the Oxford Bibliographical Society[26] and Harry Carter's *History of the Oxford University Press*[27]. Blackstone made book-making at the Press significantly more efficient; he improved its quality as well.[28] Not long after he had helped secure the Pomfret bequest of classical statuary for the University, the Clarendon Press published an elegant catalogue of these and other Oxford marbles.[29] Blackstone also took pride in the printing of his own work. His edition of what he called the Great Charter and the Charter of the Forest is particularly fine, and perhaps his hand may be discerned in at least the first version of Buckler's *Stemmata Chicheleana* (attempting to free All Souls from the preference for founder's kin) which included elaborate tables of pedigrees.[30] Even the *Commentaries* themselves, which were intended for a general, lay readership, were handsomely, even if not elaborately, produced. And Blackstone applied this keen, expert knowledge to the old

[22] See Doolittle, *Blackstone* 12–14; P Neill, 'Blackstone, Oxford and the Law', in SJD Green and P Horden (eds), *All Souls under the Ancien Régime: Politics, Learning, and the Arts, c.1600–1850* (Oxford, 2007) 272–4; and, generally, E Craster, *The History of All Souls College Library*, ed EF Jacob (London, 1971) chs 5–6.

[23] I have analysed and reconstructed his reading from the relevant Bodleian Library entry books (3/11–12, 4/1 and 5/2–3) and the All Souls Library borrowing register. I listed some of his reading in 'Sir William Blackstone and his *Commentaries on the Laws of England* (1765–69): A Biographical Approach '(1983) 2 *Oxford Journal of Legal Studies* 106fn.

[24] For example, for his work on the contentious issue of founder's kin. The Bodleian Entry books show him consulting the Tanner MSS. Buckler referred to his work in *Stemmata Chicheliana* (Oxford, 1765) iv (where Blackstone is not named but is readily identifiable). For the secondary literature, see GD Squibb, *Founders' Kin* (Oxford, 1972) and J Davis, 'Founder's Kin' in Green and Horden (n 22) ch 11.

[25] See Doolittle, *Blackstone*, ch 5.

[26] *William Blackstone and the Reform of the Oxford University Press* (Oxford, 1956). Philip prints key Blackstone documents, showing how he 'first studied and mastered the many intricate technical problems which the work of the Press involved' (1). See especially his 'Some Thoughts on the Oxford Press, 1756' (23–38).

[27] Harry Carter, *History of the Oxford University Press. Volume 1: to the Year 1780* (Oxford, 1975). Carter reproduces some of Blackstone's expert notes (392–3).

[28] See Philip's verdict in *HUO* 755. Note also Blackstone's remark in 1758 that 'we [ie the Press] are meditating a very handsome edition of Theocritus': *Letters* 55.

[29] R Chandler, *Marmora Oxoniensia* (Oxford, 1763). For a description see Carter, n 27 above, 392–5.

[30] First edition 1765; a second, expanded version appeared in 1775.

books he acquired. He added learned notes to a number of the books he left to All Souls, dealing with arcane matters of dating and printing.[31]

It was therefore as a bibliophile that Blackstone collected the works of William Prynne. He did not simply list the works he bought from the James West sale and thereafter. As we have seen, he compiled a catalogue of all Prynne's works, first by date and then by title. It was 21 pages long. The fact that Blackstone got to 184 or so items in his chronological list and 191 in his alphabetical one demonstrates diligence and knowledge. He was working from Prynne's own publisher's 'exact catalogue' of 1660, which listed 160 works,[32] and from Anthony Wood's compilation, which extended to 180 or so.[33] Even allowing for those works which, as Blackstone himself noted, were of doubtful attribution or clearly by third parties, Blackstone got admirably close to the 174 separate works which the most definitive bibliographical study attributes to Prynne.[34] It was a striking achievement. And Blackstone did not simply list the works and cross refer to his own volumes; he also identified where some of the other works could be found. He located a number in the Lincoln's Inn Library and others, apparently, in the Middle Temple Library.[35] (He seems to have been unaware of Oriel's holdings.)[36] The descriptions of each work were precise, with careful distinctions between editions and close attention to the vagaries of seventeenth-century title pages.

Blackstone clearly enjoyed a bibliographical challenge; and the extent and complexity of Prynne's publishing history afforded him plenty of scope. But was this all there was to it? It seems doubtful that the mere existence of a large number of multi-editioned, multi-part Civil War and Restoration tracts explains Blackstone's hard labour. It is certainly worth assuming that Blackstone thought Prynne and his writings were worth the effort. In other words, why Prynne?

[31] The best example is Littleton's *Tenures* (19.1). See also *Nova Statuta* (above n 20)

[32] Fry and Davies (n7) 56, 65.

[33] This is my total (actually 177) from the list in *Athenae Oxonienses* (Oxford, 1721 edn) vol 2, pp 441–53.

[34] Fry and Davies (n 7) 53.

[35] Blackstone explained that 'L' meant Lincoln's Inn Library; but he did not explain 'M'. There is however a reference against a 1660 catalogue to the Middle Temple Library (see also the Appendix to this chapter).

[36] The collection there seems to have been extensive enough by 1780 to have deserved Blackstone's attention. I am very grateful to the College Librarian, Marjory Szurko, for most helpful research on the acquisition history. Perhaps College collections were then so private as to escape the notice of even such a curious and influential 'insider' as Blackstone? There was certainly no general catalogue of Bodleian *and* College books, despite at least one initiative: *HUO* vol 5, p 746. (Blackstone's work in the College *archives* is mentioned below.)

III PRYNNE THE LAWYER

Prynne, of course, was a lawyer. He described himself, proudly, on the title pages of his works as first 'utter [*sc.* junior]' barrister and later bencher and reader (of Lincoln's Inn). The fact that Prynne's law was a century-old will have mattered little to Blackstone. He was acutely aware of the historical foundations of the common law. In fact, critics argued that he paid too much attention to antecedents and too little to practice. It might be expected therefore that the *Commentaries* would make extensive use of Prynne's works. And so they do, but not really for their *legal* content. Many of the references are to Prynne's historical compilations, especially his chronological account of the ecclesiastical power of the Kings of England and his registers of royal writs. Blackstone used them simply to explain the development of royal and parliamentary power.[37] It is interesting that some of the most sustained references were to Prynne's arcane account of the 'Queen's Gold', ie the queen consort's right to revenue during her marriage with the king. The passages are more historical, even antiquarian, than legal in nature.[38] There is also a citation of Prynne's revision of Sir Robert Cotton's abridgement of the records in the Tower of London.[39] Even Blackstone's references to Prynne on the Fourth Part of Coke's *Institutes* dealt with, in one case, writs to summon Parliament and, in another, the office of the Lord High Steward.[40] There is nothing to suggest that as a lawyer, even an historically-minded lawyer, Blackstone was attracted to Prynne.

IV PRYNNE THE POLITICIAN

Perhaps there was interest in Prynne as a parliamentarian? The term is a little misleading. Constitutionalist might be better, even at the cost of anachronism. Many of Prynne's publications were contributions to the fraught debates between king, parliament and army in the 1640s. Blackstone will not have found much of relevance in Prynne's attack on Laud and Court Catholicism: his own Anglicanism may or may not have been

[37] For citations of the former, see *Commentaries* vol 1, pp 99, 369; vol 3, p 408 and vol 4, p 339, and for the latter, vol 1, p 168. All but one of the citations distinguish explicitly between the works. The only one that does not (3 Pryn 1264) has been checked. Here and elsewhere I have used the University of Chicago facsimile edition. (A modern edition of WG Hammond's 1890 variorum edition would be very useful.)

[38] See *Commentaries* vol 1, pp 214–16. It was this section which attracted the attention of Melville in *Moby Dick* (ch 90).

[39] *Commentaries* vol 3, p 52.

[40] *Ibid* vol 1, p 170 and vol 4, p 259.

cautious and conservative,[41] but he will have felt a great deal more comfortable with the later, unambiguously monarchist, Prynne than with the earlier, apparently Presbyterian, Prynne. Of greater relevance were Prynne's repeated, passionate interventions in the controversy over parliamentary sovereignty. At one level the issues were immediate and real, not least because they involved the fate of Charles I and in due course the restoration of Charles II. At another level, the issues were long-term and theoretical, as Professor Pocock demonstrated so strikingly many years ago in his account of the 'Ancient Constitution'.[42] Pocock showed how Prynne played a key role in proving the Commons's relatively recent origins, thus undermining its right to equal status with the king and lords. In the formulation of two post-Pocock historians, Prynne attacked the 'co-ordination principle'.[43] Given the importance of the constitution in the *Commentaries* and given its centrality in critiques of Blackstone's work from Bentham onwards, it is tempting to expect to find Blackstone following Prynne into the thickets of his king-lords-commons arguments. There would certainly be some excitement if he did. Pocock's arresting views on Burke and the adaptive constitution cry out for application to Blackstone.[44] But the expectations are dashed. Blackstone leaves the thickets to the intrepid Prynne. Indeed, he distances himself from the controversy with indecent pusillanimity. He lightly rehearses the argument, and then sums up as follows:

> Hence it indisputably appears that parliaments, or general councils, are coeval with the kingdom itself. How those parliaments were constituted and composed is another question which has been matter of great dispute among our learned antiquarians and, particularly, whether the Commons were summoned at all or, if summoned, at what period they began to form a distinct assembly. But it is not my intention here to enter into controversies of this sort.[45]

[41] See Prest (n 15), which uses this writer's assessment (*Blackstone*, 103–4) as a starting point for his argument that Blackstone may have espoused High Church views which cooled in later years. As indicated earlier, he does so on the basis of the New Inn Hall Library and Professor Prest acknowledges the fragility of this source. There is indeed plenty of Low(ish) Church material too; and it is also now very clear that Oxford churchmen were certainly not all the zealots of Gibbon-derived caricature.

[42] JGA Pocock, *The Ancient Constitution and the Feudal Law. A Study of Historical Thought in the Seventeenth Century. A Reissue with a Retrospect* (Cambridge, 1987) 155–62. The book first appeared in 1957. In the reissue Pocock responded to Lamont's biography at 315–18.

[43] CC Weston and JR Greenberg, *Subjects and Sovereigns. The Grand Controversy over Legal Sovereignty in Stuart England* (Cambridge, 1981) ch 5.

[44] See Jeffrey Smitten's brief, allusive but suggestive analysis of Blackstone as a Pocock humanist: 'Blackstone's *Commentaries* as Constitutive Rhetoric' (1987) 17 *Studies in Eighteenth-Century Culture* 173. Smitten was building on JGA Pocock, 'Burke and the Ancient Constitution: a problem in the History of Ideas' in his *Politics, Language and Time* (London, 1972) ch 6. RJ Smith made a similar point, contemporaneously with Smitten, in *The Gothic Bequest* (Cambridge, 1987) 91–4.

[45] *Ibid* vol 1, p 145

Nor is he prepared to address the allied question of prescription. Prynne was only prepared to start the history of the Commons as a representative body in 1265; others wanted to take it back to at least 1189, when the death of the 'law-giver' Henry II served as the required starting-point for time immemorial. Here too Blackstone declined to debate the point. He simply rehearsed the narrow legal rule (stipulating 1189) in brisk fashion: 'Now time of memory hath been long ago ascertained by the law to commence from the reign of Richard the first'. And he attached a footnote which made clear how little he cared:

> This rule was adopted, when by the Statute of Westminster I (3 Edw. I c.39) the reign of Richard I was made the time of limitation in a writ of right. But since by the statute of 32 Hen. VIII c.2 this period (in a writ of right) hath been very rationally reduced to sixty years it seems unaccountable that the date of legal prescription or memory should still continue to be reckoned from an era so very antiquated.[46]

All he allowed himself was a defence of Prynne's actions as a MP. He took trouble, in a footnote, to point out that it was John Pym, not William Prynne, who promoted the first excise in 1643.[47] The exception speaks volumes. Blackstone was prepared to rescue Prynne from an obscure historical mistake (involving a tax whose unpopularity had recently been revived);[48] he was not ready to take a stance on fundamental features of Prynne's scholarship.

V PRYNNE THE SCHOLAR

Then there is Prynne the historian or antiquarian. Perhaps we should aim a little lower and focus on less controversial aspects. It is noteworthy that Blackstone once described Prynne as a 'painful and judicious antiquarian.'[49] (Interestingly this was in the course of the description of the Queen's Gold: further evidence that Blackstone did not really regard Prynne as a *legal* authority.) The description was apt. Prynne was no mere pamphleteer and controversialist. He compiled historical works of real originality and value. Chief among these were his four part *Brief Register of Parliamentary Writs* (1659–64) and his three volume *Exact Chronological Vindication of the King's Supreme Ecclesiastical Jurisdiction* (1665–72).[50] As their scope and length indicate, serious archival labours underpinned these

[46] *Ibid* vol 2, p 31

[47] *Ibid* vol 1, p 309

[48] Especially by the introduction of a cider excise.

[49] *Commentaries* vol 1, p 216.

[50] Like other multi-volume or reiussed Prynne publications, the titles of both works varied. Bibliographical details are given in Fry and Davies (n 7).

publications. The latter, at least in the posthumous re-worked third volume, was described as 'collected out of the ancient records in the Tower'. Hence its usual shorthand title, 'Prynne's Records'. Prynne was keeper of the records in the Tower of London for the last nine years of his life.[51] When he referred to the 'heroic study of antiquities and records' (at the end of the preface to the fourth part of his 'Writs') he could have been describing his own struggles with dust and dirt, which for one eminent legal historian (Maitland) were indeed 'heroic'.[52] All this will undoubtedly have resonated with Blackstone. Historical and antiquarian studies were close to Blackstone's heart. Admittedly his most elaborate work of history, on Magna Carta, seems to have been intended to advance his claim to what he anticipated to be an imminent vacancy for the Oxford Professorship in Ancient History.[53] But that work was no ordinary calling card. It was a serious textual analysis, prefaced by a long introduction replete with numerous references to primary (including manuscript) sources. The archival labour was extensive and painstaking. There was a great deal of personal effort, and not just in Oxford (in the Bodleian and also at Oriel College and evidently Christ Church).[54] Blackstone also devoted time to various London collections: in the (new) British Museum, Lambeth Library, the Inner Temple, the Heralds' Office, the Guildhall, (possibly) Westminster Abbey and (interestingly, given Prynne's own work there) the Tower of London.[55] He also organised collations and made enquiries at Salisbury, Durham, Cambridge, Norwich and Dublin.[56] The leading modern commentator on the subject has written that 'the modern study of Magna Carta begins with Blackstone . . . His edition is a classic and now requires very little amendment'.[57] Blackstone's other publications also reveal an intense interest in history and historical records. There are footnote references to the Winchester College archives in his *Essay on Collateral Consanguinity*[58] and to researches in the British Museum in the *Commentaries*.[59] The old records may have been used with a lawyer's determination to prove a point, but they were still used with skill and

[51] There appears to be no extended account of Prynne's work in the Tower. It is a particular shame that in his prize-winning book, *English Scholars, 1660–1730* (London, 1951), DC Douglas treated Prynne (a little oddly) as a pre-Restoration figure (see 267–8). Nor did G Parry study Prynne in *The Trophies of Time* (Oxford, 1995).

[52] Quoted in Lamont (n 1) 206.

[53] The evidence is rehearsed in Doolittle, *Blackstone* 105–6. Professor Prest supported the conjectures in a recent Selden Society lecture.

[54] Blackstone, *The Great Charter* (n 21) xxxv, xxxix, lii, lvi, and lxxiv; lxx; lxxiv.

[55] Blackstone (n 21) v, viii, xvi, xx, xxi, xxxix, lix and lx; xv; xxxix; viii; xxxiv; lxx; xvii, xxiii, xxiv, lxi and lxvii.

[56] Blackstone (n 21) xvii and xxi; xxviii, xlvii, l and lxx; xxxviii and xxxix; xlvi; and xxxii.

[57] Quoted by Neill (n 22) 288.

[58] W Blackstone, *Essay on Collateral Consanguinity* (1750) 81 and 82.

[59] *Commentaries* vol 4, p 119.

familiarity. And Blackstone enjoyed ancient texts for their own sake. In his work for the university press he took enormous trouble to facilitate the archival collation required for the second edition of Bishop Gibson's magisterial Codex of ecclesiastical law.[60] He also personally collected a number of fifteenth- and sixteenth-century books and manuscripts, studied them with care and (as we have seen) left them to All Souls College, where his expert annotations can be admired.[61] And his *Commentaries* referred, with some relish, to rare treatises in his own collection[62] and elsewhere.[63] His restless reforming mind prompted him to consider how best the university's and the colleges' manuscripts could be made available to scholars. He compiled and presented a serious proposal to use the Radcliffe Camera for this purpose.[64] His Codrington reforms extended to the college's archives as well as its books.[65] Blackstone also shared Prynne's taste for antiquarian pursuits. He engaged in learned correspondence with like-minded scholars and both presented and published his findings (for example, a Prynne-related discourse on an old seal).[66]

It is certainly notable that Blackstone made particular use of Prynne's historical (or antiquarian) works. We have already noticed this from the Prynne citations which appear in the *Commentaries*. There are also extensive footnote references in Blackstone's edition of Magna Carta to Prynne's 'Records'.[67] And there are two footnote citations of Prynne's register of parliamentary writs in the copyholder treatise.[68] But Blackstone was not simply interested in Prynne the 'painful and judicious antiquarian'. He did not confine himself to Prynne's later, archive-based works. He collected as much as he could find, from the earliest to the latest, from the ephemeral to the scholarly, from the scurrilous to the painstaking.

[60] *Letters* 73–4.

[61] Notably (as already noted) in Littleton's *Tenures* (which incidentally displays knowledge of Brasenose College Library holdings), but also the *Registrum Brevium* and *Magna Carta cum aliis antiquis statutis* (which described researches in the Oriel College archives). See above, n 20 and n 31.

[62] See vol 1, p 229 (Littleton) and vol 4, p 264 (Star Chamber cases).

[63] See vol 4, pp 119 and 264.

[64] I printed his proposal in 'William Blackstone and the Radcliffe Camera, 1753' (1982) 11 *Bodleian Library Record* 47. See also Philip (26) 15.

[65] Neill (n 22) 274.

[66] See the summary in Doolittle, *Blackstone* 106.

[67] Blackstone (n 21) xii, xxvi, xxxii, lxi, lxvii, lxviii, lxix, lxx, lxxi and lxxiv. (Again the over-abbreviated '2 Pryn 345' etc has required verification to establish that in all cases the references are to 'Records', not 'Writs'.) It would be interesting to know the reason for the 1775 index in vol 3 of the 'Records'. It was printed by T Payne of London. Could Blackstone possibly have been involved?

[68] *Considerations on the Question whether Tenants by Copy of Court Roll .. .are Qualified to Vote . . .* (London, 1758) 50.

CONCLUSION

There is one further possible explanation for Blackstone's outwardly puzzling interest in Prynne. We know that Blackstone was familiar with Anthony Wood's account, in *Athenae Oxonienses,* of Prynne's extraordinary career of unremitting labour.[69] It is bound to have made a deep impression. Popular history may focus on Prynne's attack on Laud and his cropped ears, but more 'discerning optics' (to borrow a term from a college friend's tribute[70]) will concentrate on his work on the medieval records in the Tower of London. Even allowing for Prynne's characteristic dramatization, these were remarkable efforts, especially for a mutilated 60 year old who took no care of himself. Anyone, like Blackstone, who had wrestled with old records (including those in the Tower) will have been impressed, even humbled. The sheer determination was extraordinary. And it is worth recalling just how hard Blackstone himself worked throughout his life, especially in the 1750s when he was promoting wholesale reforms of university institutions, steering Oxford away from political disaster, delivering the lectures which became the *Commentaries* and, it must be admitted, manoeuvring hard to create a Vinerian professorship suited to his purpose.[71] The efforts took a heavy toll and both Blackstone's popularity and his health suffered badly. The parallels with Prynne can be overdone. Blackstone simply took a 'sabbath as to mental employment'[72] and made his way to London where official preferment and promotion awaited. Prynne had no such options. But there *is* one common feature. Prynne famously sustained himself in his drudgery with alcohol. Wood's account was obviously taken from Aubrey. It reads:

> His custom when he studied was to put on a long quilted cap which came an inch over his eyes, serving as an umbrella to defend them from too much light and, seldom eating a dinner, would every three hours or more be munching a roll of bread and now and then refresh his exhausted spirits with ale brought to him by his servant[73]

Blackstone, equally famously, is said to have written the *Commentaries* with the aid of port. He 'found his mind invigorated and supported in the fatigue of his great work by a temperate use of it.'[74] The comparison may be facile: the social, let alone alcoholic, equivalence of ale and port may be doubted; but the impression the pictures create does not mislead. Both

[69] The edition Blackstone used was the second (Oxford, 1721), at vol 2 cols 434–53.

[70] Richard Graves in *The Triflers* (Bath, 1805) 55.

[71] These exhilarating Oxford years are described in Doolittle, *Blackstone* Pt II.

[72] *Letters* 57.

[73] Wood (n 69) vol 2, p 439.

[74] *Boswell's Life of Johnson*, ed GB Hill, (rev) LF Powell (Oxford, 1934–50) vol 4, p 91 and fn. For William Scott as the source of the anecdote and his insistence that Boswell stress Blackstone's sobriety, see *The Correspondence of James Boswell with Certain Members of the Club*, ed CN Fifer (London, 1976) 348 and fn.

Prynne and Blackstone deserve to be remembered for their extraordinary energy and resourcefulness. They were indefatigable. And it may well have been a recognition of this shared characteristic, an admiration for Prynne's sheer hard work, which attracted Blackstone. Even it were not, the links between the two men and their work are such as to make an exploration of those links helpful for a better understanding of both Blackstone and Prynne. An unlikely association? Perhaps, but it is nevertheless an association which repays examination.

APPENDIX: A BIBLIOGRAPHICAL NOTE

There are a number of uncertainties surrounding the Prynne tracts in All Souls. They do not affect the conclusions of this essay but they are rehearsed here in the hope they are of interest and to encourage further investigation. The Blackstone bequest is usually thought to comprise 19 volumes, but the last volume is bound differently from the rest and its contents were added later to Blackstone's lists. Volume 19 therefore does not appear to have been donated by Blackstone. The James West sale included a number of Prynne's works, but apart from item 1839 the lots for sale were either clearly too small to form Blackstone's own collection or were purchased by third parties. Item 1839 comprised 18 volumes, containing 104 pieces. This surely was Blackstone's starting point; but it is difficult to get the numbers to correspond with the present collection. Evidence of West's ownership (including some indexes) can be established for volumes 2–9 and 11–13, ie 11of the 18 (19) volumes. In some cases the index is signed by West, in others it is simply in his hand. Blackstone's own indexes appear in volumes 1, 10 and 14–18.

It therefore cannot easily be concluded that these are the same volumes as sold in 1773. Perhaps they were simply re-bound (with the All Souls arms): volume 5 has two additions to the index in Blackstone's hand which suggests that he was simply working with West's volumes. And Blackstone's two known post-1773 purchases (*Jus Patronatus* and *Quakers Unmasked*) appear in volume 18 (with the latter tract, acquired just before his death, forming the last piece of all). Volume 18 also contains a tract evidently in previous ownership in 1775. (It can probably be assumed that the Steevens purchase was not another version of the same work which appears in volume 17.) But if they *were* the same volumes as West's, then for some reason West indexed some volumes but not others and/or Blackstone replaced some but not all of the indexes with his own. There are in fact some signs of Blackstone or All Souls re-numbering the volumes: as witness a change from '10' in volume 12.

The number of tracts also presents a puzzle. By Blackstone's apparently full reckoning the 18 (not 19) volumes comprised 129 works (or 'pieces' in the terminology of the sales catalogue). The first 16 volumes (i.e. the number sold in 1773) comprised 98 (not 104). The older indexes, including West's, missed some items but these lower figures again do not tally with the 104 in the sale.

The West sale items were evidently quarto only. The catalogue has separate listings for folio and for octavo or smaller books. This explains, presumably, otherwise odd entries in Blackstone's listings. Most of the references are to the volumes of his All Souls bequest or to items in the libraries of Lincoln's Inn or (it is surmised) Middle Temple. But there are some which simply state 'folio'. All these can be identified in the Codrington Library's other holdings of Prynne's works, so perhaps this was Blackstone's way of indicating where the books were to be found elsewhere in the College collection. It will be recalled that Blackstone left All Souls only those Prynne tracts which were not already held by the College. There certainly seems to be little overlap between the 18 (19) volumes and those other Prynne works listed separately in the Codrington card index and clearly in the Library (and catalogued) before 1780. Of the three works which were in the Blackstone/West collection, two were acquired as part of a bequest in 1772; the other, from internal evidence, was obtained after 1754, possibly long after. This may reflect a conscious effort and in turn indicate that the volumes were a post-rationalization compilation (and not a re-bound set of West's volumes); but it may simply be fortuitous, with All Souls having few Prynne tracts before Blackstone's bequest. It is also worth appreciating that one of Prynne's most useful works, his 'Records', was folio in size. And we know from the Codrington borrowing register that Blackstone himself used volumes 2 and 3 of the College's own 'Records' for some months in 1759 (no doubt in connection with his edition of Magna Carta). Apart from the 'Writs', there are in fact only four Prynne tracts in the Codrington's other holdings which are *not* folios.

Blackstone clearly retained some of Prynne's works himself. His listings have 'per se' against the four volumes of the 'Writs'. These can perhaps be presumed to have been in the West sale (they were quarto in size), but All Souls can be assumed to have owned copies of this important work already. They may be the same volumes which appeared as item 274 in the 1845 sale of Blackstone's grandson's property. The sale also included Prynne's revision of Cotton's abridgement of records in the Tower (item 277). This could well be the copy, with Blackstone's bookplate, now housed under reference LC4 90 in the Free Library of Philadelphia.

The 1773 sale entry referred, in addition to 16 volumes and 104 pieces, to three catalogues of Prynne's publications. Those for 1643 (which listed 31 works) and 1653 (68) are recorded by Blackstone in his listings. So too is one for 1660 (with an unexplained reference to the Middle Temple Library in the chronological list), but the manuscript list (stated to show in alphabetical order 173 ‘books’), with some unconnected, possibly antiquarian, notes attached, does not seem to have found its way into the All Souls volumes.

A last point. There is little to show the provenance of West’s tracts; but one of his indexes is dated 1727, so at least one of the Prynne tracts (it was a single-work volume) survived the fire in 1737 which destroyed much of West’s early collections.

Part II Thought

SINCE THEIR FIRST publication controversy and debate have swirled around Blackstone's *Commentaries*. This collection of essays can provide at best only an impressionistic and incomplete introduction to what is now a very large, heterogeneous and still growing literature. Many of its themes may, however, be traced back to the initial confrontation between Jeremy Bentham and his former teacher, which indeed continued throughout Bentham's long life, since at the age of 80 he busied himself in adding some 300 manuscript pages to the critique of the *Commentaries* on which he had first embarked half a century before. Besides testifying indirectly to the remarkable influence and status which the *Commentaries* had by then acquired, the obsessive quality of Bentham's preoccupation with Blackstone may actually reflect as well as disguising the extent to which the two shared similar reformist goals, for example in relation to the administration of criminal justice and the penal system generally. Of course they were also separated by major intellectual and psychological differences, as well as a substantial generation gap, since Bentham was born a quarter-century after Blackstone, and lived on for more than fifty years after the latter's death.

Bentham's initial attack on the *Commentaries* and their author in his *Fragment on Government* (1776) made much of Blackstone's unthinking veneration for the common law, and consequent rooted opposition to any change in the country's legal arrangements. Of course this accusation is easily countered by producing contrary instances, where Blackstone did indeed criticise specific legal rules and advocate significant changes in their content or application (as with the game laws, the doctrine of corruption of blood, and the proliferation of capital offences, to take three specific examples). On the other hand it is undeniable that, as the young Edward Gibbon put it in his first published book review, Blackstone does generally speak 'with uncommon respect of the old common law'.[1]

Given that Blackstone's main purpose was to provide an accessible and comprehensive overview of the laws and government of his native land, it may seem hardly surprising that he adopted a broadly positive stance towards his subject. The six following essays on Blackstone's jurisprudence fall into three groups, and reach rather different conclusions about the effects of what John Orth terms Blackstone's 'traditionalism'. In examining Blackstone's scattered pronouncements on the role of the judiciary, John

[1] *The Miscellaneous Works of Edward Gibbon, Esq* (London, 1814) vol 1, pp 214–15, vol 5, p 546.

Langbein convicts the Commentator of superficiality, formalism, and even dishonesty in presenting an excessively idealised account of how common-law judges discharged their weighty responsibilities. Orth takes a less censorious view in analysing and contextualising Blackstone's account of a major judicial function, that of construing statutes, despite concluding that 'while up to date in his constitutional law, Blackstone was behind the times in other respects'. Mary Sokol and Tim Stretton then discuss Blackstone's exposition of the law of marriage. Sokol traces areas of difference and similarity in the views of Blackstone and Bentham on the legal status of marriage and the respective rights and duties of husband and wife, while Stretton concentrates on Blackstone's role in crystallising the doctrine of coverture as the chief defining characteristic of the married state. Finally, two Australian scholars scrutinise specific aspects of Blackstone's jurisprudence which retain particular contemporary relevance. The judicial use made of Blackstone as authoritative expositor of the doctrines of feudalism, with reference to large areas of northern Australia still farmed under long-term pastoral leases from the Crown, is examined by Thalia Anthony. Nicole Graham then turns to yet another aspect of the Bentham–Blackstone polarity, arguing for a return to Blackstone's less abstract and 'dephysicalised' concept of property, at a time when humanity appears in urgent danger of over-exploiting many natural resources, if not the planet itself.

5

Blackstone on Judging

JOHN H LANGBEIN

BLACKSTONE WAS SENSITIVE to the intrinsic danger of adjudicative power. He published the *Commentaries* only about 70 years after the Glorious Revolution.[1] The subservience and misbehaviour of the late Stuart bench, notably Justices Scroggs and Jeffreys, had figured prominently in the events precipitating the Revolution.[2] In Book III of the *Commentaries*, treating civil justice, Blackstone cautioned about 'the arbitrary caprice of the judge'.[3] In Book IV, regarding the administration of the criminal law, he observed that 'if judgments were to be the private opinions of the judge, men would then be slaves to their magistrates'.[4]

Although Blackstone was alert to the danger of judicial arbitrariness, he was confident that English law had put adequate safeguards in place to correct for it. Blackstone spoke of this subject in passages that are scattered through the *Commentaries*. In this chapter, I have tried to pull this material together, and to ask whether it was sound.

Blackstone identified four major limitations on judicial power: (i) legal doctrine, that is, the binding content of legal rules; (ii) the jury system, which denied English judges the power to adjudicate questions of fact; (iii) judicial independence; and (iv) appellate review. My theme in this essay is that Blackstone overestimated the strength of all four.

I LEGAL DOCTRINE

Blackstone claimed incessantly that the fixed or settled character of the substantive law restricted judicial discretion and thereby prevented

[1] *Commentaries* [ie 1765–69 edn]. Regarding the preference of some scholars for citing later editions that Blackstone revised, see AW Alschuler, 'Rediscovering Blackstone' (1996) 145 *University of Pennsylvania Law Review* 1, 3 fn 1.

[2] I have discussed these events, with citation to the scholarly literature, in JH Langbein, *The Origins of Adversary Criminal Trial* (Oxford, 2003) 79–83.

[3] *Commentaries* vol 3, p 396.

[4] *Ibid* vol 4, p 371.

arbitrariness. Writing in Book III, he claimed that the judgment of a common-law court, 'though pronounced or awarded by the judges, is not their determination or sentence, but the determination and sentence of *the law*'.[5] Accordingly, the 'judgment or conclusion depends not . . . on the arbitrary caprice of the judge, but on the settled and invariable principles of justice'.[6]

Regarding equity jurisdiction, Blackstone thought that there had been a time in the early history of the Court of Chancery when '[i]ts powers would have become too arbitrary to have been endured in a country like this, which boasts of being governed in all respects by law and not by will'.[7] Thanks, however, to the 'set of great and eminent lawyers' who subsequently served as Chancellors, Blackstone contended that equity had become 'a regular science' as precise as the common law.[8]

It might well be asked of Blackstone, if the law was as straightforward as he alleged, why were there all those lawsuits that sustained the courts and the lawyers?[9] Blackstone had an answer. Most lawsuits, he wrote, are about the facts, not about the law. '[E]xperience will abundantly show, that above a hundred of our lawsuits arise from disputed facts, for one where the law is doubted of.'[10] Speaking of cases involving 'contracts, conveyances, and testaments',[11] Blackstone contended that 'the dubious points . . . arise chiefly from . . . ascertaining the intentions'[12] of the parties. 'The law rarely hesitates in declaring it's own meaning; but the judges are frequently puzzled to find out the meaning of others.'[13]

Blackstone was surely right to emphasise the central importance of fact-finding in the adjudicative work of the legal system. Now as then, most litigation turns on establishing matters of past fact. Was the traffic light red or green? Was it OJ Simpson or somebody else who stabbed Mrs Simpson? Find the facts and the law is often easy. But Blackstone's distinction between law and fact, and his effort to confine concerns about judicial arbitrariness to fact-finding, was problematic for two quite distinct reasons.

[5] *Commentaries* vol 3, p 396. The passage strongly resembles Montesquieu's contention that judges are 'only the mouth that pronounces the words of the law, inanimate beings who can moderate neither its force nor its rigor': *The Spirit of the Laws* (ed & tr) AM Cohler et al (Cambridge, 1989; 1748) 163.

[6] *Commentaries* vol 1, p 396. Speaking about the merits of the jury system, Blackstone worried that judges, 'in spite of their own natural integrity, will have frequently an involuntary bias towards those of their own rank and dignity': *Commentaries* vol 3, p 379.

[7] *Commentaries* vol 3, p 440.

[8] *Commentaries* vol 3, pp 440–41.

[9] Regarding fluctuations in the levels of litigation in the early modern period, see CW Brooks, *Pettyfoggers and Vipers of the Commonwealth* (Cambridge, 1986) 54–5.

[10] *Commentaries* vol 3, p 330.

[11] *Commentaries* vol 3, p 329.

[12] *Commentaries* vol 3, p 329.

[13] *Commentaries* vol 3, p 329.

First, in the non-jury courts, notably Chancery, the judicial power embraced fact-finding as well as matters of law.[14] Blackstone left equity jurisdiction quite undefended against his imputation of the danger of partiality in the work of fact-finding. That was a very large omission, because much of what mattered to propertied persons was the preserve of equity—the trust, land finance through the mortgage, partnership and other modes of business organisation, married women's property, account, guardianship and so much more.[15]

Second, as regards the common law, Blackstone's depiction of the clarity of the substantive law as a safeguard against judicial excesses was formalistic and simplistic. Then as now, there were plenty of murky areas of law, in which outcomes were uncertain. Judges are not automatons and were not in Blackstone's day. Laws do not apply themselves. Rules and principles routinely come into tension and conflict with other rules and principles, which is why in collegial courts we find that able and conscientious judges often disagree about the proper outcome or rationale in a case.[16]

Interestingly, although he knew that all three superior courts—King's Bench, Common Pleas, and Exchequer—were collegial courts that decided by majority vote,[17] Blackstone did not make the evidently sound argument that the collegiality of these courts served as a corrective to eccentricity or arbitrariness on the part of any single judge. It may be that the reason he neglected the point is that he had trapped himself into the improbable assertion that the law was so clear that it stripped the judge of any field for eccentricity or arbitrariness.

In modern circumstances, Blackstone's claim that the clarity of the laws leaves the judge no room for discretion[18] finds few adherents. The central

[14] The Chancellor commonly delegated certain disputes of fact to jury trial in the common law, but any suggestion that the Chancellor lacked fact-finding authority is mistaken. I have discussed the point in JH Langbein, 'Fact-Finding in the English Court of Chancery: A Rebuttal' (1974) 83 *Yale Law Journal* 1620, correcting H Chesnin and GC Hazard Jr, 'Chancery Procedure and the Seventh Amendment: Jury Trial of Issues in Equity Cases Before 1791' (1974) 83 *Yale Law Journal* 1007.

[15] See generally G Spence, *The Equitable Jurisdiction of the Court of Chancery* (London, 1846, 1850); J Story, *Commentaries on Equity Jurisprudence as Administered in England and America* (Boston MA, 1836). For evidence that most high stakes matters were litigated in Chancery rather than at common law, see D King, 'Complex Civil Litigation and the Seventh Amendment Right to a Jury Trial,' (1984) 51 *University of Chicago Law Review* 581, 605 (focusing on the generation after Blackstone).

[16] For discussion of Blackstone's role as the dissenter in a celebrated tort case, *Scott v Shepherd* (1773), see P Neill, 'Blackstone, Oxford, and the Law' in SJD Green and P Horden (eds), *All Souls under the Ancien Régime: Politics, Learning, and the Arts, c.1600–1850* (Oxford, 2007) 268, 291–4.

[17] When describing these courts, Blackstone noted the numbers of their judges: *Commentaries* vol 3, p 41.

[18] In a similar vein, Blackstone contended that judges were bound 'to abide by former precedents', except in the case in which 'the former determination is most evidently contrary

message of the twentieth-century realist critique of common-law decision-making is that many factors affect the process of adjudication, including 'the procedural posture of a case, its factual elements, its social context, the inclinations of the judge who decided it, and the doctrinal options available to advocates and to the court'.[19] Often many conflicting rules bear on a legal problem, especially a problem of sufficient difficulty that it has resisted settlement and had to go to adjudication. An account based solely on legal doctrine does not adequately explain how and why judges decide cases. The realist view is 'that judges—stimulated, primarily by the facts before them rather than by the rules to which those facts might be fitted—work backwards "from a desirable conclusion to one or another of a stock of logical premises"'.[20]

Blackstone's claim that judges were harmless because the rules of law left them no discretion was not only a misperception according to modern notions, it was a myth in his own day. Blackstone well knew how much room for discretion the judges had. As Daniel Boorstin has emphasised, Blackstone boasted repeatedly about the adaptability of the common law in responding to changing conditions across time.[21] Albert Alschuler has argued that Blackstone's sensitivity to the adaptability of the common law protects Blackstone from '[t]he claim that Blackstone regarded the law as fixed for all time'.[22] If so, however, it convicts Blackstone of the inconsistency, indeed, the plain dishonesty, of resting his defence of judicial power on the supposed binding force of legal rules whose plasticity he well knew.

The greater candour that modern observers bring to the study of the adjudicative process by comparison with Blackstone is, however, hardly responsive to the problem of judicial arbitrariness. We have removed Blackstone's polite doctrinal fig leaf, but the reality that we have revealed, especially in the pre-trial process where most civil litigation is now discharged, is that twenty-first-century judges often do have very considerable unchecked authority. I shall say more about that phenomenon after looking at Blackstone's treatment of jury trial, to which I now turn.

to reason' in which case 'the subsequent judges do not pretend to make a new law, but to vindicate the old one from misrepresentation': *Commentaries* vol 1, pp 69–70. The disfavoured rule was not '*bad law*,' rather 'it was *not law*': vol 1, p 70 (italics in original). Bentham rightly castigated Blackstone's distinction; for Bentham's critique (and Cross's effort to rehabilitate Blackstone), see R Cross, 'Blackstone v. Bentham', (1976) 92 *Law Quarterly Review* 516.

19 GE White, 'The American Law Institute and the Triumph of Modernist Jurisprudence' (1997) 15 *Law & History Review* 37 . For striking evidence that the political orientation of American judges affects their adjudicative work, see C Sunstein et al, *Are Judges Political?: An Empirical Analysis of the Federal Judiciary* (Washington DC, 2006).

20 N Duxbury, *Patterns of American Jurisprudence* (Oxford, 1995), quoting H Oliphant, 'A Return to Stare Decisis' (1928) 14 *American Bar Association Journal* 71, 161.

21 D Boorstin, *The Mysterious Science of the Law* (Cambridge MA, 1958) 62–84, remarked by Alschuler, 'Rediscovering Blackstone' (n 1) 38.

22 *Ibid* 43.

II THE JURY SYSTEM

The division of adjudicative responsibility between judge and jury was for Blackstone a central safeguard against judicial arbitrariness. In his self-styled 'panegyric'[23] to the civil jury 'as the glory of the English law',[24] Blackstone emphasised the danger of leaving responsibility for the administration of justice 'entirely'[25] to the bench. He thought that the jury corrected for potential class bias of the judge,[26] and that the system precluded judicial 'partiality'[27] by keeping the judge away from fact-finding.

In connection with the allocation of power between judge and jury, Blackstone reiterated his claim that the substantive law was so clear that it largely foreclosed abuse. Judicial 'partiality can have little scope [in applying the law, because] the law is well known . . .'.[28] However, if the responsibility for

> settling and adjusting a question of fact [were] intrusted to any single magistrate, partiality and injustice [would] have an ample field to range in; either by [the judge] boldly asserting that to be proved which is not so, or more artfully by [his] suppressing some circumstances, stretching and warping others, and distinguishing away the remainder.[29]

Accordingly, Blackstone concluded that 'sensible and upright jurymen . . . will be found the best investigators of truth'.[30]

This account of the merits of jury trial is deeply problematic. Blackstone simply asserted, that is, he made no attempt to demonstrate, that the work of fact-finding was as easily done by inexperienced amateurs as by experienced and legally trained professionals. In the nineteenth century, when the civil jury came under attack in England, just this assumption was challenged. For example, in 1848 a writer in the *Law Times* asked regarding the civil jury:

> Would this humble, uneducated class of men be selected by anyone enjoying the ordinary share of reason to be the umpires in a question requiring skill, delicacy, and tact? A man unaccustomed to surgical operations is surely not the man

[23] *Commentaries* vol 3, p 385.
[24] *Ibid* vol 3, p 379.
[25] *Ibid*, p 379.
[26] *Ibid* ('an involuntary bias towards those of their own rank and dignity').
[27] *Ibid*, p 380.
[28] *Ibid*.
[29] *Ibid*.
[30] *Ibid*.

> whom you would allow to operate upon a fracture in your leg . . ..The jury is here what quack doctors are in the medical world—they have not the training for the duty.[31]

Blackstone's account left civil jury trial quite undefended when the functional competence of jurors came to be questioned in this way.

There was, however, a much deeper flaw in Blackstone's account of the allocation of power between judge and jury. As so often in the *Commentaries*, Blackstone's account was formalistic, in the sense of describing the nominal power relationships, while failing to acknowledge what he and other lawyers of his day knew to be the actual division of power and influence. In practice the trial judge exercised immense influence over the jury's verdict by means of his power to sum up and comment on the evidence. Earlier in Blackstone's chapter on civil jury trial, he described this process, remarking that at the conclusion of the trial the judge 'sums up the whole [of the evidence] to the jury; omitting all superfluous circumstances, observing wherein the main question and principal issue lies, stating what evidence has been given to support it, with such remarks as he thinks necessary for their direction, and giving them his opinion in matters of law arising upon that evidence'.[32]

The last words of the passage I have just quoted were quite inaccurate. The judge gave his opinion not simply 'in matters of law arising upon [the] evidence', but also upon the facts. I have elsewhere emphasised how extensive was this practice of judicial comment on the merits of the evidence presented at trial (in both civil and criminal cases) before,[33] during[34] and long after[35] Blackstone's day. Jurors welcomed the guidance of the trial judge and were commonly anxious to follow his views. As a result, the views of the judges pervasively shaped and influenced jury verdicts that turned on disputes about facts. Moreover, as Blackstone elsewhere acknowledged, if a jury returned a verdict contrary to the views of the trial judge, the judge could and commonly did reject the verdict and order a new trial before a new jury at the next session of the court.[36]

[31] Quoted in C Hanly, 'The Decline of Civil Jury Trial in Nineteenth-Century England' (2005) 26 *Journal of Legal History* 253, 262 and fn 62.

[32] *Commentaries* vol 3, p 375.

[33] JH Langbein, 'The Criminal Trial Before the Lawyers' (1978) 45 *University of Chicago Law Review* 263, 285–7.

[34] JH Langbein, 'The Historical Foundations of the Law of Evidence: A View from the Ryder Sources' (1996) 96 *Columbia Law Review* 1168, 1190–3.

[35] Hanley (n 31) 258–9; Langbein (n 2) 321–3.

[36] *Commentaries* vol 3, pp 390–4. Lord Mansfield spoke in 1757 of the 'numberless causes of false verdicts', which made it imperative that the judges be able to correct the jurors' 'mistake[s]': *Bright v Enyon* (1757), 1 Burr. 390, 393, 97 ER 365–6. The emergence and development in the seventeenth and eighteenth centuries of the technique of quashing a verdict and ordering a new trial is the subject of ch 7 of JH Langbein et al, *History of the Common Law: The Development of Anglo-American Legal Institutions* (forthcoming 2009).

Return now to Blackstone's account of the supposed danger of letting the judge decide the facts, that is, his concern that the judge would be able 'artfully . . . [to] suppress[] some circumstances [while] stretching and warping others, and distinguishing away the remainder'.[37] In truth, the jury system did not eliminate this supposed danger, it simply caused the danger to operate by indirection, channelling the judge's role in adjudicating fact into comment and instruction to the jury rather than formal judgment.

The reality of judicial domination of civil jury trial was openly discussed in the middle of the nineteenth century when the first steps were taken to authorise juryless trials in civil matters in the superior courts. For example, an editorial in *The Times* in 1850 'suggested that ninety-nine times out of 100, the verdict turned more on the judge than the jury, [because the juries] . . . understood that the "Judge advocates the cause of truth alone"'.[38]

Once again the puzzle about Blackstone is why he was so content to tell myths. He knew that English trial judges dominated English trial juries, especially in civil matters. Instead, he told his readers a fairy tale about how 'sensible and upright jurymen' were serving as 'the best investigators of truth and the surest guardians of public justice'.[39]

Most of Blackstone's chapter about jury trial[40] is not about judge/jury relations as such, but about the procedures for conducting a jury trial—who qualifies to serve;[41] how veniremen are chosen; the grounds on which prospective jurors can be challenged;[42] and most importantly, the taking of evidence at oral public trial.[43] Blackstone concluded his description of trial procedure with a passage, heavily derived from Matthew Hale's *History of the Common Law*,[44] which celebrates the superiority of jury trial by comparison with the fact-finding procedures in the ecclesiastical and other civilian-derived courts,[45] of which Chancery was by far the most important.

Blackstone's theme was that the 'open examination of witnesses *viva voce*, in the presence of all mankind, is much more conducive to clearing up of truth'[46] than the civilian practice of examining witnesses on party-propounded interrogatories administered in the absence of counsel

37 *Commentaries* vol 3, p 380.
38 Hanly (n 31) 259, citing *The Times* (29 March 1850) p 4, col D.
39 *Commentaries* vol 3, p 380.
40 *Ibid*, pp 349–85 (ch 23, 'Of the Trial by Jury').
41 *Ibid*, p 357.
42 *Ibid*, pp 353–67.
43 *Ibid*, pp 367–75.
44 M Hale, *The History of the Common Law of England*, ed CM Gray (Chicago IL, 1971; 1713) 164–5.
45 *Commentaries* vol 3, pp 373–4.
46 *Ibid*, p 373.

for either party. Following Hale,[47] Blackstone emphasised that the common-law procedure of having judge, jurors, and counsel 'propound [questions] to the witnesses on a sudden', that is, orally and somewhat spontaneously, 'will sift out the truth much better than a formal set of interrogatories previously penned and settled'.[48] Moreover, Blackstone continued, 'the confronting of adverse witnesses is also another opportunity of obtaining a clear discovery, which can never be had upon any other method of trial'.[49]

We see in these statements that Blackstone, like Hale before him, was straining to identify a concept, which we recognise as cross-examination, that had not yet quite found expression in his day. Toward the end of the eighteenth century and across the nineteenth century that concept would become the basis of a new body of law, the modern law of evidence. Indeed, cross-examination would become the basis for what in retrospect appears to have been quite a radical retheorisation of the nature of safeguard in Anglo-American law: from oath (fear of God) to cross-examination (fear of lawyers).[50] Once that re-theorisation had taken place, the contrast between common-law trial, which was increasingly centred on cross-examination, and equity's interrogatory-based procedures, which wholly lacked cross-examination, became intolerable. The Chancery Procedure Act of 1852 extended common-law trial procedure to Chancery. That development was an essential precondition for the subsequent path of fusing law and equity. It has been said that fusion entailed the conquest of common law by equity,[51] in the sense that the fused procedures of the nineteenth and twentieth centuries were heavily based on equitable pre-trial investigation and the extension of equitable remedies to common law courts. It is less appreciated that before equity conquered law, law first conquered equity, when oral examination and cross-examination of witnesses became an option in equity.

Blackstone was right to emphasise the centrality of oral public trial in the civil jury system of his day, but he made what turned out to be a mistake in assuming that the trial procedures he admired were in any way integral to the jury courts in which he found these procedures operating in

[47] Hale praised common-law trial procedure for providing the 'Opportunity for all Persons concerned, *viz.* The Judge, or any of the Jury, or Parties, or their Counsel or Attorneys, to propound occasional Questions, which beats and bolts out the Truth much better than when the Witness only delivers a formal [statement] without being interrogated . . ..': Hale (n 44) 164.

[48] *Commentaries* vol 3, p 373.

[49] *Ibid.*

[50] See TP Gallanis, 'The Rise of Modern Evidence Law' (1999) 84 *Iowa Law Review* 499, 533; Langbein (n 34) 1201–2; Langbein (n2) 246.

[51] See SN Subrin, 'How Equity Conquered Common Law: The Federal Rules of Civil Procedure in Historical Perspective' (1987) 135 *University of Pennsylvania Law Review* 909; see also D Laycock, 'The Triumph of Equity' (1993) 56 *Law & Contemporary Problems* 53.

his day. They were not. Rather, as I have just mentioned, these procedures were imported into the non-jury equity courts as an option in the 1850s. Moreover, in 1854, the Common Law Procedure Act[52] began the process of disassociating common-law trial procedure from the jury system, by allowing the parties to waive the jury and have their case tried to the judge alone, what Americans call bench trial. This was a momentous step. In our post-fusion world, it is too often forgotten that until the Common Law Procedure Act of 1854 no English common-law judge had ever made a finding of fact, whereas today in England it is only judges who are permitted to make findings of fact in civil litigation (laying aside a few inconsequential enclaves such as defamation in which civil jury trial is still permitted).[53] Fusion turned every trial judge into a mini-Lord Chancellor.

Although the civil jury is gone, most of the procedures that caused Blackstone to admire it remain, but only so far as trial remains. What has happened in recent decades, both under the American Federal Rules of Civil Procedure, and even more dramatically in England under the Woolf Reforms of the late 1990s, has been the ever more pronounced trend toward the disappearance of the trial. Twenty-first-century civil procedure is becoming not only non-jury, but also non-trial. So-called pre-trial procedure is increasingly a misnomer for non-trial procedure. More and more of what we do is conduct discovery and then dispose of cases through pre-trial dismissal or through settlement agreements engineered in consequence of pre-trial adjudication. Most civil business today is resolved in the pre-trial process by a single judge from whose rulings our tradition of hostility to interlocutory relief precludes effective appeal.[54]

I cannot leave Blackstone's troubled treatment of trial procedure without remarking on his acuity in identifying and recommending reform of the two worst features of the procedure of his day, the testimonial disqualification of the parties for interest, and the lack of pre-trial discovery for documents and certain forms of testimonial evidence.[55] The parties to civil litigation were incompetent to testify at common law until the nineteenth century, ostensibly for fear of perjury.[56] This rule, among many other

[52] 17 & 18 Vict. c 125 (1854).

[53] Regarding the history of that change, see Hanly (n 31) 253.

[54] This is the theme of notable scholarship on modern American civil procedure: see SC Yeazell, 'The Misunderstood Consequences of Modern Civil Process' (1994) 1994 *Wisconsin Law Review* 631; J Resnik, 'Managerial Judges' (1982) 96 *Harvard Law Review* 374.

[55] *Commentaries* vol 3, pp 382–3.

[56] The historical background to the rule of testimonial disqualification of the parties, civil and criminal, is discussed in JH Wigmore, *A Treatise on the Anglo-American System of Evidence in Trials at Common Law*, 3rd edn (Boston MA, 1940) 2, ss 575–6 at 674–93; regarding the nineteenth-century abolition movement in England and the US, see G Fisher, 'The Jury's Rise as Lie Detector' (1997) 107 *Yale Law Journal* 575, 659–97.

consequences, almost singlehandedly stunted the development of the law of torts, by forbidding victims to tell how they were injured.[57]

III JUDICIAL INDEPENDENCE

After the Revolution of 1688–89 there was revulsion about the subservience of the late Stuart bench.[58] Efforts commenced to distance the bench from dependence on the government, in order to protect the judges from pressure for political subservience. The Act of Settlement of 1701 protected judges from removal from office other than for cause, and legislation in 1761 protected their tenure against expiration on death of the monarch.[59] Blackstone lauded both Acts and praised judicial independence.[60] He wrote that '[n]othing . . . is more to be avoided, in a free constitution, than uniting the provinces of a judge and a minister of state',[61] although Blackstone made no effort to reconcile that principle with the office of the Lord Chancellor, who was both a high officer of state and the sole judge in Chancery. Uneasiness about that overlap of functions has now, in the early years of the twenty-first century, finally brought the Chancellor to the edge of extinction.[62]

Recent scholarship has underscored that despite the legislation advancing the cause of judicial independence, the crown retained throughout the eighteenth century many channels of influence in selecting and promoting judges agreeable to crown policy.[63] About these practices, which limited the effectiveness of judicial independence, Blackstone was characteristically silent.

As a safeguard against arbitrariness, judicial independence is a two-edged sword. It protects judges against the worst sorts of interference from the government, but it also insulates judges against justified criticism. The question, in other words, is whether judicial independence strikes the right balance between providing safeguards against subservience and preserving incentives for good performance. The case can be made that in the United

57 Regarding this and other factors that retarded the development of tort law, see Langbein (n 34) 1178–9.

58 See Langbein (n 2), 81–2.

59 Geo III c 23 (1761).

60 *Commentaries* vol 1, pp 267–8.

61 *Ibid*, p 269.

62 See Department of Constitutional Affairs Consultation Paper, *Constitutional Reform: Reforming the Office of the Lord Chancellor* (London, 2003); www.dca.gov.uk/consult/lcoffice/index.htm.

63 D Lemmings, 'The Independence of the Judiciary in Eighteenth-Century England' in P Birks (ed), *The Life of the Law* (London, 1993) 125, 127–9; see also S Jay, 'Servants of Monarchs and Lords: The Advisory Role of Early English Judges' (1994) 39 *American Journal of Legal History* 117.

States, the geriatric revolution has upset the balance, with life-tenured but impaired judges teetering along, causing delay and mischief.

IV APPELLATE REVIEW

Perhaps the least developed strand of Blackstone's thought about restraining judicial arbitrariness concerned appellate review. He took the legal system as he found it, and appellate relief in English law was still primitive in his day, especially by contrast with the emphasis on appeal in ecclesiastical and European legal systems.[64] Blackstone describes the writ of error,[65] for review by a superior court, including its two critical limitations. The writ lay only for a so-called error of record, meaning an error appearing on the face of the official court record, which excluded relief for matters such as the conduct of the trial and the taking of evidence that were not recorded; and the writ lay only for errors of law, not fact.[66] Blackstone did not acknowledge what he must have known, that these limitations rendered the writ largely useless.

We have already seen that Blackstone did take account of review of civil verdicts on motion for new trial. He was oddly silent about the technique of review that the judges had developed for criminal cases. At least from the sixteenth century, the judges devised the so-called Twelve Judges procedure for reviewing criminal convictions. If a trial judge was concerned about a point of law that arose in a case resulting in conviction, the judge could reprieve execution and refer the case for consultation with the other common-law judges, customarily twelve in number, who met regularly in London at the conclusion of each of the two annual assize circuits. 'If [they] thought the conviction wrong, a pardon was recommended . . . By the eighteenth century it had become customary for the trial judge to prepare a written "case"' (a note of the evidence and of the question) for circulation to his brethren.'[67] By comparison with the new trial for reviewing doubtful civil cases, the procedure of reserving a case for the Twelve Judges had serious shortcomings. It was 'limited to supposed questions of law. The reasonableness of the verdict remained unreviewable'.[68] Moreover, the decision of whether or not to reserve a point for the Twelve Judges was in the absolute discretion of the trial judge; the

[64] See RC van Caenegem, 'History of European Civil Procedure' (1973) 16 *International Encyclopedia of Comparative Law*, ss 2-15/16 at 17–19 .

[65] *Commentaries* vol 3, pp 407–11, vol 4, pp 390–2.

[66] *Ibid*, p 407.

[67] JH Baker, 'Criminal Courts and Procedure at Common Law 1550–1800' in JS Cockburn (ed), *Crime in England 1550–1800* (London, 1977) 15, 47.

[68] BL Berger, 'Criminal Appeals as Jury Control: An Anglo-Canadian Historical Perspective on the Rise of Criminal Appeals' (2005) 10 *Canadian Criminal Law Review* 10. Proposals to extend new trial procedure to criminal cases were recurrently made across the

convicted person had no right to review.[69] Although the Twelve Judges met in private, it became 'customary for judges to make their notes available to reporters',[70] and accordingly, published reports of many of the decisions of the Twelve Judges became available, helping to shape criminal law, criminal procedure, and the law of criminal evidence.

There is no ready explanation for why Blackstone, who devoted an entire volume of the *Commentaries* to the administration of the criminal law, neglected to discuss the Twelve Judges procedure, except to recall his pervasive premise that the clarity of the law ought to leave scant room for error.

Blackstone was at his most disingenuous when discussing the House of Lords, which had managed to establish itself as the court of last resort during the constitutional struggles of the seventeenth century.[71] In Blackstone's day, review by the Lords had not yet been delegated to the Judicial Committee; rather, every member of the House could sit and vote.[72] Blackstone closed his eyes to the shortcomings of a supreme court composed of aristocrats and bishops ignorant of the law, and instead praised it as 'a court composed of prelates selected for their piety, and of nobles advanced to that honour for their personal merit, or deriving both honour and merit from an illustrious train of ancestors, who are formed by their education, interested by their property, and bound upon their conscience and honour, to be skilled in the laws of their country'. Just how Blackstone came to his conclusion that these people were 'skilled in the laws of their country' he did not explain. In truth, '[t]he vast majority of peers were totally incompetent to recognize distinctions in the law'.[73]

nineteenth century, but the judges resisted, contending that errors occurred too rarely in criminal cases to justify an appellate process: *ibid* 23–9. It took a pair of notable wrongful convictions that came to light at the turn of the twentieth century to precipitate the creation of the Court of Criminal Appeal in 1907, with powers to review verdicts for unreasonableness and to order new trial: *ibid* 30.

69 JF Stephen, *A History of the Criminal Law of England* (London 1883) vol 1, p 312.

70 DR Bentley (ed), *Select Cases from the Twelve Judges' Notebooks* (London, 1977) 1, 21, noting that Leach made the first extensive effort to collect and publish such case reports; see T Leach, *Cases in Crown Law, Determined by the Twelve Judges* (Dublin 1789); the fourth edn (1815) is reproduced in 168 ER 103.

71 See generally JS Hart, *Justice upon Petition: The House of Lords and the Reformation of Justice, 1621–1675* (London 1991).

72 In 1844 the rule was established that lay peers could not vote on judicial business: R Stevens, *Law and Politics: the House of Lords as a Judicial Body, 1800–1976* (Chapel Hill NC, 1978) 32–4.

73 JS Flemion, 'Slow Process, Due Process, and the High Court of Parliament: A Reinterpretation of the Revival of Judicature in the House of Lords in 1621' (1974) 17 *Historical Journal* 15.

V THE PUZZLE OF BLACKSTONE

Reading Blackstone's *Commentaries* is an exasperating experience. In one dimension he appeals powerfully to the sensibilities of the modern reader. Blackstone was the first professor of the common law,[74] he took the first steps toward opening the common law to university legal education.[75] All of us who teach law in the Anglo-American world find in him our progenitor. The didactic spirit suffuses his work, he wants us to learn. Moreover, Blackstone was a legal intellectual, much influenced by the natural law tradition of the day. The question that pervades the *Commentaries* is 'why': why did the common law take shape as it did, what is the logic of this rule or that, why does the system work as it does? More than anyone before him, Blackstone sought to give reasons for the character and content of English law. But the disappointment is that Blackstone's reasons were so often shallow, formalistic, indeed sometimes plain dishonest.

Part of Blackstone's immense influence in American law is that, on account of the timing and seeming comprehensiveness of the *Commentaries*, the work became a beguilingly accessible source for understanding what appeared to be the state of the common law at the point of American separation. One scholar has computed that the *Commentaries* were cited in about six and a half percent of American cases, state and federal, reported in the years up to 1828.[76] Alschuler remarked in 1996 that the US Supreme Court 'still cites the *Commentaries* approximately ten times a year.'[77] I am uneasy about this reliance upon Blackstone as a proxy for the common-law tradition. As this chapter illustrates, despite all the strengths of Blackstone's *Commentaries*, the work is simply too unreliable to merit the deference it tends to be accorded.

[74] Regarding Blackstone's career, see now Prest, *Blackstone*; also LS Sutherland, 'William Blackstone and the Legal Chairs at Oxford' in R Wellek and A Ribiero (eds), *Evidence in Literary Scholarship* (Oxford, 1979) 229–40.

[75] I have discussed this point in JH Langbein, 'Blackstone, Litchfield and Yale: The Founding of the Yale Law School' in AT Kronman (ed), *History of the Yale Law School: The Tercentennial Lectures* (New Haven CT, 2004) 17, 21–3.

[76] DR Nolan, 'Sir William Blackstone and the American Republic: A Study of Intellectual Impact' (1976) 51 *New York University LawReview* 731, 753.

[77] Alschuler (n 1), 16.

6

Blackstone's Rules on the Construction of Statutes

JOHN V ORTH

IN WORDS THAT echo from antiquity, Blackstone defined law in the introduction to his *Commentaries* as 'a rule of civil conduct prescribed by the supreme power in a state, commanding what is right, and prohibiting what is wrong'.[1] The deficiencies of this definition need not detain us. They are daily before me as I teach the rules (dare I say the laws?) concerning the drafting and interpretation of deeds, wills and trusts—instruments that one may, but need not, execute. On this dubious foundation Blackstone erected the structure of his *Commentaries:* two volumes on rights, of persons and things respectively; two volumes on wrongs, public and private. Again, a jurisprudential lapse: things have no rights, only persons do. Yet, for all its flaws, Blackstone's arrangement actually works. I usually experience no difficulty finding where in the *Commentaries* he discussed any particular subject I am looking for.

Also in his Introduction Blackstone listed ten 'rules to be observed with regard to the construction of statutes' as follows:

1 There are three points to be considered in the construction of all remedial statutes; the old law, the mischief, and the remedy . . .
2 A Statute, which treats of things or persons of an inferior rank, cannot by any *general words* be extended to those of a superior.
3 Penal statutes must be construed strictly.
4 Statutes against frauds are to be liberally and beneficially expounded.
5 One part of a Statute must be so construed by another, that the whole may if possible stand . . .
6 A saving, totally repugnant to the body of the act, is void.

[1] *Commentaries* vol 1, p 44. *Cf* Cicero, *De legibus* vol 1, p 6: lex est ratio summa insita in natura, quae iubet ea, quae facienda sunt, prohibetque contraria.

7 Where the common law and a statute differ, the common law gives place to the statute; and an old statute gives place to a new one.
8 *If a statute, that repeals another, is itself repealed afterwards, the first statute is hereby revived, without any formal words for that purpose.*
9 Acts of parliament derogatory from the power of subsequent parliaments bind not.
10 *Lastly, acts of parliament that are impossible to be performed are of no validity. . .*[2]

By my count, three of these remain in active use today: number 1, the well-known mischief rule, and numbers 3 and 4 on, respectively, the strict construction of penal statutes and the liberal construction of statutes against fraud. Two are largely anachronistic: number 2 concerning the narrow construction of statutes applying to social inferiors and number 8 concerning the effect of repeal on a statute that itself repealed a prior statute.

Three are almost too obvious for modern mention: numbers 5 and 6, that statutes must be construed as a whole but that a saving clause totally repugnant to the rest of the statute is void, and number 7, that the common law gives place to a statute and an old statute to a new one. One rule of construction—number 9, that Acts of one Parliament cannot bind another—looks today more like a matter of constitutional law. And one is distinctly odd, with a long past and a curious future: number 10, 'acts of Parliament that are impossible to be performed are of no validity'. Reflections on these rules and a comparison of them with Blackstone's seven requisites 'to make a particular custom good',[3] that is, to make it enforceable by the judges as common law, illuminate the commentator's uncomfortable straddle of the old world of case law and the new world of statute.

Of the two rules concerning the construction of statutes to which I wish to direct attention, one was old in Blackstone's day and is now all but forgotten, the other new and seemingly hardly worth mention. The old rule is number 8, concerning the effect of repeal on a statute that itself repealed a prior statute. The new rule is number 10, concerning acts impossible to be performed.

Number 8: '*If a statute, that repeals another, is itself repealed afterwards, the first statute is thereby revived, without any formal words for that purpose*'. This rule addresses the following situation: (i) Parliament

[2] *Commentaries* vol 1, pp 87–91.

[3] 'To make a particular custom good, the following are necessary requisites': (1) 'used so long, that the memory of man runneth not to the contrary', (2) 'continued', (3) 'peaceable, and acquiesced in', (4) 'reasonable; or rather, taken negatively…, not… unreasonable', (5) 'certain', (6) 'compulsory', and (7) 'consistent' with other customs: *Commentaries* vol 1, pp 76–8.

adopts Statute Alpha; (ii) Parliament later adopts Statute Beta, which repeals Statute Alpha; (iii) finally, Parliament adopts Statute Gamma, which repeals Statute Beta. What law should a court apply? Answer: whatever Statute Alpha provided, because the repeal of Statute Beta revived Statute Alpha regardless of whether it said so or not. In consequence, when the notorious British Combination Acts against trade unions were repealed in 1824 and then the repealing statute was itself repealed and replaced a year later, all the repealed Acts had to be re-repealed.[4] Modern lawyers would probably find this rule nonsensical, if they had ever heard of it, which most likely they have not, since Parliament repealed this rule of construction in 1850,[5] and American states, so often a museum of discarded common-law rules, seem to have repealed, abandoned or simply ignored it.[6] Lawyers from the American state of Louisiana, with its more rigorous civil law system, may recall the succinct formulation of the state's Civil Code: 'The repeal of a repealing law does not revive the first law'.[7]

But the old rule has a modern analogue in the law of wills. If a testator makes Will Number 1 and later makes Will Number 2 which revokes Will Number 1, but then revokes Will Number 2 before dying, which will (if any) is valid? The answers vary in American state courts, the majority holding that the second will *eo instante* revoked the first, but that the revocation of the second will revived the first, if that was what the testator intended—the position of the latest version of the Uniform Probate Code.[8] A minority of states, including my own state of North Carolina, hold to the contrary that the first will was forever revoked by the second regardless of the fate of the second will or the intention of the testator.[9] But the common-law rule is simply that Will Number 1 is to be given effect.[10] The parallelism with Blackstone's rule of statutory construction is not, to be sure, exact. The theory of the common law in the wills case is that Will Number I was never actually revoked at all. Wills are not effective until death, so the recognition of a power in the second will to revoke the first immediately on execution would give it *inter vivos* effect. (The difficulty

[4] 5 Geo 4, c 95 (1824); 6 Geo 4, c 129 (1825). See JV Orth, *Combination & Conspiracy: A Legal History of Trade Unionism, 1721–1906* (New York NY, 1991) 68–87.

[5] 13 & 14 Vict, c 21, s 5 (1850): '[W]here any Act repealing in whole or in part any former Act is itself repealed, such last Repeal shall not revive the Act or Provisions before repealed, unless Words be added reviving such Act or Provisions.'

[6] Kent faithfully repeated the rule but noted state statutes abolishing it. James Kent, *Commentaries on American Law*, ed OW Holmes, 12th edn (Boston, 1873) vol 1, p *446 and fn 1. Holmes glossed the passage with the cryptic 'it is not infrequently provided that the repeal of a repealing act shall not have the effect mentioned in the text': *ibid* fn 1, 12th edn (1873).

[7] La Civ Code, art 8.

[8] Uniform Probate Code s 2–509 (1990).

[9] NC Gen Stat s 31–5.8 :'No will or any part thereof that has been in any manner revoked can… be revived other than by a reexecution thereof'.

[10] See J Dukeminier et al, *Wills, Trusts, and Estates*, 7th edn (New York NY, 2005) 267–8.

with this view, of course, is that the revocatory act on Will Number 2 was effective *inter vivos*.) By contrast, statutes are effective on adoption, unless otherwise indicated.

There is, however, a more exact parallel. If a common-law court overrules a case that itself overruled a still earlier case, the law as it was *ab initio* is restored. If Parliament were a court, its overruling of itself would have that effect. And, of course, when it really was the High Court of Parliament, this is exactly what it was. As Parliament ceased to be thought of as a court finding good customs and became a legislature making new law, the parallelism broke down. In American terms, what had happened was simply the final step in the 'separation of powers': legislatures exercise legislative power, courts judicial power, and the difference is (or rather still was when the first American constitutions were adopted) the difference between making and finding law.

Number 10: '*Acts of Parliament that are impossible to be performed are of no validity* …'. As stated, the rule hardly makes sense. What is impossible to be done, cannot be done. A statute that ordered the impossible would be of null effect. As if to acknowledge the rule's inanity, Blackstone departed from his practice with the other rules of construction and offered no illustration of this rule. Dicey later filled the gap, quoting De Lolme to the effect that 'Parliament can do everything but make a woman a man, and a man a woman'.[11] Blackstone would no doubt have agreed. He said elsewhere in the *Commentaries* that Parliament 'can do everything that is not naturally impossible'.[12] Before the advances of modern medicine, the idea of changing sex was absurd, and even today courts (at least in America) still refuse to give legal effect to surgical alterations.[13] But, of course, Parliament need never attempt to make a woman a man or a man a woman. Why should it? It can get the same legal effect—all that really matters—by simply requiring the courts to treat women as if they were men and vice versa.

Why did Blackstone bother to state the obvious? The reason, as he patiently explained, was that there was a competing rule that was much more sweeping: 'Acts of Parliament contrary to reason are void.' The *locus classicus* of this rule is, of course, Bonham's Case from a hundred and fifty years earlier, in which so high an authority as Sir Edward Coke had said just that: 'When an Act of Parliament is against common right and reason, or repugnant, or impossible to be performed, the common law will

[11] AV Dicey, *Introduction to the Study of the Law of the Constitution* (London, 1908) 41. Holdsworth could not locate the source: *HEL* vol 12, p 344 fn 5.

[12] *Commentaries* vol 1, p 160.

[13] *Estate of Gardner*, 42 P3d 120 (Kan 2002) (holding marriage of a man to transsexual woman invalid); *Kantaras v Kantaras*, 884 So2d 155 (Fla App 2004) ('We agree with the Kansas, Ohio, and Texas courts in their understanding of the common meaning of male and female, as those terms are used statutorily, to refer to immutable traits determined at birth.')

controul it, and adjudge such Act to be void'—or, elided to its bare essentials, 'an Act of Parliament... against... reason... [is] void'.[14] And English judges had repeated it into the eighteenth century.[15] In America, as reformulated by John Marshall, it became 'a law repugnant to the constitution is void', but of course by then the referent had changed.[16]

What value there is in Blackstone's tenth rule of construction is not actually in the rule itself but in the qualification he added to it: 'and if there arise out of [acts of Parliament] collaterally any absurd consequences, manifestly contradictory to common reason, they are, with regard to those collateral consequences, void'. Coke's ringing affirmation of judicial review, as reformulated by Blackstone, had become the rather lame collateral: consequences contrary to reason are void. The hypothetical case Blackstone posed to illustrate the rule, or rather the rule's qualification, was an old chestnut: 'if an act of Parliament gives a man power to try all causes, that arise within his manor of Dale, [and] if a cause should arise in which he himself is party', what then? Should the man judge his own cause? Long before Blackstone or Coke, Littleton had asked the very same question in his little book on tenures. Coke was, of course, thoroughly—even obsessively—familiar with 'Littleton on Tenures' and himself had posed the question in the identical words Blackstone used.[17] A hundred and fifty years later Chief Justice Taft of the US Supreme Court would ask essentially the same question. Like the mythical law-school exam, the question remains the same but the answer changes.

At a time when statutes were few and far between, Littleton worried about a hypothetical manor in which it was the custom for the lord to distrain cattle that strayed onto his land and hold them until their owner paid a fine in the amount he assessed for the damage. This would make the lord a judge of his own cause and open the door for abuse: 'If he had damages but to the value of a halfpenny', Littleton reasoned, 'he might assess and have therefore an hundred pound, which should be against reason'. What is unreasonable is not a good custom, that is, not one to be enforced by the king's judges as common law.[18] Law is reason; what is contrary to reason cannot be law.

Three hundred years later this was still the rule, as Blackstone noted when he came to list the seven requisites 'to make a particular custom good': Number 4 is that it must be reasonable, or rather—with a typical

[14] 8 Co Rep 113b, 118a, 77 ER 646, 652 (CP 1610). See JV Orth, 'Did Sir Edward Coke Mean What He Said?' (1999) 16 *Constitutional Commentary* 33.

[15] *Day v Savadge* (1615) 80 ER 235, 237 (Hobart, J); *City of London v Wood* (1701) 88 ER 1592, 1603 (Holt, CJ).

[16] *Marbury v Madison* (1803), 5 US (1 Cranch) 137, 180.

[17] Holdsworth thought Coke worked on his *Commentaries* on Littleton for his entire life: *HEL* vol 5, p 466.

[18] *Littleton's Tenures in English*, ed and tr E Wambaugh (Washington DC, 1903) 99.

Blackstonian qualification—that it must 'not be unreasonable'.[19] Although citing Littleton for the proposition, the Commentator ignored Littleton's example of a man judging his own cause, choosing instead a hypothetical parish custom that no cattle be put in the common pasture till the lord of the manor has first put in his. This is unreasonable and therefore bad, Blackstone explained, 'for peradventure the lord will never put in his; and then the tenants will lose all their profits'.[20] Littleton would doubtless have agreed, but the unreasonableness of the parish custom is a general unfairness, not (as with the manorial custom concerning distress) a failure of due process of law.

The judge in his own cause seemed to haunt the imagination of Shakespeare, Coke's great contemporary, who brought it up, not once but twice. In *Twelfth Night,* premiered before the benchers of Middle Temple in 1602, Olivia comforts the wronged Malvolio:

> Prithee be content.
> This practice hath most shrewdly passed upon thee;
> But when we know the grounds and authors of it,
> Thou shalt be both the plaintiff and the judge of thine own cause.[21]

That is, when the lady knows the facts of the matter, her steward will have certain justice because he will administer it himself. And in *Measure for Measure*, which premiered two years later before King James I and his court—an audience that may well have included Sir Edward Coke, then the King's Attorney General—the dramatist actually staged the unreasonable trial. Duke Vincentio entraps Angelo, the hypocritical deputy who governed Vienna in the Duke's absence, by ordering an immediate trial of the corruption charge brought against him:

> Come, cousin Angelo
> In this I'll be impartial; be you judge
> Of your own cause.[22]

That is, the Duke will stand by and let Angelo condemn himself by his ready acceptance of the assignment to be both defendant and judge.

[19] *Commentaries* vol 1, p 77 (citing Littleton s 212). Reasonableness remains a requirement in courts still willing to recognise custom as a source of legal rights: *State ex rel Thornton v Hay*, 462 P2d 671 (Or 1969).

[20] *Commentaries* vol 1, p 77 (citing Coke's Compleat Copyholder s 33: see E Coke, *Three Law Tracts* (London, 1764) 61).

[21] V.i.341–4. Earlier, in *The Merchant of Venice* (1596–97), Portia, in the casket scene, not the courtroom scene, observes that '[t]o offend and judge are distinct offices, [I] And of opposed natures': II.ix.60–1.

[22] V.i.167–9. There is something similar in *Othello* (1604): The Venetian Duke comforts Brabantio, who had accused the Moor of seducing his daughter Desdemona: 'Whoe're he be that in this foul proceeding |Hath thus beguiled your daughter of herself, | And you of her, the bloody book of law |You shall yourself read in the bitter letter | After your own sense': I.iii. 67–9.

When half a dozen years later Coke posed the 'manor-of-Dale' hypothetical in Bonham's Case he, of course, rejected poetic justice and concluded matter-of-factly (in words he himself reported), 'If any Act of Parliament gives to any to hold, or have conusans of all manner of pleas arising before him within his manor of D., yet he shall hold no plea, to which he himself is party.' Law is reason, so what is contrary to reason cannot be law. What is true of customs is true of statutes as well. 'An Act of Parliament… against… reason… [is] void.' Just how sensitive Coke was to the risk of abuse in such a case, he demonstrated a few years later by deferring to a colleague to judge a dispute that had arisen between him and some of his tenants at Stoke.[23]

When Blackstone took up the question a century and a half later, he distinguished custom from statute and demoted Coke's dictum to a relatively minor matter of statutory construction, a mere qualification on an otherwise meaningless rule. If a statute seemed to produce the absurdity of making a man a judge of his own cause, the court would to this extent disregard it. But Blackstone did not leave the matter there. Resolutely, he imagined the worst:

> If we could conceive it possible for the Parliament to enact, that he should try as well his own causes as those of other persons, there is no court that has power to defeat the intention of the legislature, when couched in such evident and express words, as leave no doubt whether it was the intent of the legislature or no.[24]

The language itself is halting, a break in the Commentator's stately periods, as if wrung from him against his will, and the concession is strictly limited. It is a matter not of law but of power: 'there is no court [in England] that has power to defeat the intention of the legislature'.

Statute could do things that the common law could not. It could, Blackstone had to admit, 'enact a thing to be done which is unreasonable'.[25] It could make a man a judge of his own cause. It could even make him a slave, a condition unknown to the common law, as Mansfield had held in Sommersett's Case only a few years earlier.[26] At the beginning of the century Holt had joked about it from the bench:

[23] *Liber Famelicus of Sir James Whitelocke*, ed J Bruce (London, 1858) 50: 'Thear grew sum smale questions between him and sum of his tenants at Stoke about copies. He sent for me, prayed me to keep his court, and to order all things as I sholde see cawse in justice, upon view of his rolles and that he wolde be contented with what I determined withe him or against him.' Sir James Whitelocke served with Coke on the Court of King's Bench. Coke's conscientiousness is the more remarkable because at the time, in the autumn of 1616, he had other things on his mind, what Whitelocke referred to as 'his unfortunate businesses at the court', when he was forbidden to go on circuit and ordered to revise his *Reports*. Later in the year he was dismissed from his judicial and conciliar offices.

[24] *Commentaries* vol 1, p 91.

[25] *Commentaries* vol 1, p 91.

[26] *Somerset v Stewart* (1772) 98 ER 499. Mansfield's decision, reprinted from Lofft, and expanded reports of the arguments of counsel are given in 20 Howell's *State Trials* 1, where

> An Act of Parliament can do no wrong, though it may do several things that look pretty odd; for it may discharge one from his allegiance to the Government he lives under, and restore him to the state of nature,[27]

that is, it could make him an outlaw in the old sense of the word.[28]

In the New World, James Kent, hailed as the American Blackstone,[29] followed the Englishman's lead in his Commentaries on American Law:

> When it is said in the books, that a statute contrary to natural equity and reason, or repugnant, or impossible to be performed, is void [just what Coke had said], the cases are understood to mean that the courts are to give the statute a reasonable construction'.[30]

This is Coke filtered through Blackstone. But Kent had not yet fully worked out the implications of America's invention of written constitutions. Unlike Coke, common-law judges in America did not need to rely on the fading light of natural reason when confronted with an unjust statute.[31] 'With us,' as a Virginia judge had pointed out in 1793, 'the constitution is not an "ideal thing, but a real existence: it can be produced in a visible form"'.[32] So long as a textual basis can be found—and the judges have been very good at that—American courts do have the power to defeat the intention of the legislature no matter how clearly expressed.

When the case presented itself in 1928 of a statute that provided for a judge to be paid out of the fines he levied, the US Supreme Court, speaking through Chief Justice Taft, declared it unconstitutional and void, not (to be sure) as a violation of 'common right and reason', but as a violation of the right to 'due process of law'—a phrase, incidentally, that Coke had himself popularised if not invented, and a right expressly guaranteed by the Fifth

the name of the plaintiff is spelled Sommersett. Even a pro-slavery judge in the ante-bellum American South agreed with Mansfield that slavery was unknown to the common law: *State v Mann* (1829) 13 NC 263 (Ruffin, J).

[27] *City of London v Wood* (1701) 88 ER 1592, 1603. Nonetheless, Holt still thought parliament could not make 'one who lives under a Government Judge and party'. See JV Orth, 'When Analogy Fails: The Common Law & State v Mann' (2009) 87 *North Carolina Law Review* 979.

[28] Blackstone admitted that 'anciently an outlawed felon was said to have *caput lupinum*, and might be knocked on the head like a wolf, by any one that should meet him; because having renounced all law, he was to be dealt with as in a state of nature, when everyone that should find him might slay him, [but he observed that in his day] to avoid such inhumanity, it is holden that no man is intitled to kill him wantonly and willfully; but in so doing is guilty of murder, unless it happens in the endeavour to apprehend him.' *Commentaries* vol 4, pp 314–15.

[29] Kent stands to Blackstone very much as James Fennimore Cooper stands to Sir Walter Scott: a careful imitator of considerable talent.

[30] Kent (n 6) vol 1, p 447.

[31] See *Calder v Bull* (1798) 3 US 386 (Iredell, J) for a precocious statement of the need for a textual basis for constitutional decision-making: 'The ideas of natural justice are regulated by no fixed standard: the ablest and the purest men have differed on the subject'.

[32] *Kamper v Hawkins* (1793) 3 Va (1 Va Cas) 20, 78 (Tucker, J quoting T Paine, *The Rights of Man* (London,1791).

and Fourteenth Amendments to the US Constitution (as well as by the various state constitutions).[33] To Blackstone's seventh rule of statutory construction, 'Where the common law and a statute differ, the common law gives place to the statute',[34] Americans added, 'and a statute gives place to the constitution'[35]—just as they also modified Blackstone's rule Number 9, 'Acts of Parliament derogatory from the power of subsequent parliaments bind not'—at least insofar as one legislature initiates a constitutional amendment that goes on to final ratification.

Did Blackstone realise how he was situated, astraddle the old world of the common law and the new world of statute, the world in which Parliament like the courts tried customs to see if they were good, and the world in which the will of the Parliament is law? To a degree, he must have. After all, he defined law as a rule commanding what is right and prohibiting what is wrong, and built his *Commentaries* around the distinction between rights and wrongs. He piously repeated, and no doubt sincerely believed with Coke, that 'law is the perfection of reason', 'what is not reason is not law'.[36] But he went out of his way to contradict the master concerning the respective roles of court and Parliament, using Coke's own manor-of-Dale example to illustrate the new reality. Coming after Coke, Blackstone knew who had won the civil wars. Nor could he have underrated the concession he made. At the end of the *Commentaries* he returned to the judge-in-his-own-cause problem: 'In a state of society', he said, 'men are prevented from being judges in their own causes, which is one of the evils that civil government was intended to remedy'.[37] If Parliament could, even in theory, allow that, then the law's perfection was in jeopardy, and the state of nature threatened. Could this be 'the little rift within the lute |That by and by will make the music mute'?

Although up-to-date in his constitutional law, Blackstone was behind the times in other respects. The oft-noted absence of commercial law from the

[33] *Tumey v Ohio* (1928) 273 US 510, 534 :'a situation in which an officer perforce occupies two practically and seriously inconsistent positions, one partisan and the other judicial, necessarily involves a lack of due process of law'. See JV Orth, *Due Process of Law: A Brief History* (Lawrence, KS 2003) 7–8. A few state constitutions expressly prohibit the practice. See NC Const art IV, s 21 ('In no case shall the compensation of any Judge or Magistrate be dependent upon his decision or upon the collection of costs.').

[34] *Commentaries* vol 1, p 89. See JV Orth, *The North Carolina State Constitution, with History and Commentary* (Chapel Hill NC, 1995) 117–18.

[35] As to whether the common law must give place to the constitution, see JV Orth,' Can the Common Law Be Unconstitutional?' in his *How Many Judges Does It Take to Make a Supreme Court? And Other Essays on Law and the Constitution* (Lawrence, KS 2006).

[36] *Commentaries* vol 1, p 70, paraphrasing E Coke, *The First Part of the Institutes of the Lawes of England. Or, A Commentarie upon Littleton* (London, 1629; 1628) fo 97v.

[37] *Commentaries* Vol 4, p 8 (restating J Locke, *Two Treatises of Government*, ed P Laslett (Cambridge, 1960; 1689) 294: 'Civil Government is the proper Remedy for the Inconveniences of the State of Nature, which must certainly be Great, where Men may be Judges in their own Case').

Commentaries, or even of any serious discussion of contract, was at that moment being remedied by the reformist Lord Mansfield, who sought to do 'substantial justice' and effectuate intention even at the expense of long established rules.[38] Critics from Junius and Jefferson through Langdell to Hayek have denounced such judicial activism,[39] although American judges applauded.[40] As we know, Blackstone himself was outraged by Mansfield's willingness to disregard the venerable Rule in Shelley's Case and helped to prolong its life for another century or two.[41] It was still the law in North Carolina when I began teaching there.[42]

Blackstone did not foresee the dramatic changes English society was beginning to undergo. He had steeped himself too deeply in tradition, lived too long among the landed classes. In any event, he preferred whatever legal improvements lay ahead, to be—as those in the past had been—only matters of degree, gradual.[43] And time was running out. Nor did Blackstone foresee that the initiative in legal development was about to pass from court to Parliament, or that by the mid-nineteenth century it would be conceded that only Parliament could overturn a common-law rule, even such a recent and ill-considered rule as Lord Ellenborough's holding in 1808 that a cause of action in tort did not survive the life of the victim, a rule with the outrageous consequence that it was cheaper for the defendant to kill the victim than to injure him.[44] By contrast, in America the judges carried on in the old way: as Justice Story observed a quarter-century later, judicial precedents there were 'often re-examined, reversed, and qualified by the Courts themselves, whenever they are found to be either defective, or ill-founded, or otherwise incorrect'.[45] Ironically it was the country

[38] *Alderson v Temple* (1768) ER 165, 167; *Eaton v Jacques* (1780) 99 ER 290, 292.

[39] J Cannon (ed), *The Letters of Junius* (Oxford, 1978) 209–10 (Letter 41, 14 November 1770); Thomas Jefferson to Philip Mazzei (November 1785) in JP Boyd (ed), *Papers of Thomas Jefferson* (Princeton NJ, 1954) vol 9, p 71; CC Langdell, *Summary of the Law of Contracts* (Boston MA, 1880) 20–21, s 15; FA Hayek, *The Road to Serfdom* (Chicago IL, 1944) 92 fn 3.

[40] See *Livingston v Jefferson* (1811) 15 F Cas 660, 664 (No 8,411): John Marshall CJ, who described Mansfield as 'one of the greatest Judges who ever sat on any bench, and who has done more than any other to remove those technical impediments which grew out of a different state of society, and too long continued to obstruct the course of substantial justice'. It is probably not a coincidence that Marshall praised Mansfield so lavishly in a decision involving President Jefferson, who abominated the English judge. *Cf* RK Newmyer, *Supreme Court Justice Joseph Story: Statesman of the Old Republic* (Chapel Hill NC, 1985) 246.

[41] *Perrin v Blake* (1772) 98 ER 355; F Hargrave (ed), *Collectanea Juridica* (London, 1792) vol 1, p 283.

[42] NC Gen Stat s 41–6.3 (1987) (Rule in Shelley's Case abolished). See JV Orth, 'Requiem for the Rule in Shelley's Case' (1988) 67 *North Carolina Law Review* 681.

[43] See *Commentaries* vol 4, ch 33: 'Of the Rise, Progress, and Gradual Improvements, of the Laws of England'.

[44] *Baker v Bolton* (1808) 170 ER 1033; rule replaced by the Fatal Accidents Act, 9 & 10 Vict c 93 (1846) (Lord Campbell's Act).

[45] *Swift v Tyson* (1834), 41 US (16 Pet) 1, 18.

without a written constitution and its embodiment of the doctrine of separation of powers that witnessed a more complete separation of law-making and dispute-resolution than the newly constituted United States.

If Blackstone had a particular strategy to preserve the common law from its perils, it was to defend the law's reasonableness by shifting the burden of proof. 'Law is the perfection of reason'. 'What is not reason is not law'. To which he added a characteristic qualification:

> not that the particular reason of every rule in the law can at this distance of time be always precisely assigned; but it is sufficient that there be nothing in the rule flatly contradictory to reason, and then the law will presume it to be well founded.[46]

The law presumes its own reasonableness and places on its critics the burden of proving the contrary.

With respect to statutes, Blackstone warned that they often did more harm than good:

> Whenever a standing rule of law, of which the reason perhaps could not be remembered or discerned, hath been wantonly broke in upon by statutes or new resolutions, the wisdom of the rule hath in the end appeared from the inconveniences that have followed the innovation.[47]

And indeed, abolition of the Rule in Shelley's Case, for example, has resulted in the recognition of interests in unascertainable persons, an inconvenience that has necessitated further legislation. The same may be said of the abolition of the so-called Doctrine of Worthier Title. A North Carolina statute gives a power to the grantor of a deed that creates a contingent remainder in persons not yet ascertained to revoke the grant at any time prior to the vesting of the remainder,[48] and a New York statute provides that a trust may be revoked by the settlor and the ascertained beneficiaries when the only other interested persons are the settlor's heirs[49]—an uncomfortable reminder that Blackstone might have had a point.

With respect to Coke's extravagant claim in Bonham's Case that reason—or, rather, the artificial reason of the law—could trump Parliament, Blackstone salvaged what he could. Without a written constitution to restrain the legislature, the judges were thrown back on their skills of

[46] *Commentaries* vol 1, p 70.

[47] *Ibid.* Blackstone faulted even the seemingly benign attempt begun with the Statute of Wills to allow freedom of testation: 'Innumerable frauds and perjuries were quickly introduced by this parliamentary method of inheritance.': *Commentaries* vol 2, p 376. For a review of modern efforts to turn the clock back, see JV Orth, 'Wills Act Formalities: How Much Compliance is Enough? '(2008) 43 *Real Property, Trust & Estate Law Journal* 73.

[48] NC Gen Stat s 39–6.

[49] NY Est, Powers & Trusts Law s 7–1.9 (b).

statutory construction, which are not inconsiderable. That and the fact of a reasonable Parliament dominated by the landed interest postponed the problem until, more than a century later, Professor Dicey (Blackstone's successor in the Vinerian chair) bewailed the fact that a parliamentary majority could rubbish the 'rule of law'.[50]

Perhaps more than anything else, what Blackstone did to secure the common law was, of course, simply to restate it in elegant Augustan prose. For the first time in five hundred years the law found its eloquent voice. And, as Professor Milsom reminded us in his Selden Society Lecture, 'In trying to give laymen a view from above the procedural technicalities, he had given lawyers a new vision of the law'.[51] At the end of the day, as Blackstone knew, the common law would survive because its rules and procedures are, well, reasonable—or at least not unreasonable.

[50] AV Dicey, *Lectures on the Relation between Law and Public Opinion in England during the Nineteenth Century* (London, 1914) xlvii. Holdsworth agreed: *HEL* vol 2, p 446.

[51] SFC Milsom, *The Nature of Blackstone's Achievement*, 1980 Selden Society Lecture, reprinted in (1981) 1 *Oxford Journal of Legal Studies* 10.

7

Blackstone and Bentham on the Law of Marriage

MARY SOKOL

I INTRODUCTION

IN THE FIFTEENTH chapter of the first book of his *Commentaries on the Laws of England* (1765) William Blackstone outlined the eighteenth-century law of marriage. He set out the formalities necessary to make a valid marriage, distinguishing disabilities (incapacities) imposed by common law from those at canon law. He also discussed recent legislation (Hardwicke's Marriage Act) designed to end clandestine marriages, the doctrine of coverture, the legal status of a married woman and the law of divorce. Then in Book Three of the *Commentaries* marriage appears again in a discussion of the jurisdiction of the church courts.

Blackstone's law of marriage was not narrowly focused on legal rules, although he certainly provided many of these. He also gave his readers a broad theoretical basis for an arguably secular law of marriage. He made reference to contemporary European debates on marriage which in part continued seventeenth-century controversies about natural law and the secularisation of marriage. Blackstone explained the existing law of marriage in terms of its historical development from earliest times. His famous metaphor of legal fictions as a Gothic castle fitted up for modern inhabitants applies equally to his account of the law of marriage.

By the time the young Jeremy Bentham began to write on marriage Blackstone had long been a successful and well-known public figure. We know that Bentham owned a first edition of Blackstone's *Commentaries*, and some of his work has been said to echo Blackstone's phraseology and arrangement, making Blackstone 'a pervasive factor in Bentham's early thought'.[1] Is this equally true about Bentham's thought on the law of marriage?

[1] J Bentham, *A Comment on the Commentaries and A Fragment on Government*, ed JH Burns and HLA Hart (London, 1977) xxi.

Surprisingly enough, there seems at first glance much in common between Bentham's and Blackstone's writings on marriage. Besides clear similarities in the structure and content of their work, both were evidently indebted to Hale, Locke and Montesquieu. There are also obvious differences. Bentham's writings are both more extensive and discursive than Blackstone's, partly because much of Bentham's work on marriage remains in manuscript. Bentham's friend and editor Etienne Dumont did publish some of this material as part of Bentham's *Traités de Législation Civile et Pénale* (1802). However Dumont's version of Bentham on marriage is not always reliable, because Dumont exercised his editorial role vigorously to exclude or rewrite material he thought contentious.[2] While Bentham left it to others to publish, or mangle, his work, Blackstone himself carefully undertook the revision and publication of his university law lectures as the *Commentaries*.

Other differences between Blackstone's and Bentham's work are more fundamental and include, most importantly, different purposes in writing about marriage. Blackstone's aims were those of a pioneering expositor and would-be reformer of English law. Writing for an educated public as well as for lawyers, he set out to reveal a constitution and laws founded on natural law and moulded by history. Bentham also considered himself a reformer and an expositor, but he intended his reforms to be incorporated in a wholly new codified law of marriage based on the principle of utility, which holds that all human actions are governed by a wish to avoid pain and gain pleasure. Bentham instructed his ideal legislator to draft a law of marriage based on the principle of utility and told him how and why he should do so.[3]

In order to consider how far Blackstone's *Commentaries* influenced Bentham's writing on the law of marriage I have chosen to examine particular aspects of the law of marriage that were addressed by both authors, rather than providing a general overview of their work. These are canon law and the jurisdiction of the church courts, forming a valid marriage, and the doctrine of coverture, all of which were the subject of legal and popular controversy during the course of the eighteenth century.

II OXFORD AND AFTER

It is more than likely that Bentham first heard the English law of marriage explained from Blackstone's own mouth, because in 1763 Bentham, then

[2] L Campos Boralevi, 'Jeremy Bentham's Writings on Sexual Non-Conformity: Utilitarianism, Neo-Malthusianism, and Sexual Liberty' (1983) 2 *Topos* 138.

[3] Bentham's marriage code was to be given to couples when they married, so they should be aware of their respective rights and duties: see UC lxxvii 18, lxxvi 152.

sixteen years old and an undergraduate at Queen's College, Oxford, attended Blackstone's lecture course on the common law. Bentham's undergraduate notebook is still extant. But it contains only notes on the first 10 lectures, and not on those later classes which included the law of husband and wife under the heading of 'Private Rights'.[4] Yet it is likely that Bentham heard these, for he later told John Bowring that he attended the lectures with two other students both of whom took copious notes 'which I attempted to do, but could not continue it, as my thoughts were occupied in reflecting on what I heard'.[5]

In 1774 Bentham began writing a general criticism of the *Commentaries*, taking over a work first begun by his friend John Lind. He subsequently abandoned this project in favour of a far more narrowly focused critique, published anonymously in 1776 as *A Fragment on Government*. His main assault on Blackstone, *A Comment on the Commentaries*, remained unpublished until nearly a century after Bentham's death in 1832. But here Bentham concentrated his criticisms on the second and third sections of Book One, ('Of the Nature of Laws in General', and 'Of The Laws of England'), with no discussion at all of Blackstone's writing on marriage.[6]

There was a strange irony in this omission. Bentham's immediate purpose in drafting *A Comment on the Commentaries* was to further his plans to marry Polly Dunkley, a young woman from Colchester with no private fortune. Bentham, now aged 26, lived on an inheritance from his mother which he thought inadequate to support a family. Jeremiah Bentham, his father, refused financial help and opposed the marriage on the grounds that it could bring his son neither fortune nor social advantage.[7] Jeremiah's behaviour was not unusually avaricious for the age, although perhaps he was more obdurate than many contemporary fathers faced with emotional appeals from their children. Bentham wrote bitterly to his brother Samuel that despite indications to the contrary, most probably their father did love him, or at least 'next to his money'.[8]

Deciding to marry without his father's help, Jeremy planned to raise money by renting out his chambers in Lincoln's Inn and moving into his friend John Lind's house in Holborn, where Polly would join him. There he would support his wife by writing for profit. Bentham did move house. But what he called his 'great marriage scheme'[9] failed, and Bentham remained

[4] I Doolittle, 'Jeremy Bentham and Blackstone's Lectures' (1982) 6 *Bentham Newsletter* 23–5.

[5] *The Works of Jeremy Bentham*, ed J Bowring (Edinburgh, 1838–43) vol 10, p 45.

[6] Bentham, *Comment on the Commentaries* (n 1) xxiv.

[7] Bentham, *Correspondence* vol 1, pp 232–4.

[8] Bentham, *Correspondence* vol 1, pp 232–4; see generally A Vickery, *The Gentleman's Daughter: Women's Lives in Georgian England* (London, 1998) 39–44, 52.

[9] Bentham, *Correspondence* vol 1, pp 185, 235.

a bachelor throughout his long life, actively promoting a picture of himself as a reclusive celibate scholar, the 'hermit of Queens Square'.

By contrast Blackstone had personal, as well as professional and academic experience of the law of marriage. Professionally, Blackstone heard and made careful notes on many Poor Law cases argued in Westminster Hall between 1746–79, cases which often turned around the validity of a marriage in order to claim a right to settlement. Records of Blackstone's personal life are few, but we know that once he achieved some degree of financial security he married Sarah Clitherow in May 1761. During the nineteen years of reputedly happy marriage that followed, Sarah and William raised a family of seven surviving children.[10]

III BLACKSTONE AND BENTHAM AS INSTITUTISTS

The law of marriage appears in Book One of Blackstone's *Commentaries,* as the second of four 'private relations of persons'. The first such 'private relation' is that of master and servant, followed by husband and wife, then parent and child, and lastly guardian and child. Similarly Bentham's published work set out four forms of private and domestic relationships, although marriage appears last of all, reversing the order in the manuscripts where 'Husband and Wife' appear first, and master and servant last.[11]

Despite these differences in order, Blackstone and Bentham were both following the model set out in Book One of Justinian's *Institutes* (AD 533), which examined the nature and sources of law, and then of persons, including husband and wife.[12] It has been convincingly argued that Blackstone used an 'institutional' framework to forward his aim of producing a 'map' of the common law, but that Bentham too could be considered as an institutist is more controversial. Others before Blackstone had attempted to fit the common law into an institutional framework. Eighteenth-century institutists always introduced their work with essays on laws in general, discussing law as a theory of justice derived from either God or nature. Unlike Roman law the common law did not easily fit into an institutional framework because 'its intrinsic nature as a system of remedies' involved no moral definitions, or resort to principle.[13] But for

[10] Doolittle, *Blackstone* 96–7; Prest, *Blackstone* 179–80, 208–9, 278–9.

[11] *Commentaries* vol 1, p 421; J Bentham, *The Theory of Legislation*, ed CK Ogden (London, 1931) 199. UC lxxi 90.

[12] A Watson, *The Making of the Civil Law* (Cambridge MA, 1981) 12, 16; A Watson, 'The Structure of Blackstone's *Commentaries*' (1988) 97 *Yale Law Journal* 796.

[13] *Ibid.* See *OED*, sv 'Institutional', which cites Blackstone and Bentham as the first users of the term in this sense. See also J Cairns, 'Blackstone, An English Institutist: Legal Literature and the Rise of the Nation State' (1984) 4 *Oxford Journal of Legal Studies* 318–40; AWB

Blackstone the theoretical structure of an institute allowed him to attempt a reconciliation between analytical method and substantive common-law content, a reconciliation that he achieved with great success.[14]

Although he rejected theories of natural law, Bentham certainly recognised and acknowledged Blackstone's achievement, especially in his 'technical arrangement' of English law, which he praised, maybe not so faintly, as 'the best that a technical nomenclature will admit'.[15] More generally, Bentham thought that Blackstone had taught jurisprudence to speak the language of the scholar and the gentleman, enlivened by classical erudition, metaphors and allusions.[16] Arguably, Bentham then followed Blackstone's example and used the same recognisable order, or structure, when he wrote on marriage in the 1780s. If so, Bentham's use of an institutional structure owed more to the 'pervasive' influence of Blackstone's successful *Commentaries* than to any other cause.

Despite his praise for Blackstone's structural model, Bentham's purpose in using it differed from Blackstone's. Rather than Blackstone's reformed national common law, Bentham worked for a codified system of law based on the principle of utility which would have universal application. This 'Pannomion', or comprehensive code was to be divided into constitutional, civil and penal codes, with subsidiary particular codes including a marriage code: and so Bentham would be the 'legislator of the world'.[17]

The most conclusive illustration of Bentham's departure from Blackstone's institutional model is provided in his lengthy discussion about the origins of marriage. Here Bentham looked to the principle of utility and Hobbesian contractual theory, rather than to divine or natural law, or jurisdictional claims. He held that a marriage contract was 'beyond comparison' the most important of any in law. Love, by which Bentham here meant physical love, was a pleasure within a utilitarian scheme of law, and therefore the legislator had a duty to establish and then enforce such marriage contracts.[18]

Bentham admitted that restricting love to marriage was 'harmful' because it reduced pleasure, but maintained that the benefits for men, women, children, and all society from marital fidelity far outweighed any

Simpson, *Legal Theory and Legal History* (London, 1987) 281–3, 293, 296; M Lobban, *The English Common Law and English Jurisprudence 1760–1850* (Oxford, 1991) 14, 19, 22–8.

[14] Lobban, *English Common Law* (n 13) 27.

[15] D Lieberman, *The Province of Legislation Determined: Legal Theory in Eighteenth-Century Britain* (Cambridge, 1989) 258, 219–40; Lobban (n 13) 124–7.

[16] G Jones, *The Sovereignty of the Law: Selections from Blackstone's Commentaries on the Laws of England* (Toronto, 1973) xxvii–xxviii.

[17] See J Bentham, *'Legislator of the World': Writings on Codification, Law and Education*, ed P Schofield and J Harris (Oxford, 1998); also J Dinwiddy, *Bentham* (Oxford, 1989) 14–16, 58–61.

[18] UC xxxii 124, 103.

transitory inconvenience. In order to illustrate this he wrote a fable about a group of six people living a miserable existence in a state of nature. This story begins when a man leaves his wife and ends when a child, deserted by his mother, is devoured by a wolf. Evoking Hobbes's *Leviathan*, Bentham's story concludes that without government, which here includes a form of marriage, man's nature must inevitably lead to conflict.[19]

Blackstone, however, completely rejected the notion that there was ever a time without 'society'. He found quite implausible the belief of 'theoretical writers' that society originated with a meeting on a large plain of individuals who then entered into an original contract. Any such scenario was contrary to historical evidence of early civilisations.[20] Nevertheless Blackstone did believe that '[t]he only true and natural foundations of society are the wants and fears of individuals', whose sense of their weakness and imperfection would then keep them together.[21]

IV MARRIAGE AND THE CHURCH COURTS

Blackstone and Bentham both described marriage as a civil or secular contract, rather than a religious sacrament. That they shared this conclusion reflected, in part, the Enlightenment's interest in non-European cultures, a perspective which in turn allowed for a new scrutiny of English institutions. It also reflected the particular history of the English law of marriage and English political thought. Until 1857 the English church courts, applying canon law, had a broad jurisdiction over marriage. Solemnisation of marriage using the marriage service set out in the Book of Common Prayer had been prescribed since the Elizabethan Act of Uniformity (1559). Calling banns had been part of the ecclesiastical law of marriage even longer. The Canons of 1603–4 prohibited marriage without parental consent for minors (although they were never formally enacted). But in effect civil registration of marriage had been required since 1694, under the Marriage Tax and Marriage Registration Acts.[22] Lord Hardwicke's Act of 1753, enacted as Blackstone began his Oxford lectures, gave statutory force to most previous canon law requirements. Stressing recent statutory change, Blackstone wrote in 1765 that:

[19] UC lxxi 91–2; T Hobbes, *Leviathan* (London, 1962; 1651) 143; J Wolfe, *An Introduction to Political Philosophy* (Oxford, 1996) 8.

[20] *Commentaries* vol 1, p 47.

[21] *Ibid.*

[22] 20 & 21 Vict c 85; see JH Baker, *An Introduction to English Legal History Fourth Edition* (London, 2002) 496; RB Outhwaite, *The Rise and Fall of the English Ecclesiastical Courts, 1500–1860* (Cambridge, 2006) 104–5. 6 & 7 Wm III c 6 and 6 & 7 Wm III c 35.

> Our law considers marriage in no other light than as a civil contract. The *holiness* of the matrimonial state is left entirely to the ecclesiastical law: the temporal courts not having jurisdiction to consider unlawful marriage as a sin, but merely as a civil inconvenience.[23]

So English law treated a contract of marriage as it did any other. It was valid where the parties were willing and able to contract, and then did so contract in the required form.

At pains to accommodate canon law into his common-law system, Blackstone needed to explain canon law's inferior position. Civil and canon laws, he wrote, had 'no force or authority in this kingdom; they are no more binding in England than our laws are binding in Rome'.[24] 'Foreign', that is canon law, only had force in so far as it was permitted to operate in certain courts. He firmly reiterated this position in a subsequent passage, writing that 'eccentrical tribunals' (such as the church courts), 'are admitted in England, not by any right of their own, but upon bare suffrance and tolerance from the municipal laws'.[25]

Blackstone then produced historical evidence to support his claim that canon law depended on common law for its authority, so countering any suggestion that a religious ceremony was necessary for the validity of a marriage. Until papal intervention in the middle ages, he wrote, marriage had been 'totally a civil contract'. Later, during the 'grand rebellion', or Interregnum, marriages could only take place in a civil ceremony before a justice of the peace. After the Restoration these civil marriages were validated by statute, without requiring a second, religious, ceremony.[26]

Blackstone accepted that the church courts had jurisdiction to declare marriages as void *ab initio* if certain impediments were disclosed. But, he said, as far as the common law was concerned, these marriages were only 'voidable, and not *ipso facto* void', remaining valid unless and until avoided by an ecclesiastical court. In addition, the common-law courts could prohibit and annul proceedings in the church courts.[27] He argued that because the ecclesiastical Canons of 1603–04 had never been confirmed by Parliament they lacked legal authority, and that when Lord Hardwicke's Act stipulated that marriage must be performed by a priest, this requirement reflected positive, not divine or natural law.[28]

Blackstone's insistence on the civil rather than divine nature of marriage formation was not an attack on either the Established Church or its courts. He later managed to upset many Dissenters, most famously Joseph

[23] 26 Geo II c 33; *Commentaries* vol 1, p 421.

[24] *Commentaries* vol 1, pp 14–15.

[25] *Ibid* vol 3, pp 86–7.

[26] *Ibid* vol 1, p 427; RB Outhwaite, *Clandestine Marriage in England, 1500–1850* (London, 1995) 11–13.

[27] *Ibid*, pp 422, 14–15.

[28] *Ibid*, pp 83, 427.

Priestley, with various derogatory comments in Book IV of *Commentaries*. In that context Blackstone clearly considered himself an upholder of the Church of England.[29] Yet in some other respects, as we shall see below, Blackstone's writing on marriage indicates a 'reformed protestant' inclination. He remained consistently rude about 'monkish clergy', and 'popish ecclesiastics', even describing pre-reformation England as 'those days of bigotry'.[30] But when Blackstone wrote of the civil as opposed to religious nature of marriage he was not making a theological point. His intention was rather to proclaim the ascendancy of English common law over all 'foreign' laws, not least the canon law. He did not argue for the abolition of the church courts, despite his insistence that their authority depended on the common law. Quite to the contrary, he maintained that it was

> to the honour of the spiritual courts, that though they continue to this day to decide many questions which are properly of temporal cognizance, yet justice is in general so ably and impartially administered in those tribunals, (especially of the superior kind) and the boundaries of their power are now so well known and established, that no material inconvenience at present arises from this jurisdiction continuing in the antient chanel.[31]

If changes were made to a system that had lasted seven centuries the consequence would be 'great confusion'.[32] Such opinions, especially about the excellent working of the 'superior tribunals', were certainly shared by others.[33]

For Bentham, too, marriage was a secular contract. But unlike Blackstone, Bentham's secularism was not the result of historically based arguments about classical or early medieval marriage ceremonies, and so owed little to Blackstone. Instead Bentham's main interest was to promote utilitarian codification of the law of marriage, rather than reform of the existing law.

V MAKING A VALID MARRIAGE: POLYGAMY

A valid marriage was made between a man and a woman who consented to the marriage and who married according to the requirements of canon law and of Hardwicke's Marriage Act which set out the necessary formalities.

Despite Blackstone's typically English focus, in writing about the requirements for a valid marriage and the legal disabilities which prevent

29 Prest, *Blackstone* 246–50.
30 *Commentaries* vol 1, pp 18, 20–21.
31 *Ibid* vol 3, p 99.
32 *Ibid*, p 99.
33 *Ibid*, pp 98–9; Outhwaite (n 22) 125.

marriage he made a sudden, surprising, digression into comparative law. Polygamy, he said, was 'condemned both by the law of the new testament, and the policy of all prudent states, especially in these northern climates'.[34] Bentham had even more than Blackstone to say about polygamy, and also made reference to polyandry (where one woman has several husbands). For both, the context was an explanation of why the existence of a prior marriage should make a subsequent marriage void. Bigamy had been an offence in English law since 1604. But in the eighteenth century public concern was more likely to be about concubinage, and the scandals of clandestine marriages, rather than polygamy, with its suggestions of exotic seraglios and multiple concurrent domestic arrangements.

How then is Blackstone's surprising and unnecessary rejection of polygamy to be explained? English law texts did not usually discuss polygamy. There are no references to polygamy, nor mention of 'northern climates', found in Giles Jacob's *New Law Dictionary* (1772), or Thomas Wood's *Institute of the Laws of England* (1775). But a discussion of polygamy does appear in Thomas Salmon's *A Critical Essay Concerning Marriage* (1724). Salmon's popular treatise examined polygamy and concubinage in some detail, concluding with an extensive survey of historical and contemporary marriage customs from around the world.[35]

Salmon, and Blackstone too, made frequent reference to the work of Samuel Pufendorf (1632–94), the Protestant German jurist and philosopher. Pufendorf saw marriage as necessary for the preservation of order in states. Natural law dictated a natural equality between men and women; neither divine law nor their superior strength gave males sovereignty over females. While God punished Eve by ordering her to be subject to the will of her husband, that was 'a mere provision of [divine] positive law', and not of natural law. So the husband's authority over his wife derived solely from the contract they entered into upon marriage.[36]

Blackstone also referred to Montesquieu, who seems to have set an agenda for discussions about marriage and male–female relations in eighteenth century England, in both his *Persian Letters* (1721) and *The Spirit of the Laws* (1748). Montesquieu's theory about the effect of climate on the character, laws and customs of nations included details about marriage customs, polygamy and polyandry. He concluded that 'the law permitting only one wife' had more relation to the physical aspect of the

[34] *Ibid*, p 424.

[35] T Salmon, *A Critical Essay Concerning Marriage* (London, 1724) 81–108.

[36] *The Political Writings of Samuel Pufendorf*, ed CL Carr, tr MJ Seidler (Oxford, 1994) 151, 199.

climate of Europe than that of Asia[37] Also, very controversially, Montesquieu compared the laws of domestic servitude with those of domestic slavery. Slavery was of two kinds, real and personal. Personal slaves are domestic slaves: '[I]n Asia' he wrote, 'domestic servitude and despotic government have been seen to go hand in hand in every age', while he claimed that wives in seraglios were but personal slaves.[38] Montesquieu's conflation of slavery and domestic servitude was not extended to the poor. Simple people, he wrote (quoting Tacitus), have no need of personal slaves because their women and children will carry out the domestic work.[39]

Clearly Blackstone had in mind Montesquieu's climate theory when he wrote of 'northern climates'. Cultural comparisons and climate theory were ubiquitous in literary and philosophical texts at the time.[40] Bentham composed seven pages of manuscripts on polygamy and polyandry which do not appear in the published version of his marriage work, Dumont's *Traités*. Starting with the cryptic question 'how many people?' Bentham defined polygamy as an offence where one person marries another during the continuation of a previous marriage, making the later marriage void. He had little to say on polyandry, but found the practice of polygamy unacceptable, as typically an aggravated species of fraud used to gain the person and sometimes fortune of a deluded woman. It subsumed two other crimes, defraudment and seduction, but did not fit perfectly with either because the disgrace brought on a woman by polygamy was not as great as by seduction.[41]

No doubt Bentham was familiar with Blackstone's discussion of polygamy, but he was not primarily indebted to Blackstone for his own comments on multiple marriages, rather to Montesquieu directly. For when Bentham wrote of polygamy and repudiation of a marriage the language he used was that of Montesquieu. In choosing to discuss polygamy at all both Blackstone and Bentham were responding to the same ideas and writings of the *philosophes* of the European Enlightenment, and in particular to Montesquieu. But any further similarity quickly disappears with the reasons advanced by Bentham and Blackstone respectively for rejecting polygamy. Bentham completely rejected Montesquieu's climate theory and consequent explanations for the variety of human laws. He insisted, on the

[37] FTH Fletcher, *Montesquieu and English Politics 1750–1800* (London, 1939) 17–33; *Commentaries* vol I p 6; P Kra, 'Montesquieu and Women' in SI Spencer (ed), *French Women in the Age of Enlightenment* (Bloomington IN, 1984) 272–84. C Montesquieu, *The Spirit of the Laws* (tr & ed) AM Cohler et al (Cambridge, 1989; 1748) 264–77.

[38] Montesquieu, *Spirit of the Laws* (n 37) 254, 264, 270.

[39] *Ibid* 254.

[40] Fletcher (n 37) 62; W Paley, *The Principles of Moral and Political Philosophy* (London, 1785) 167–8, 182–6; *Political and Philosophical Writing of William Godwin, ed* M Philp (London, 1993) 32–42; M Wollstonecraft, *A Vindication of the Rights of Woman* (London, 1985; 1792) 6.

[41] UC lxxi 106.

contrary, that he would not look at comparative social and legal customs when drafting his code of law but only consult the principle of utility.[42] Blackstone also rejected polygamy, but on the basis of Christian teaching which forbade it, and because of what he described as the political prudence found in northern countries which did not allow such multiple marriages.[43]

VI LORD HARDWICKE'S MARRIAGE ACT

Blackstone and Bentham concurred that forming a valid marriage should be publicly regulated by means of legislation. The Clandestine Marriages Act of 1753, better known as Lord Hardwicke's Act, sought to regulate the formation of marriages by requiring compliance with certain formalities, including recording each marriage in a parish register.[44] It thereby put an end to the notorious scandals of runaway and secret clandestine marriages, because if its provisions for publicity, registration and solemnisation were not met, such a 'marriage' was automatically void.

Traditional marriage customs and practices, such as marriage by hand-fasting, had once been popular, although exactly how common they were is unclear. Neither Blackstone nor Bentham showed much sympathy for claims that Lord Hardwicke's Act interfered with supposed traditional folk customs such as marriage by handfasting. By the eighteenth century clandestine marriage was likely to be an irregular marriage which took place before a priest, but failed to comply with canon law in some way, as by omitting to call the banns. Such clandestine marriages often took place in extra-parochial churches or 'peculiars', and undoubtedly had been common before the Act.[45] Peculiars existed outside the normal jurisdiction of a bishop, claiming their own rights to issue marriage licences and to conduct marriage ceremonies. Some prison chapels, most notoriously that at the Fleet debtors' prison, enjoyed this status, and had carried on a profitable trade in clandestine marriages (which moved to the 'liberty' just outside the Fleet when marriages within the prison itself were blocked by

[42] Bowring (n 5) X 54; see also Fletcher (n 37) 13–14.

[43] *Commentaries* vol 1, p 424.

[44] 26 Geo II c 33; see generally L Stone, *Road to Divorce England 1530–1987* (Oxford, 1990) 121–8.

[45] *Ibid* chs 4–5; M Ingram, *The Church Courts, Sex and Marriage in England, 1570–1640* (Cambridge, 1987) 132–4; RL Brown, 'The Rise and Fall of the Fleet Marriages' in RB Outhwaite (ed), *Marriage and Society: Studies in the Social History of Marriage* (London, 1981) 118–19; Anonymous, *A Treatise of Feme Coverts* (London, 1732) 27; S Parker, *Informal Marriage, Cohabitation and the Law, 1750–1989* (London 1990) 17; R Probert, 'The Impact of the Marriage Act 1753: Was it really "A most Cruel Law for the Fair Sex"?' (2005) 38 *Eighteenth-Century Studies* 249–50.

legislation in 1712).[46] Before the Act the problem was that those who took part in clandestine marriage ceremonies were subject to punishment by the church courts, but the marriage itself was valid.

Blackstone made it quite clear that the parties must contract in the form required by the Act to make a good civil marriage. Therefore any verbal contract or agreement between the couple accompanied with cohabitation, which 'was before the late act deemed to be a valid marriage to many purposes' could no longer be enforced by the church courts.[47] He emphasised, however, that neglecting some of the formalities prescribed by the Act did not actually invalidate the marriage. He saw the Act as an 'innovation upon the antient laws and constitution', with both good and bad effects.[48] The Act was still so new that Blackstone included a section on the prior, no longer relevant, canon law provisions on underage marriage without even mentioning the Act. The Act's requirement for parental consent if the parties to the marriage were under 21 years of age then appears in the following section. Blackstone deplored clandestine marriages as 'often a terrible inconvenience to those private families where they happen', so preventing such marriages was beneficial. But, on the other hand, putting restraints on marriage could have adverse effects, particularly for the lower classes, by inhibiting population growth and encouraging licentiousness and debauchery.[49]

Blackstone's dislike of restraints on marriage went beyond fears about any consequent economic or social evils. He expressed concern about the concept of parental control of marriage, noting that in France a son could not marry without parental consent until the age of 30, while for daughters the age was 25. In Holland the respective ages were 25 and 20. Blackstone thought that Lord Hardwicke's Act had followed the French example, because underage marriage without parental consent was now void. Roman law, he pointed out, while forbidding marriage without parental consent, had been less rigorous 'on that very account with regard to other restraints'. If a parent failed to find a husband for his daughter by the time she reached 25, 'and she afterwards made a slip in her conduct, he was not allowed to disinherit her on that account'.[50]

Long after Blackstone wrote the mandatory formalities in the Act met with much criticism in Parliament, and the merits of parliamentary regulation of marriage were questioned. The Act had imposed Anglican marriage ceremonies on all, including Dissenters and Catholics, although

46 Stone (n 44) 110–14; see also Outhwaite (n 26), Brown (n 45) 17–36

47 Parker (n 45) 18; *Commentaries* vol 1, p 427.

48 *Commentaries* vol 1, pp 425–6; DF Lemmings, 'Marriage and the Law in Eighteenth Century England: Hardwicke's Marriage Act of 1753' (1996) 39 *Historical Journal* 340.

49 *Ibid*, pp 424–6.

50 *Ibid*, p 425.

not Quakers and Jews, which made it unpopular and difficult to enforce. In 1771, in order to comply with statute, Thomas Paine married twice in one day; first in a non-conformist chapel in Lewes in Sussex, and then at the nearby Anglican church.[51] Even 30 years later opposition to the Act continued, sometimes quoting Blackstone's *Commentaries*. Repeated bills to repeal the Act were brought to Parliament. Henry Fox, who had eloped with the young Lady Caroline Lennox in 1774 much to the fury of her father, the Duke of Richmond, was particularly critical of the Act, and claimed it mainly benefited aristocratic patriarchs. Echoing Blackstone, Fox and others also thought the Act discriminated against the poor because the residence and solemnisation requirements added a mandatory financial burden on marriage, making it difficult and expensive.[52]

Bentham wrote some 30 years after the passing of Lord Hardwicke's Act and so did not regard the Act in the same 'innovatory' light as Blackstone. Neither did he have the same reservations as Blackstone about its possible consequences. Like Blackstone, Bentham considered statutory regulation of marriage formation beneficial. He rejected the unwritten common law as 'dogs law' (where men were punished after the event just as dogs are beaten) because it provided no clear written rules. As a result Bentham did not support Fox's attempts to amend the 1753 Act, supporting retention of the crucial section which rendered void any marriage which did not comply with the Act. In fact, Bentham supported moves to extend the Act to Scotland, complaining that the law in Scotland was far too accommodating because it allowed impatient English minors to 'relieve themselves by an offhand marriage at a village on the Scotch frontier, called Gretna Green'.[53]

VII LORD HARDWICKE'S ACT AND THE SEDUCTION OF WOMEN

When Lord Hardwicke's bill was first debated in Parliament alarming predictions were made that the Act would have a particularly detrimental effect on women by leaving them more vulnerable to seduction, because promises to marry could no longer be enforced by the church courts. To modern sensibilities these concerns can look like exaggerated political opposition to the Act, but at the time women were severely disadvantaged in finding paid employment and marriage brought with it financial support.

[51] Outhwaite (n 26) 75–95; Lemmings (n 48) 340; J Keane, *Tom Paine A Political Life* (London, 1995) 76.

[52] Outhwaite (n 26) 101–12; Lemmings (n 48); R Probert, 'The Judicial Interpretation of Lord Hardwicke's Act 1753' (2002) 23 *Journal of Legal History* 143–6; Parker (n 45) 40–7.

[53] Bentham (n 1) 197–9; Lobban (n 13) 116–17; UC lxxi 113; Bentham (n 11) 235.

It has been said that in the event the Act did not bring about such dire consequences for women.[54] Yet in 1765, 12 years after the Act, Blackstone still had misgivings. He wrote that one consequence of the 1753 Act was that it might inadvertently revive part of an earlier 1540 statute of Henry VIII (32 Hen VIII c 38). This statute was a post-Reformation attempt to remedy an abuse due to the 'usurped Power of the Bishop of Rome', whereby the church courts would find void long-standing consummated marriages with children if a prior unconsummated pre-contract with someone else was disclosed. So it prevented church courts from invalidating a marriage (as bigamous) if it had been solemnised within the Church of England and consummated, despite the existence of any earlier unconsummated marriage contract, or spousals. Quite soon, and perhaps inevitably, it became apparent that the 1540 statute itself led to abuse; the pretext of an invalid prior marriage was used for seduction, and so the statute was repealed in 1548.[55] Blackstone thought that Hardwicke's Act, by prohibiting all suits in church courts to compel marriage, could have the unwanted consequence of abolishing the impediment of pre-contract, but he left this, he said, 'to be considered by the canonists'.[56] He did not explain his concerns further, but it seems he feared a return to the cynical exploitation of marriage law by unscrupulous seducers that was supposedly seen in the sixteenth century.

Blackstone's forensic experience gave grounds for his fears about unscrupulous seducers. For example, his *Reports* noted the details of a scandalous case (*The King v Delavel and others*) where an incensed father, who had apprenticed his daughter to a theatre manager, claimed damages against the latter, and against the egregious 'gentleman' who had set her up as his mistress. The case was tried before Lord Mansfield, who commented that although the church courts heard some cases of 'Indecency and Immorality . . . yet the general Inspection and Superintendence of the Morals of the People belongs to this Court, as *Custos Moram* of the Nation'.[57]

Blackstone showed sympathy too for the uncertain fate of mistresses in the case of *Walker v Perkins Administrator*, which he argued as counsel before King's Bench in 1764. Here a bond for the upkeep of a mistress was eventually held to be void (because of its immoral purpose). Blackstone had proposed that while the bond for cohabitation during life was invalid, yet after a man's death the maintaining of his mistress, 'the virtuous part of the contract' should be upheld. He argued that if such bonds were always annulled it would be as much an encouragement to seduction in one sex (the man), as finding the contract valid might encourage incontinence in

[54] Probert (n 45) 254 and passim.

[55] 2 & 3 Edw VI c 23.

[56] *Commentaries* vol 1, p 423.

[57] *Reports* vol 1, p 439; see also *ibid* pp 410–13, 439–40.

the other (the woman). Of these two wrongs, 'seduction was the more odious crime'.[58] Blackstone had recognised the woman's need for financial support, but his case failed to persuade the court.

Bentham too was concerned about vulnerable women and seduction. The offence of seduction is defined in his Penal Code as 'where a man by false promises of marriage attains carnal knowledge of an unmarried woman who is of good fame of chastity'. Then in defining the offence of fornication Bentham distinguished between what he called 'promiscuous venery', and settled cohabitation, remarking that cohabitation was politically discouraged.[59] He referred here to contracts for the support of 'common prostitutes' which were void for immoral purposes; yet by the second half of the eighteenth century evidence of past cohabitation did on occasion allow the court to uphold a contract made in favour of a mistress.[60] Blackstone's discussion of the perils of seduction did just possibly cause Bentham to think about commenting on the problems for women of irregular unions in his own law of marriage, although he probably did not have access to Blackstone's *Reports*, which remained in manuscript until 1781. Bentham's somewhat startling proposed alternative to cohabitation – short-term marriages which would give mistresses the legal rights and some of the respectability enjoyed by wives – owed nothing at all to Blackstone.[61]

VIII COVERTURE

A married English woman's legal status was governed by the doctrine of coverture, which Blackstone set out in concise, elegant and much quoted language.[62] Once married, a woman's legal status changed from *feme sole* to *feme covert*, with significant consequences. She could no longer enter into contracts, or sue or be sued in her own name; her personal property vested absolutely in her husband, and he had a life interest in all her real property. Her liability in criminal law was also affected.[63]

In the seventeenth and early eighteenth centuries marriage was often described as mirroring an ordered commonwealth, with the husband as head and governor of his household exercising authority over his wife, children and servants, just as the king ruled his subjects. A man 'must govern his wife' wrote William Whately in 1619: 'Nature hath framed the lineaments of his body to superiority, and set the print of government in his

[58] *Reports* vol 1, pp 517–19
[59] UC lxxii 207, lxxxvi 197.
[60] See 26 ER 191 (*Earl of Chesterfield et al v Janssen*, 1750).
[61] UC xxxii 111.
[62] *Commentaries* vol 1, p 430; see also ch 8 below.
[63] Baker (n 22) 483–9; Anonymous (n 45) 52–77.

very face', and God's authority was invested in his person.[64] By the time Blackstone published the *Commentaries* the relationship between husband and wife was more likely to be described as contractual, in the sense of the Hobbesian social contract. Whatever authority men possessed over women was seen as derived from nature, that is to say from men's greater physical strength, rather than being divinely ordained.

Blackstone did not mention physical strength as a basis for masculine authority, but argued that the law of husband and wife was founded in nature and modified by civil society. According to Pufendorf, whom Blackstone cited, natural law was understood to suppose an original equality in faculties between men and women. That original equality was then modified by the laws of state and civil society.[65] So Blackstone acknowledged that sometimes the civil (ie in England, common) law might appear to disadvantage married women by imposing various legal disabilities. But these he then sought to justify by writing that 'even the disabilities . . . are for the most part intended for her protection and benefit. So great a favourite is the female sex of the laws of England.'[66]

For Blackstone a husband's sovereignty over his wife was limited, and certainly did not extend to the right to beat her. He wrote that 'The husband also (by the old law) might give his wife moderate correction. For, as he is to answer for her misbehaviour, the law thought it reasonable to instruct him with this power of restraining her, by domestic chastisement.' Blackstone doubted this was any longer valid at common law, but many of Blackstone's contemporaries did not agree, and upheld the supposed customary right to 'correct' wives. For instance the anonymous author of *The Treatise of Feme Coverts, or the Ladies Law* claimed that although a husband 'shall neither do nor procure to be done to her, any Bodily Damage' this did not exclude blows that 'appertains to the Office of a Husband, and for lawful Correction. She has no right of action at common law.'[67]

The right of husbands to beat their wives had long been fiercely debated in England. The Protestant idea of a 'companionate marriage' appeared in the marriage service set out in the 1559 Book of Common Prayer prescribed by the Elizabethan Act of Uniformity in 1559 (1 Eliz 1 c 2), and in 1613 Edward Coke, a puritan sympathiser, refused to accept the existence of any such right. Then in 1674 in *Lord Leigh*'s case Lord Chief Justice Hale found that a husband had a right to admonish his wife and to

[64] W Whately, *Directions for Married Persons* (Bristol, 1768; 1619) 46–8.

[65] *Commentaries* vol 1, p 410; Pufendorf (n 36) 199–200; I Hunter, *Rival Enlightenments: Civil and Metaphysical Philosophy in Early Modern Germany* (Cambridge, 2001) 182–3, 333; Paley (n 40) 194–5.

[66] *Commentaries* vol 1, pp 432–3.

[67] *Ibid*; Anonymous (n 45) 81.

confine her to the house if she was 'extravagant', but no unlimited right to beat her. Blackstone relied particularly on *Lord Leigh*'s case for his own claims that the right to beat was not good law. Although wives had long been able to complain to the church courts about cruel husbands such an action usually formed part of an action for divorce *a mensal et thoro*. Blackstone pointed out that an abused wife could also seek security of the peace from the justices against her husband, or apply by writ of supplicavit to the courts of Chancery and King's Bench which took recognizances from her husband. And 'yet' Blackstone commented wryly, 'the lower orders of people, who were always fond of the old common law, still claim their antient privilege'.[68]

Surprisingly, Bentham made little mention at all of the doctrine of coverture, nor Blackstone's definition of it. Of course this doctrine was a legal fiction and as such Bentham would have rejected it on that basis alone.[69] But Bentham was not alone in ignoring coverture. Other contemporary writers on marriage made no mention of it either. William Paley, for example, wrote that 'nature . . . [has] left the sexes of the human species nearly equal in their faculties, and perfectly so in respect of their rights', with no discussion at all of the doctrine of coverture. For Mary Wollstonecraft and Hannah More the abysmal lack of education for women, and not the largely economic operation of the doctrine of coverture, was the significant factor in the subjection of women.[70]

In any event, the fiction that husband and wife were one person, with the husband as head, was never applied consistently in law. As a common-law doctrine it was simply ignored in some other jurisdictions. The church courts and local courts 'unlike the courts of common law . . . did not observe the doctrine of coverture', while the central equity courts allowed married women rights of audience.[71] As Margot Finn writes, there was also a 'disjuncture between legal theory and social practice'; coverture existed in a state of 'suspended animation' so far as married womens' debt and credit relations were concerned, for many women could live quite unaffected by it until some event brought it sharply into consideration.[72]

[68] Lord Seymour's Case (1613) 72 ER 966; 84 ER 807; *Commentaries* vol 1, pp 432–3.

[69] Dinwiddy (n 17) 55–6. Blackstone, of course, thought legal fictions 'highly beneficial and useful': *Commentaries* vol 3, p 43.

[70] Paley (n 40) 194–5. H More, *Strictures on the Modern System of Female Education* (London, 1834); Wollstonecraft (n 40).

[71] T Stretton, 'Women, Property and Law' in A Pacheo (ed), *Early Modern Women's Writing* (Oxford, 2002) 48; T Stretton, 'Women, Custom and Equity in the Court of Requests' in J Kermode and G Walker (ed), *Women, Crime and the Courts in Early Modern England* (London, 1994); M Finn, 'Women, Consumption and Coverture in England c.1760–1860' (1996) 39 *Historical Journal* 714–16; but note also E Spring, *Law, Land and Family: Aristocratic Inheritance in England, 1300 to 1800* (Chapel Hill NC, 1993) 117–22.

[72] Finn (n 71) 717, 705–6.

Perhaps, then, our present understanding of the effect of the doctrine is over-simplified, and has tended to obscure its bizarre nature and uneven application in earlier times.

As a barrister Blackstone was familiar with the practical operation of coverture. In 1766 he noted the case of a married woman who traded in her own name as a fan-maker. She was able to do so by the custom of London, despite being under coverture. When sued by her creditors the question before the court was whether they had priority over her husband's creditors in the event of her bankruptcy.[73]

Bentham had firsthand experience of the way in which coverture could disadvantage women. He tried, unsuccessfully, to help a family friend abandoned by her husband. In the face of financial ruin she committed suicide, leaving several orphaned children.[74] Bentham also recognised the historical and contemporary importance of married women's access to the law of equity and the Court of Chancery. So when in 1825 he drafted a petition to be presented to Parliament seeking a new court of Chancery, which he named the Equity Dispatch Court, he addressed this document to women as well as men.[75]

Bentham's failure to discuss coverture was not because he was unaware of the problems the doctrine posed in family and property law. Instead his manuscripts make clear that he dealt with the question of married women's legal status by drafting a whole new legal regime, which would apply to both men and women. This made no reference to either divine authority or to nature. Bentham listed several different domestic relations; husband and wife, parent and child, master and servant, and guardian and ward. Reciprocal rights and duties attached to each relationship, and any particular relationship, such as husband and wife, could be subject to a different regime according to the circumstances that applied. So if a husband was under an express obligation to have regard for the welfare of his wife, then the relation between them was that of guardian and ward.[76]

Bentham's replacement of the doctrine of coverture by a new legal regime owed nothing to Blackstone. Bentham based his law of marriage, including his proposed new legal regime for relations between married men and women, on equality and the principle of utility. While Blackstone had read Pufendorf who had found men and women to be equal, these views are not explicitly expressed in the *Commentaries*.[77]

Rather than repeating more typical eighteenth-century reasoning on man's rights to authority over woman resting on greater strength, Bentham

[73] *Reports* vol 1, pp 570–5 (*LaVie and other Assignees v Phillips and another Assignees*).
[74] Bentham, *Correspondence* vol 2, pp 7–10.
[75] Bowring (n 5) vol 3, p 319.
[76] UC lxviii 271.
[77] Pufendorf (n 36) 199.

reversed that argument. If the greatest happiness principle was used as a measure of true worth of a rule of law, he wrote, then females should take precedence. This is because 'As between male and female, in regard to strength, the less the care taken by nature the greater should be that taken by law'.[78] He then cut short appeals to history by agreeing that customary laws like primogeniture, which preferred males to females, had indeed a historical origin in the military system set up after the Norman Conquest. It had been politically expedient then to prefer male succession to land because of 'the universal national interest of military self defence'; men who held land were in return obliged to form an army. But these historical necessities had long gone and the only remaining reason to prefer males to females was the fact that males possessed political power. He concluded, ironically, that the legal rule that currently prevailed was 'the greatest happiness' of men, the stronger of the two sexes, excluding women, the weaker of the two sexes.[79]

XI CONCLUSION

Blackstone's *Commentaries* were indeed a 'pervasive factor' in Bentham's thought on the law of marriage, particularly in his choice of an institutional structure for his own work. That Blackstone wrote in the middle of the eighteenth century and Bentham much later must account for some difference in their respective approaches to the law of marriage. Blackstone died in 1780, before the French Revolution and before some of the more radical late eighteenth- century ideas on marriage and the relations between men and women had found expression. He could hardly have imagined the cultural changes that were to take place by the end of the century, and no doubt he would have disapproved of some of them. Leaving conjecture aside, as we have seen Blackstone's text makes clear that he did not take a narrow view of the law of marriage. His writings on marriage, although limited to one part of a more comprehensive text on English common law, mean that he should indeed be recognised as a 'leading representative' of the English Enlightenment.[80]

By contrast, Bentham, who lived on until 1832, was acquainted with radical ideas in England and France.[81] Like Blackstone he too was an inheritor of the European Enlightenment. But he lived through the French

[78] UC lxxvii 22.

[79] UC lxxvii 155–6, 158; see also Bowring (n 5) vol 1, p 335. Compare Dumont's published version of Bentham's description of the legal relations between men and women during marriage, stipulating that women are subject to their husband during marriage: see Bentham (n 11) 230–1.

[80] Prest, *Blackstone* 308–9.

[81] Bentham, *Correspondence* vol 1, pp 138–48, vol 4, p xxvii.

Revolution and English reactions to the Terror, the war with France and the peace, and he died just before the 1832 Reform Bill. His extensive work on marriage was carried out mainly in the 1780s, and it reflects a very different world from that inhabited by Blackstone in the 1760s.

Nevertheless time alone cannot account for all the divergences from the model of Blackstone's *Commentaries* found in Bentham's work. A difference in purpose is clear. Bentham hoped that a utilitarian, reformed, law of marriage would bring with it a social reform of marriage, including legal equality between men and women. Such an aim is not found implied or expressed in Blackstone's *Commentaries*.

8

Coverture and Unity of Person in Blackstone's Commentaries

TIM STRETTON*

ONE OF THE most quoted passages of William Blackstone's *Commentaries on the Laws of England* comes from the chapter on 'the Law of Husband and Wife', describing the nature and effects of the common-law idea of coverture:

> By marriage, the husband and wife are one person in law; that is the very being or legal existence of the woman is suspended during the marriage, or at least incorporated and consolidated into that of the husband: under whose wing, protection and cover she performs everything . . . Upon this principle, of an union of person in husband and wife, depend almost all the legal rights, duties, and disabilities that either of them acquire by the marriage.[1]

Blackstone's description of married women's position at common law influenced generations of English and American jurists, enraged nineteenth- and early twentieth-century feminists and continues to colour the interpretations of modern historians.[2] For many of the commentators and judges who followed Blackstone the simple logic of unity of person, or marital unity, was compelling. A husband could not give a gift to his wife because he would be giving a gift to himself and he could not contract with her because he would be contracting with himself.[3] A married couple could not be guilty of conspiring to commit a crime because it takes at least two people for a conspiracy, and spouses could not testify for or against each

* Tim Stretton thanks the Faculty of Graduate Studies & Research at Saint Mary's University for financial assistance and audiences at the North American Conference on British Studies, Dalhousie University and the Blackstone Symposium in the Adelaide Law School for their feedback on earlier versions of his essay.

[1] *Commentaries* vol 1, p 430.

[2] See M Beard, *Woman as Force in History: A Study in Traditions and Realities* (London, 1976; 1946) chs 4 and 5.

[3] H Broom and E Hadley, *Commentaries on the Laws of England* (London, 1869) vol 1, p 543.

other in criminal proceedings for fear of undermining the cherished maxims that no one is bound to accuse him or herself and no one ought to be witness in his or her own cause.[4] Unity of person also helped explain why the law regarded a wife's domicile as her husband's, even if they were living apart, and why a man could not marry his deceased wife's sister, on the grounds that it would constitute incest.

An impartial observer might expect unity of person, the fusing together of two distinct legal personalities, to involve equal sharing of the new identity. After all, the most prevalent example of unity of person in the English imagination was not husband and wife, but the holy trinity of God the father, the son and the holy spirit.[5] Sadly, if predictably, equality was never a feature of marital unity. Writing in the *Law Quarterly Review* in 1891, JEG De Montmorency described how prior to the mid nineteenth century,

> the doctrine obtained that the husband and wife were but one person possessing but one will and that that will resided in the mind of the husband as the person 'fittest and ablest to provide for and govern the family'. It was a doctrine of elegant simplicity and one capable of remarkable results. It was a doctrine that removed, in theory, the burdens of responsibility and the sanctions of morality from any woman that entered the holy state of matrimony. Logically considered, all her crimes and all her sins emanated from the duplicated brain of her husband and her lord. Not only did she convey to him her person and her worldly goods, but she added the entire responsibility of her personality to the weight of his own. The Creator took from Adam a rib and made Eve; the common law of England endeavoured to reverse the process, to replace the rib and to re-merge the personalities.[6]

The fiction of marital unity has here been raised to the status of an all-encompassing doctrine. Not only were married women not considered legal persons for most purposes, but they also lacked independent wills.

To Blackstone's disciples unity of person was and always had been the lynchpin of coverture, to the point where many commentators regarded the two terms as synonymous.[7] However, unity of person was not the lynchpin of coverture prior to the eighteenth century. In his *History of English Law Before the Time of Edward I,* published in 1898, FW Maitland was unequivocal: 'the main idea which governs the law of husband and wife is not that of an "unity of person"'. Instead, it was the power a husband wielded over his wife or 'the guardianship, the *mund*, the profitable

[4] *Commentaries* vol 1, p 431. Possible exceptions to these rules included treason and instances of personal violence within marriage.

[5] Unity of person also applied to executors, trustees and corporations.

[6] JEG De Montmorency, 'The Changing Status of a Married Woman' (1897) 13 *Law Quarterly Review* 197.

[7] T Stretton, *Women Waging Law in Elizabethan England* (Cambridge, 1998) chs 2 and 5.

guardianship, which the husband has over the wife and over her property'.[8] Maitland's forensic dismantling of interpretations of coverture organised around marital unity slowly took hold in legal and academic circles.[9] Where the second and third editions of *Lush on the Law of Husband and Wife*, edited by Walter Hussey Griffith and published in 1896 and 1910, confidently asserted that 'From the earliest times' marital unity 'has been laid down as a fundamental principle of law, a principle upon which the whole law relating to husband and wife has hitherto depended', the fourth edition, published in 1933, barely mentioned it, except to repeat Maitland's warning that it was not the main idea behind coverture.[10]

Writing in 1947, Glanville Williams agreed that commentators who invoked unity of person in situations where common-law rules or judgments shaped or restricted married women's rights were generally mistaken. Married women clearly remained legal persons throughout marriage, for example in relation to their interests in real property, when fulfilling duties as executors or administrators of deceased person's estates, when named as co-plaintiffs or defendants in litigation, and for many matters concerning criminal responsibility. Furthermore, there were better ways to account for most limitations on married women's rights. The inability of a wife to make contracts without her husband's consent was often a natural consequence of her inability to own or control movable property.[11] The reason for the rule that 'the law will not suffer a wife to be a witness for or against her husband' was not unity of person, Lord Hardwicke argued in 1735, but rather the need 'to preserve the peace of families'. Other justices believed it was 'inequitable or repugnant to condemn a man on the evidence of those who share the secrets of his domestic life'. The prohibition against a man marrying his deceased wife's sister came from ecclesiastical law, not common law, and stemmed from the biblical idea of unity of flesh and the prohibited degrees of consanguinity and affinity listed in Leviticus, not from the legal fiction of unity of person. This was also more a policy decision than a strict legal principle, as ecclesiastical law permitted a husband and son to marry a mother and daughter, or two sisters to marry two brothers. Examining the rule that a wife who hides her felon husband is not guilty as an accessory, unlike a husband who hides his wife, Williams concluded that this discrepancy

[8] F Pollock and FW Maitland, *The History of English Law Before the Time of Edward I*, 2nd edn (Cambridge, 1898) vol 1, p 485.

[9] Maitland did not mention Blackstone by name, but warned that 'we must be on our guard against the common belief that the ruling principle is that which sees an "unity of person" between husband and wife': *ibid* vol 2, pp 405–6.

[10] M Lush, *Lush on the Law of Husband and Wife*, 2nd edn with W H Griffith (London, 1896) 3; 3rd edn (London, 1910) 3; 4th edn with SN Grant-Bailey (London, 1933) 8, 58.

[11] See *HEL* vol 3, p 528.

could not be 'a deduction from the idea of a unified personality'. As he explained, 'If there is a technical doctrine behind it, it is the doctrine of the man's *potestas* over his wife, not the doctrine that the wife has no separate personality'.[12]

More recently, Henrik Hartog has followed the lead of Norma Basch and Mary Beard in charting the effect Blackstone's skewed vision of the history of coverture had on law and practice in colonial America.[13] Judges and legislators in various colonial jurisdictions hailed Blackstone's musings on unity of person and quickened the process of transforming this curious fiction into a guiding principle and then an inflexible doctrine. In England a similar transformation occurred, so that in 1876 in Queen's Bench Justice Field calmly referred to unity of person as 'a fundamental maxim of the common law'.[14] Yet while a growing chorus of voices finds fault with Blackstone's depiction of married women's rights, few have asked why he came to endow the fiction of unity of person with 'the warrant of holy writ', to borrow Maitland's phrase.[15] The exceptions are Beard, who chastised Blackstone for almost single-handedly extinguishing the married woman's legal personality (even though she acknowledged the influence of other legal voices, such as Sir Edward Coke) and Maeve Doggett, who recognised Blackstone's role in helping to engineer a transformation in legal understandings of unity of person, but speculated that the key shift occurred in the seventeenth, not the eighteenth, century.[16]

Common-law rules affecting married women changed little between the sixteenth and the eighteenth century. Yet as Beard and Doggett recognised, justifications for those rules underwent a subtle but significant transformation. This chapter examines Blackstone's role in that process, asking how, why and to what extent he reshaped justifications for coverture, and why he placed so much faith in the common law on this question, to the neglect of equity.

Owing an obvious debt to the biblical idea that husband and wife were one flesh, the fiction of unity of person appears to have arrived in England with the Normans. References to it can be found in legal writings in every century from the twelfth to the twenty-first. However, its most consistent application prior to the eighteenth century concerned the share a married couple held in interests in land. Under common law if a feoffment was

[12] G Williams, 'The Legal Unity of Husband and Wife' (1947) 10 *Modern Law Review* 19, 26.

[13] H Hartog, *Man and Wife in America: A History* (Cambridge MA, 2000) 115–22; Beard (n 2) ch 5; N Basch, *In the Eyes of the Law: Women, Marriage and Property in Nineteenth-Century New York* (Ithaca NY, 1982) ch 2.

[14] *Phillips v Barnet* (1876) 1 QB 436, 441: as quoted in M Doggett, *Marriage, Wife-Beating and the Law in Victorian England* (Columbia SC, 1993) 61.

[15] Pollock and Maitland (n 8) vol 2, p 406.

[16] Beard (n 2) 88; Doggett (n 14) 77–86.

made to a husband and wife and a third person, the husband and wife's share was not two thirds, but one half, because the law considered them one person ('*quia una persona*').[17] They held what Blackstone later described as a tenancy in entireties, in which both owned the whole interest.[18] Apart from that specific usage, invocations of unity of person were rare in early texts and had little to do with restrictions on a wife's autonomy. The author of the twelfth-century tract known as Glanville acknowledged that a wife could accuse her husband's murderer 'because husband and wife are one flesh ('*quia una caro sunt vir et uxor*') but the reason a wife experienced restrictions at law was because 'legally a woman is completely in the power of her husband' ('*in potestate viri*') and therefore 'it is not surprising that her dower and all her other property are clearly deemed to be at his disposal'. A husband's power was so great that he could alienate his wife's dower and she was 'bound to consent to this as to all other acts of his which do not offend against God'.[19]

For Bracton, writing in the thirteenth century, it was also self-evident that wives lived 'under the rod' ('*sub virga*') as well as the power of their husbands, a chilling allusion to the extent of patriarchal authority. He acknowledged that husband and wife 'are one flesh, though different souls' or 'so to speak one body and blood' and it is possible to see how later writers could discern from his use of this language a link between unity of person and the limiting of women's rights, but such a link was not central to the legal world Bracton was describing. For example, the reason why a husband and wife could not give each other gifts 'is lest they be made because of the lust or excessive poverty of one of the parties', which might lead 'one of them [to] be destroyed by want and poverty, which cannot be tolerated'. For Bracton, unity of flesh and blood was a useful way of describing the marital state and a practical fiction where certain property interests were concerned. However, a wife was capable of wager of law, and various other acts that would be impossible if she were not a legal person.[20]

Blackstone's authority for his statement that husband and wife were one person at law was Coke's commentary on Littleton's *Tenures*, the first part of his *Institutes of the Laws of England*, published in 1628. Littleton, writing at the end of the fifteenth century, stated in his chapter on tenure in burgage, one of the most obscure forms of tenure in English law, that 'a

[17] T E[dgar] (ed), *The Lawes Resolutions of Womens Rights* (London, 1632) 120.

[18] JV Orth, 'Tenancy by the Entirety: The Strange Career of the Common-Law Marital Estate', *Brigham Young University Law Review* (1997) 35–49. See also Blackstone's remarks in *Green on the demise of Crew v King* (1778), *Reports* vol 2, pp 1212, 1214.

[19] GDG Hall (ed and tr), *The Treatise on the Laws and Customs of the Realm of England commonly called Glanville* (Holmes Beach FL, 1983) 60, 174.

[20] Bracton, *On the Laws and Customs of England* (tr) SE Thorne (Cambridge MA, 1968–77) vol 4, pp 166, 335.

man may not grant, nor give, his tenements to his wife during the coverture, for that his wife and he be but one person in the law'.[21] Writing in Law French, rather than Latin, Littleton used the word 'coverture' and referred to a wife's status as 'feme covert' or 'covert de baron', a rather different shorthand than '*sub potestate viri*' or '*sub virga*' that could be read in expansive ways, allowing emphasis to be placed on the idea of protection as well as authority in the marital relationship. Coke expanded on Littleton's short entry on burgage tenure, asserting that at common law a husband could make no conveyance of any kind to his wife and he could not covenant or contract with his wife, all 'for the reason that Littleton here yieldeth'. However, he pointed out that a husband could achieve a conveyance to his wife by using a deed to create a use or trust for his wife's benefit, as long as he covenanted with others. To elucidate the meaning of coverture, Coke quoted Bracton. Coverture was so called because the wife is '*sub potestate viri*, and she is disabled to contract with any without the consent of the husband'.[22] Littleton and Coke made reference to unity of person, but neither author relied on it to any great extent. Some other authorities did not mention it at all. John Rastell's 1523 law dictionary went through over 20 editions and imprints in the sixteenth and seventeenth centuries, none of which mentioned unity of person in the context of husband and wife.[23]

The author of *The Lawes Resolutions of Women's Rights*, written around 1600 and published in 1632, referred to marital unity on a number of occasions, but clearly did not regard it as the central or guiding principle of coverture. His first reference to husband and wife being one person expressly linked it to the biblical idea that husband and wife were one flesh, and elsewhere the author displayed a reluctance to rely on marital unity as sole justification for particular rules of coverture.[24] He reflected with an air of puzzlement, for example, that 'I find none other cause in our Year books alleged why things may not pass by gift between Baron and feme save only unity of person' and felt obliged to explain that 'undoubtedly the restraint springeth from a politique consideration rather to breed, cherish and maintain the unity, than in judging of an impossibility because of the unity'. He also went on to note ways that lands could pass between husband and wife through 'fines, recoveries and uses', regardless of 'whatsoever Bracton say'.[25] What was at work here appears to be policy rather than doctrine. Unity was undoubtedly a legal fiction, but it was

[21] *Littleton's Tenures in English* ed E Wambaugh (Washington DC, 1903) 80; see also *ibid* 296–7, 299.

[22] E Coke, *The First Part of the Institutes of the Lawes of England. Or, A Commentarie upon Littleton* (London, 1629; 1628) fos 112–112v.

[23] J Rastell, *Exposiciones Terminorum Leges Anglorum* (1523 and subsequent editions).

[24] TE[dgar] (n 17) 120.

[25] *Ibid* 123.

employed in a series of metaphors and rarely represented the same way twice. It *described* rather than explained the nature of the power balance within the marital relationship.

According to Maeve Doggett, the mid-to-late seventeenth century was the key period in the privileging of unity of person as the defining principle of coverture. However, it is hard to detect a lasting change in legal commentaries and cases to match the transformations that occurred in political discourse.[26] *Baron and Feme. A Treatise of the Common Law Concerning Husbands and Wives*, published in 1700, contains only a scattering of references to unity of person within its 300 plus pages. The author echoed Littleton and Coke in stating that 'baron and feme are commonly said to be one person at law, which explains why a man cannot grant lands and tenements to his wife' but otherwise allowed little influence to the concept. The reason why a wife took her husband's surname and social status, for example, was that 'a wife by the law of God is *sub potestate viri*'. Elsewhere it was 'the law of Nature' that 'hath put her under the obedience of her husband, and hath submitted her will to his, which the law follows'.[27]

William Hawkins, in his *Pleas of the Crown* published in 1716, explained that a feme covert 'is not guilty of felony in stealing her husband's goods; because husband and wife are considered but as one person in law, and the husband by endowing his wife at the marriage with all his worldly goods, gives her a kind of interest in them'. On the question of marital privilege, Hawkins noted that 'It seems agreed, that the husband and wife being as one and the same person in affection and interest, can no more give evidence for one another in any case whatsoever than for themselves.' However, he wrote that the reason why courts usually refused to admit spouses giving testimony against each other was not because they were one person, but 'by reason of the implacable dissension which might be caused by it, and the great danger of perjury from taking the oaths of persons under so great a bias, and the extreme hardship of the case'.[28]

Knightley D'Anvers', *A General Abridgment of the Common Law*, the first volume of which appeared in 1722, contains repeated references to feme coverts and coverture, including a 23-page section on Baron and

[26] Discussions of the laws affecting husband and wife referred instead to the legal incapacity of married women, to the wife being at the will of her husband and to the presumption that a wife's actions were done 'for fear of the husband'; see eg J March, *Reports: Or, New Cases* (London, 1648), 90; W West, *The First Part of Symboleographie* (London, 1647 and previous edns) pt 1, bk 2, s 634; *Cary's Reports in Chancery* (London, 1650) 14.

[27] Anonymous, *Baron and Feme, A Treatise of the Common Law Concerning Husbands and Wives* (London, 1700) 3.

[28] W Hawkins, A *Treatise of the Pleas of the Crown* (London, 1716) vol 1, pp 93, 294; vol 2, pp 431–2.

Feme, but makes no reference to husband and wife being one person. Instead D'Anvers compared baron and feme at different points to an abbot and a monk and to a master and servant. He explained, for example, that an action on the case for negligent keeping of a fire in a house that leads to the burning of another's house 'lies upon the general custom of the realm against *patrem familiæ* [the patriarch or father of the family] and not against a servant or feme covert, who is but in nature of a servant.'[29] Matthew Hale made a similar comparison in his *History of the Pleas of the Crown*, written during the middle decades of the 1600s (although not published until 1736), when describing 'incapacities or excuses by reason of civil subjection'. He observed that 'this civil subjection is principally of the subject to his prince, the servant to his master, the child to his parent, and the wife to her husband'.[30] For D'Anvers, the feme's subjection to her baron explained her lack of independence, for 'by the marriage her will is submitted to her husband's: it is 'transferred to the baron' and 'the whole will of the feme is put in the Baron during the coverture'.[31]

The very first sentence of the preface to *A Treatise of Feme Coverts*, published in 1732, states that 'When a man and woman are join'd in matrimony, the woman is called a feme covert, and the law regards them but as one person.' However the following 290 plus pages contain only four other references to unity, two of which concern a married couple's share of a feoffment.[32] Even *The Hardships of the English Laws in Relation to Wives*, published in 1735 and usually attributed to Sarah Chapone, contains only oblique references to unity of person. The hardships of the title stemmed not from unity of person, but from English law permitting husbands 'the full extent of their despotic power', leaving wives in the condition of slaves.[33]

None of these works directly linked the idea that husband and wife were one person with the idea that by marriage a wife submitted her will to her husband's. Matthew Bacon was one of the first to take that leap in his *A New Abridgment of the Law by a Gentleman of the Middle Temple*, published anonymously in 1736. In a chapter on 'Baron and Feme', Bacon explained that

[29] K D'Anvers, *A General Abridgment of the Common Law*, 2nd edn (London, 1722–25) vol 1, pp 10, 716, 718.

[30] M Hale, *Historia Placitorum Coronæ. The History of the Pleas of the Crown* (London, 1736) 43, 47. Given his focus on criminal law, Hale emphasised a wife's position as *sub potestate viri*, but he noted that husband and wife were disabled from testifying against each other 'in respect of the civil unity of their persons': *ibid* vol 1, pp 47, 48, 516; vol 2, p 279.

[31] D'Anvers (n 29) vol 2, pp 504, 789. The judges in *Manby v Scott*, mentioned below, also compared a wife to her husband's servant; 83 ER 1065.

[32] Anonymous, *A Treatise of Feme Coverts: or The Lady's Law* (London, 1732) v, 129, 135, 139, 179.

[33] *The Hardships of the English Laws in Relation to Wives with an Explanation of the Original Curse of Subjection Passed upon the Woman* (London, 1732) 46, 51.

> From the time of the intermarriage, the Law looks upon the husband and wife but as one person, and therefore allows of but one will between them, which is placed in the husband, as the fittest and ablest to provide for and govern the family.[34]

It is possible to detect a similar pattern of development in the Year Books and printed case law. Prior to the mid seventeenth century judges made occasional reference to unity of person, but most quoted Littleton and restricted their attention to a husband and wife's shares in property and a wife's right to sue.[35] In *Manby v Scott*, the influential case from 1663 that limited a wife's right to contract for necessaries without her husband's consent, counsel argued on behalf of the plaintiff that a wife had a right to contract for her maintenance as it would be to his benefit, as husband and wife were 'but one person', but this plea fell on deaf ears. Those in the majority relied instead on arguments based around a husband's power over his wife, summed up in Mathew Hale's observation (as lord chief baron) that 'by the laws of God, nature, nations of England, and of reason, her will is subject to her husband'.[36]

This, then, was the state of thinking about coverture when Blackstone sat down with a sustaining glass of port to write his *Commentaries*. The growing frequency of references to unity of person, and the slow but steady expansion of the contexts in which commentators and judges employed it, mean that Blackstone's invocations of unity of person were hardly revolutionary. What made his interpretation unique was the central role he gave to the fiction, suggesting that it amounted to the key underlying principle behind married women's status, rights and obligations at common law. The question, then, is why Blackstone chose to organise his description of coverture in this novel way. Why place such emphasis on unity of person, and so little emphasis on a husband's physical power?

Blackstone directed his *Commentaries*, like the lectures they were based on, primarily at an audience of educated, property-holding English gentlemen. In privileging these men's freedoms, rights and obligations he remained infuriatingly quiet on the subject of women's place within the common law, at turns overlooking the question or else obscuring it in a syntax heavy with singular and collective male pronouns. It is therefore difficult to discern his motives for describing, or failing to describe, legal options for married women in the manner that he did. Nevertheless, it seems likely that the first explanation for his showcasing of unity of person

34 This passage provided the quote JEG De Montmorency used in his article, cited n 6 above; M Bacon, *A New Abridgment of the Law by a Gentleman of the Middle Temple* (London, 1736–66) vol 1, p 286; and see also pp 290, 291, 294, 458; vol 2, pp 49, 252, 378, 421, 452, 475, 527, 546; vol 3, pp 144, 190, 577, 695; vol 4, pp 222, 269.

35 See eg 23 ER 687, 73 ER 19, 79 ER 1039, 82 ER 922, 84 ER 557, 86 ER 917.

36 *Manby v Scott* (1663) 83 ER 902, 1043.

can be found in his desire to organise the law in a scientific and systematic manner, in contrast to the 'immethodical arrangement, too justly complained of in our ancient writers'. To Blackstone 'the law is the perfection of reason' and 'this most rational branch of learning' a science to be 'cultivated, methodized, and explained'.[37] Given this focus and aim, the attractions of unity of person become obvious, the versatility of this curious legal fiction promising a logical and almost universal explanation for most aspects of coverture—a single key capable of unlocking the complexities of what previous commentators had presented as a rag-bag of different rules and conflicting court decisions. The novelty of Blackstone's employment of unity of person in this way can be gleaned from the remainder of the *Commentaries*. For, in spite of his express declarations in volumes one and two that 'Upon this principle, of an union of person in husband and wife, depend almost all the legal rights, duties, and disabilities that either of them acquire by the marriage', his application of the principle throughout the rest of his text is rudimentary, and not nearly as coherent or comprehensive as in the works and rulings of the authors and judges who followed him.[38]

The other, related, explanation for Blackstone's emphasis on marital unity flows from his larger themes in the *Commentaries*, and in particular his focus on the liberty of the individual. Medieval commentators, writing when feudal landholding and inheritance customs supported a largely martial kingdom and the dominance of one person over another was a defining feature of society, had no qualms about tying married women's legal status to their subject condition, at the mercy, and under the authority, of their husbands. A husband's natural and God-given power over his wife justified the rules of coverture for centuries, until new ways of imagining the political nation emerged in the aftermath of the social, economic and political turmoil of the seventeenth century, making such open appeals to force less and less tenable. Promoting the familiar legal fiction of unity of person allowed Blackstone to discard or downplay other longstanding justifications for the rules affecting married women, in particular those based on the triumph of a husband's will over his wife's. The *Commentaries* are therefore notable for what they do not contain, as much as for what they do. In contrast to earlier works, it is striking how rarely in the context of the status of married women the text openly refers to masculine power. Blackstone chose to avoid the terms 'baron' and 'feme' found in 'our elder law books', with the implicit suggestion of feudal subjection, and 'man' and 'wife', preferring in most instances the simple

[37] *Commentaries* vol 1, pp 3, 4; vol 2, p 2; vol 3, p 265.
[38] *Ibid* vol 2, p 433.

and neutral 'husband' and 'wife'.[39] While he mentioned that a child, under civil law, was *in potestate parentis* [under the authority of the parent], he never used the phrase *sub potestate viri*.[40] He did acknowledge that,

> though our law in general considers man and wife as one person, yet there are some instances in which she is separately considered; as inferior to him, and acting by his compulsion. And therefore all deeds executed and acts done by her during her coverture are void, or at least voidable.[41]

However, the overall picture he painted of marriage was consistently idealistic and optimistic.

When writing about a husband's right to correct his wife he used the past tense, describing how 'the old law' allowed a husband to give his wife moderate correction 'confined within reasonable bounds' for 'as he is to answer for her misbehaviour, the law thought it reasonable to intrust him with this power of restraining her, by domestic chastisement'. He went on to note that the civil law was worse, allowing the husband a greater authority over his wife, and that 'with us, in the politer reign of Charles the second, this power of correction came to be doubted: and a wife may now have security of the peace against her husband; or in return a husband against his wife.' It is easy to pick holes in Blackstone's vision of history at this point, but his stress on the limits of husbands' legally sanctioned powers, suggesting that they belong to a dark and primitive past, while acknowledging the persistence of marital violence among 'the lower rank of people' who 'still claim and exert their antient privilege', reveals his attachment to an enlightened belief in the possibility of improvement (however patronising and misguided his stance may seem to modern readers).[42]

Despite the accusations of a number of his modern critics, Blackstone did not depict married women as their husband's property or chattels.[43] He also carefully separated discussions of slavery from discussions of married women, and rarely made direct comparisons between the autonomy of wives and of servants. Wives were not owned, they were merely dependant, just as all men and women in England except for the monarch were dependant. As Blackstone explained in volume one, 'Man, considered as a

[39] He did, on occasion, refer to a wife's husband as her 'lord', eg when explaining why the law regarded a wife murdering her husband as petty treason; *Commentaries* vol 4, p 75

[40] *Commentaries* vol 2, p 498.

[41] *Ibid* vol 1, p 432.

[42] HA Kelly has taken issue with Blackstone's contention that husbands formerly enjoyed a clear right to use force to correct their wives; HA Kelly, 'Rule of Thumb and the Folklore of the Husband's Stick' (1994) 44 *Journal of Legal Education* 341–65.

[43] See eg, H Brewer, *By Birth or Consent: Children, Law and the Anglo-American Revolution in Authority* (Chapel Hill NC, 2005) 361; T Michals, 'That Sole and Despotic Dominion': Slaves, Wives, and Game in Blackstone's Commentaries' (1993–94) 27 *Eighteenth-Century Studies* 202–3.

creature, must necessarily be subject to the laws of his creator, for he is entirely a dependant being' and 'a state of dependence' inevitably obliges 'the inferior to take the will of him on whom he depends, as the rule of his conduct'. Only the king, by virtue of statute, was 'inferior to no man upon earth, dependant on no man, accountable to no man', answering directly to God.[44] Human laws determined 'what degree every man retains of his natural liberty; what he has given up as the price of society'.[45] Blackstone made no direct mention of women in these discussions, but presumably he believed that the laws surrounding marriage worked a similar effect for wives, determining what they retained of their natural liberty and what they gave up as individuals as the price of the marital bond that made them as one with their husbands. And while their state of dependence obliged them to 'take the will' of their husbands, this did not amount to a complete erasure of their own will.

Closely linked to liberty in Blackstone's vision was the appeal of reason and rationality. Breaking ranks with many of his predecessors, he made it clear that the rules of coverture were not grounded in Nature (if they were, then presumably single women should have been be just as subject to men as married women). Neither were they grounded in biblical authority. In 1663 Edward Waterhouse had labelled scripture 'the Magna Charta of man's superiority'; but for Blackstone the sins of Eve or the admonitions of St Paul had no place in expositions of the legal position of married women.[46] As we have seen, he conceded that subjection in general came from God, but he was adamant that coverture was a product of the human ordering of civil society. In book one he distinguished 'those rights God and nature have established' from the laws the municipal legislator enacts 'for promoting the welfare of the society' and used laws affecting married women as one of his examples;

> Thus our own common law has declared that the goods of the wife do instantly upon marriage become the property and right of the husband; and our statute law has declared all monopolies a public offence: yet that right, and this offence, have no foundation in nature; but are merely created by the law, for the purposes of civil society.[47]

Marriage was a state of incapacity for women, wives or feme coverts taking their accustomed place in numerous lists that included 'infants, people of unsound mind, prisoners, people beyond the seas'.[48] But in contrast to states of incapacity resulting from nature, such as 'the want or

[44] *Commentaries* vol 1, p 235.

[45] *Ibid*, p 53.

[46] E Waterhouse, *Fortescutus Illustratus, or, A Commentary on that Nervous Treatise, De Laudibus Legum Angliae* (London, 1663) 492.

[47] *Commentaries* vol 1, pp 54–55 and see p 410; *Commentaries* vol 2, p 433.

[48] See eg *ibid* vol 2, pp 354, 356, 375, 450; vol 3, p 177; vol 4, p 340.

defect of will' in children and idiots, it was a state of incapacity created by law.[49] As Blackstone explained, 'the matrimonial subjection of the wife to the husband' could in many instances excuse a wife's criminal misconduct, but not for serious crimes such as murder, as 'since in a state of nature no one is in subjection to another, it would be unreasonable to screen an offender from the punishment due to natural crimes by the refinements and subordinations of civil society'.[50]

The fundamental point for Blackstone was that married women consented to their modified legal status when they agreed to marry. He observed that 'our law considers marriage in no other light than as a civil contract' and in common with other contracts, to be good and valid 'the parties at the time of making it' had to be 'willing, able and did contract'.[51] He made consent crucial, pointing out, for example, that previous judges and commentators were wrong to have accepted that an idiot or lunatic could marry, whereas it was now agreed 'upon principles of sound sense and reason, that an idiot cannot marry, being incapable of consenting to any contract'.[52] It was therefore the logic of contract that justified married women's particular treatment at law. However, it was a narrow concept of consent that ended abruptly at the church door, with no room for renegotiation during marriage and virtually no effective ability to escape the legal effects of marriage through separation or divorce.[53] The finality of a woman's marriage vows in fixing her subordinate position brings to mind Hale's infamous pronouncement that a husband could not be guilty of rape within marriage 'for by their mutual matrimonial consent and contract the wife hath given herself in this kind unto her husband, which she cannot retract.'[54]

The nature of Blackstone's characterisation of married women is hinted at in his much-quoted observation that 'even the disabilities which the wife lies under are for the most part intended for her protection and benefit. So great a favourite is the female sex of the laws of England.'[55] Some modern observers have detected an ironic tone behind this phrase. Wilfrid Prest, for example, speculates that it was 'perhaps merely a semi-facetious flourish' or else a 'variation on the *Commentaries*' largely positive view of the common law'. It would seem to be the latter, as many other commentators before Blackstone made reference to the favoured status of women under

[49] *Commentaries* vol 4, pp 20–1.

[50] *Ibid*, p 29.

[51] *Ibid* vol 1, p 421

[52] *Ibid* vol 1, p 130.

[53] See C Pateman, *The Sexual Contract* (Cambridge, 1988); ML Shanley and C Pateman (eds), *Feminist Interpretations and Political Theory* (Cambridge, 1991); Basch (n 13).

[54] Hale (n 30) vol 1, p 629.

[55] *Commentaries* vol 1, p 433.

English law.[56] The author of *A Treatise of Feme Coverts*, for example, stated that 'many particular privileges are belonging to married females'.[57] Most authors made a distinction between law in theory and in practice. Edward Chamberlayne, in *The Present State of England*, published in 1669, admitted that English laws affecting married women were particularly harsh, supposing 'a wife to be in so much subjection and obedience to her husband, as to have no will at all of her own'. But he went on to assert that

> their condition *de facto* is the best in the world; for such is the good nature of Englishmen towards their wives, such is their tenderness and respect, giving them the uppermost place at table and elsewhere, the right hand every where, and putting them upon no drudgery and hardship; that if there were a *bridge* over into *England*. . . it is thought all the women in *Europe* would run thither.[58]

Here optimism about the human character overcomes pessimism about English law. In the *Commentaries* such a dichotomy seems almost inconceivable, for at every turn Blackstone emphasised how the law supported and encouraged the goodwill of husbands.[59]

Elsewhere in the *Commentaries* Blackstone stressed that power depended on property, and that only those with property possessed a functioning will.[60] Given that the common law removed control of property from married women, to a modern eye the implications are clear: but Blackstone was blind to them. Liberty for Blackstone meant the right to enjoy property and the freedom to act in legally sanctioned ways, but it also meant protection.[61] Coverture therefore represented the ultimate expression of the common law's benevolent paternalism, providing wives with a blanket set of protections unique to England. During marriage a wife not only lived 'under the protection and influence of her husband', performing everything under his 'wing, protection and cover', but he also took responsibility for most of her debts and misdemeanours, which Blackstone described as 'one of the greatest privileges of English wives'.[62] In common with many other eighteenth- and nineteenth-century thinkers, Blackstone felt able to celebrate the story of English liberty, despite the common law excluding women from many or most of the freedoms that English society held so dear, thanks to the assumption that women benefited from the status and privileges of their menfolk. Blackstone's tone

[56] W Prest, 'Law for Historians: William Blackstone on Wives, Colonies and Slaves' (2007) 11 *Legal History* 108.

[57] Anonymous (n 32) 78.

[58] E Chamberlayne, *Angliae Notitia, or The Present State of England Together with Divers Reflections upon the Antient State Thereof* (London, 1669) 502.

[59] See eg *Commentaries* vol 2, p 436.

[60] *Commentaries* vol 1, pp 165–6.

[61] *Ibid*, pp 120–22, 413.

[62] *Ibid* vol 3, p 414.

of gentlemanly chivalry suggested that wives, despite the loss during marriage of 'all legal and separate existence', somehow basked in the glow of the liberty and privileges of their free-born husbands.

Blackstone displayed an unmistakable commitment to what we recognise as Enlightenment principles: acknowledging a wife's will (it was covered by her husband's, but not erased altogether), downplaying, and at times abhorring, a husband's physical power over his wife, denying a role for scripture in wifely subjection. However, he remained a man of his times. He advocated reform for many areas of the common law, but more often through a hearkening back to older and more straightforward practices unsullied by Norman innovations than through legislative initiatives. As Paul O Carrese puts it, Blackstone, like Montesquieu before him, sought the law of liberty 'not in some new Enlightenment rationalism but in the woods, with the medieval Goths' and despite his openness to reform he remained staunchly conservative when it came to the laws governing marriage and the family.[63] As a result, his descriptions of laws affecting women were strangely static, as if immune to evolution and adaptation in response to changing circumstances. He explained, for example, that the punishment for a wife who murdered her husband–petty treason, a crime against the state–was burning at the stake, 'a custom from Caesar's time' the idea of which 'seems to have been handed down to us from the laws of the antient druids'. In reference to the favouring of males in inheritance, 'or, as our male lawgivers have somewhat uncomplaisantly expressed it, the worthiest of blood shall be preferred', he stated that 'I shall not here . . . examine into the greater dignity of blood in the male or female sex; but shall only observe that our present preference of males to females seems to have arisen entirely from the feodal law.'[64] Elsewhere in the *Commentaries* Blackstone described feudalism as 'A slavery so complicated and so extensive as this called aloud for a remedy in a nation that boasted of her freedom', a remedy that came with Charles II's abolition of feudal tenures.[65] But as the cornerstone of women's diminished property and inheritance rights, the feudal past went unquestioned.

Nowhere is Blackstone's conservatism in this area more apparent than in his neglect of the options equity offered to married women.[66] He described the ecclesiastical jurisdiction at length, including the ability of a married woman to sue there in her own name and to seek a separation order and alimony if she was cursed with a violent husband, yet largely ignored the

[63] PO Carrese, *The Cloaking of Power: Montesquieu, Blackstone and the Rise of Judicial Activism* (Chicago, 2003) 117.

[64] *Commentaries* vol 2, p 213.

[65] *Ibid*, p 76.

[66] This was Mary Beard's main criticism of Blackstone, although she saw no reason to 'ascribe it to any personal animosity toward women': Beard (n 2) 102.

assistance available to married women in the equitable jurisdiction. As Holdsworth pointed out, Blackstone used the term equity in two distinct senses in the *Commentaries*, in volume one referring to justice and fairness in the broadest possible sense and in volume three referring to the particular 'laboured connected system' operating in Chancery. Holdsworth criticised Blackstone for insufficiently distinguishing these two usages, but they help to explain his particular vision of the law of husband and wife. Put simply, Blackstone saw equity as 'a mere supplement to the common law'.[67] He approved of equity when Chancellors employed it to 'supply the defects' of the law, but disapproved of equitable instruments and interventions intended to undermine or circumvent the law.[68] It can be deduced from his relative silence on the subjects of trusts designed to protect married women's property interests, and of Chancery's willingness to hear litigation involving the competing spouses' interests, that he disapproved of these usages of equity, presumably because they corroded common-law certainty. As he explained in his lectures, equity

> must not sap or weaken the fundamental pillar of the Law, in order to redress a seeming hardship in rights that are merely positive depending solely on the will of the legislature and in which conscience is not at all concerned.

The example he gave was the exclusion of the half-blood from the inheritance, which

> how so unreasonable it may seem, yet shall not be redressed by Equity, because the right of Succession is founded not on the Law of Nature but on compact, not on any primitive natural Right but on the Law of the State, and therefore this being a general rule, shall not be superseded.[69]

As we have seen, Blackstone believed that the rules of coverture were founded on contract and the law of the state, not on 'the Law of Nature' or on any 'primitive natural Right' and so did not look kindly on decisions in equity that superseded them.

Blackstone's descriptions of the actual laws affecting married women, as opposed to their history and changing rationales, are difficult to fault, although his focus on the common law led him to neglect equity. What was original was his explanation of those laws. In recognising that unashamed appeals to masculine power to justify the superior position of husbands at law were becoming harder to make (not least to women) and that the force of the Bible as an unshakeable authority was losing its grip, Blackstone jettisoned these two traditional supports for coverture. His search for alternative ways of characterising the marital relationship, not to change

[67] WS Holdsworth, 'Blackstone's Treatment of Equity' (1929) 43 *Harvard Law Review* 2, 5, 29.

[68] *Commentaries* vol 3, p 60.

[69] Holdsworth (n 67) 30.

the law but to justify the status quo, led to a concentrated focus on unity of person. As various historians have observed, from the 1780s onwards decisions in King's Bench under Lord Mansfield expanded the contractual capacity of married women at common law, in the case of separated wives pledging credit for necessaries. This move away from regarding husband and wife as one person (inspired not by the rights of wives but by the interests of creditors) might have signalled the beginning of the end for understandings of coverture built upon unity of person, but it was short-lived. Lord Kenyon swiftly returned marital unity to its position as the central pillar supporting coverture, arguably endowing it with a greater influence in the early years of the nineteenth century than it had enjoyed at any point in its history.[70] Jeremy Bentham provided a rare dissenting voice in 1827, describing unity of person as a 'grimgribber nonsensical' justification, but he noted with despair that 'on questions relative to the two matrimonial conditions this quibble is the fountain of all reason'.[71]

What had begun as a limited fiction applied in specific circumstances had grown to become a metaphor that helped to describe the marital state, then a doctrine that at first explained coverture and finally justified coverture.[72] By increasing the explanatory weight that the 'age old' fiction of unity of person should bear, Blackstone helped to shelter the rules of coverture from discussions of the liberty and freedom of the individual, allowing them to persist until the 1880s and beyond.[73]

[70] S Staves, *Married Women's Separate Property in England, 1660–1833* (New Haven CT, 1990) ch 6; K Pearlston, 'At the Limits of Coverture: Judicial Imagination and Women's Agency in the English Common Law' (unpublished PhD dissertation, York University, 2007).

[71] J Bentham, *Rationales of Judicial Evidence, Specially Applied to English Practice* (London, 1827) vol 5, pp 344–5.

[72] On this transformation, see Doggett (n 14) 99.

[73] On the longevity of coverture and unity of person see *Midland Bank Trust Co Ltd v Green* (1981) 3 All England Reports 744; A Ronner, 'Husband and Wife Are One, Him: *Bennis v. Michigan* as the Resurrection of Coverture' (1996) 4 *Michigan Journal of Gender & Law* 129–69.

9

Blackstone on Colonialism

Australian Judicial Interpretations

THALIA ANTHONY*

A DEARTH OF legal authority for Australian colonisation led New South Wales colonial courts to rely heavily on Sir William Blackstone's *Commentaries on the Laws of England*. Colonial judges relied on Blackstone when determining matters relating to land, sovereignty and technical aspects of criminal, family and tax law. The focus of this chapter is how Australian courts construed Blackstone's doctrines on the processes of and justification for Australian colonisation. It argues that Australian courts took Blackstone's writings on colonialism out of their original context in order to meet the imperatives of British sovereignty. After analysing the use of Blackstone in judgments by the New South Wales Supreme Court from the 1820s to the 1840s, this chapter will then consider how Blackstone's feudal proposition justifying British land colonisation materialised in New South Wales and northern Australia, and was eventually dealt with in native title case law.

The contribution of Blackstone to colonial legal doctrine is significant in two respects. First, it was relied on by judges to justify colonisation, in the absence of clear legal authority such as British government policy, British case law, or international law. Blackstone's doctrines were used to create the myth that there was an established legal basis for colonisation. Blackstone stated that the lawful acquisition of another territory must be by treaty, conquest or where a land is found without inhabitants (which he referred to as 'desart [sic] and uncultivated'[1]). Only when one of these pre-conditions was met could the British Crown assert its sovereignty.

* Thalia Anthony acknowledges valuable comments and feedback provided by Amanda Porter, Hannah Robert, Michelle Burgis, David Lewis and anonymous editorial referees.

[1] 'Introduction: of the countries [s]ubject to the laws of England': *Commentaries* vol 1, p 104; 'Of title by prerogative, and forfeiture: the rights of things': *Commentaries* vol 2, p 414.

The doctrine that pre-1788 New South Wales was a land without inhabitants was developed by the New South Wales Supreme Court in the 1830s and by the Privy Council in the late nineteenth century. This myth gave a legal basis for the colonisation of New South Wales that had already taken place by occupation. Blackstone stated that 'occupancy is the thing by which the title was in fact originally gained; every man seising to his own continued use such spots of ground as he found most agreeable . . . provided he found them unoccupied by any one el[s]e'.[2] However, Blackstone's *Commentaries* were interpreted as encompassing not only uninhabited land, but also inhabited yet uncultivated land, which was an innovation of the New South Wales courts.

Historians have pointed to the fact that 'the proposition that inhabited land could be dealt with as if it was uninhabited or terra nullius' had no legal basis under British common law, legislation or international law.[3] Merete Borch argues that the influential role of Justice Burton of the Supreme Court in the 1830s and the 1840s, the context of Western positivist theory and ideas of European superiority created a justification that uncultivated (although inhabited) land could be considered *terra nullius*.[4] Borch argues that contrary to the way in which New South Wales judges invoked Blackstone's doctrines, Blackstone did not intend 'desert uninhabited' to mean land uncultivated.[5] Rather, an analysis of his writings in the context of the Americas reveals that Blackstone literally meant a land uninhabited.[6] According to this interpretation of Blackstone, the only basis in British law for acquiring colonial land inhabited by Indigenous people was treaty or conquest.[7]

Blackstone's second major contribution to the legal doctrine of colonisation was his articulation of the process for colonisation—namely that the Crown acquires all land in the form of radical (or ultimate) title. He stated that this was akin to feudal tenure, where the Crown held ultimate title but granted land to lords for productive use. New South Wales judges in the mid nineteenth century pointed to the appropriateness of this doctrine in a colonial setting where feudal tenure was a means for the sovereign Crown to retain control of a distant land. In south-eastern Australia, the feudal basis for land law was highly relevant in the first 80 years of settlement—prior to the introduction of the Torrens system of land title registration between 1858 and 1875—because it retained Crown control over land titles. Indeed the feudal system of obligations in exchange for land

[2] *Commentaries* vol 2, pp 8–9.

[3] MF Borch, 'Rethinking the Origins of *Terra Nullius*' (2001) 32 *Australian Historical Studies* 222, 238.

[4] *Ibid* 236–8.

[5] *Ibid* 239.

[6] *Ibid* 225–6.

[7] *Ibid* 227.

continues to be relevant anywhere in Australia where leasehold still prevails. Thus, colonial legislatures and courts translated Blackstone's *Commentaries* to enforce feudal governance and power.

In Australia, references to Blackstone's *Commentaries* have a greater significance than mere relics of eighteenth- and nineteenth-century cases. For example, Blackstone was cited profusely in the 1992 *Mabo* decision on native title. This was because the judges in *Mabo* reconsidered many of the nineteenth-century cases which relied on Blackstone. In that case, the High Court held that judges had misapplied Blackstone's justification for occupation to Australian land. Moreover, Blackstone continues to be cited in subsequent native title cases. This chapter will interrogate Blackstone's legal justifications for colonisation, and show how a post-*Mabo* reading of Blackstone's *Commentaries* urges consideration of a treaty with Indigenous people to sustain the legitimacy of Australian colonisation.

I BLACKSTONE IN THE COLONIAL COURTS

When the British first occupied New South Wales in 1788, the legal authority for that act went unchallenged. Indeed, the New South Wales court system was not established until 1823,[8] and there were no international contests to British sovereignty, despite the Dutch having 'discovered' the Australian continent in the early seventeenth century.

The early challenges to Crown sovereignty in the 1840s were not brought by Indigenous claimants. Rather, the challenges came from squatters, miners and pastoralists who sought to acquire land by means other than Crown grant. Courts that heard these challenges would turn to Blackstone's lucid description of Crown rights where colonial lands are 'desart [sic] and uncultivated'.[9] Blackstone claimed that these lands 'are claimed by right of occupancy only', so all English laws 'are immediately there in force'.[10] Judges interpreted this claim as meaning uncultivated lands,[11] or lands where inhabitants lacked 'numbers', 'civilization', or recognised title to land.[12] Borch suggests that the courts of New South

[8] *New South Wales Act* (Imp) 1823.

[9] *Commentaries* vol 1, p 104, vol 2, p 414

[10] *Ibid.*

[11] Locke was often invoked to interpret Blackstone's statement as meaning that uncultivated lands could be appropriated without consent: Borch (n 3) 231. Locke had stated that common uncultivated lands brought into production would 'first begin a title of property'; however, Borch claims that Locke recognised the original rights of hunter-gatherers: *ibid* 232; J Locke, *Two Treatises of Government*, ed P Laslett (Cambridge, 1960; 1689) 320.

[12] eg, *R v Murrell and Bummaree* (1836), in banco: Supreme Court, Miscellaneous Correspondence relating to Aborigines, State Records of New South Wales, 5/1161, 210–16, 211 (Burton J) http://www.law.mq.edu.au/scnsw/cases1835–6/html/r_v_murrell_and_bummaree__1836.htm.

Wales, and later England, adopted this reading of Blackstone to accommodate the 'establishment of New South Wales'.[13]

However, colonial judges took Blackstone's statements about 'desert and uncultivated' out of their original context. Following his use of this phrase, Blackstone clarifies that an '*uninhabited* country' (emphasis added) can be 'planted by English subjects' with the force of English laws.[14] In making this point, Blackstone is often referring to the specific examples of colonisation in the Americas. Borch claims that Blackstone relies on a 1722 Privy Council decision in relation to Barbados as evidence of occupation of a land that 'seems to have been truly uninhabited when the British settled in 1625'.[15] By contrast, in (what became) the United States of America, the requirement that the land be truly uninhabited meant that American colonial courts treated land as having been acquired from natives by conquest or cession.[16]

Colonial judges in New South Wales in the 1830s, however, took the view that there were no legally recognised inhabitants in New South Wales at the time of colonisation. Therefore, the Crown was the lawful 'univer-[s]al lord and original proprietor' of all settled land.[17] The courts adapted Blackstone's notion of occupation to dismiss challenges to the Crown's claims to land. In 1831, the Supreme Court in the case of *R v Farrell, Dingle and Woodward* considered whether the British defence of necessity would apply to an Australian crime. In finding for the validity of this defence, Chief Justice Forbes commented that the statute, 9 Geo IV, c 84, gave the Supreme Court power to adopt English law as it stood in 1823.

In *R v Farrell, Dingle and Woodward*, Chief Justice Forbes created a myth of retrospective British sovereignty through the imposition of his court's jurisdiction.[18] Citing Blackstone's *Commentaries*, he held that British sovereignty pre-existed the 1823 statute establishing his court. Lisa Ford claims that judicial findings of retrospective sovereignty are 'the transformation of the theory of sovereignty' through the 'practice of jurisdiction'.[19] She writes that 'exercises of territorial jurisdiction' and sovereignty are contingent on 'legal personality: the legal status, the race,

Cooper v Stuart (1889) 1 AC 286, 291 (Lord Watson); *Milirrpum v Nabalco and the Commonwealth* (1971) 17 FLR 141, 201–2 (Blackburn J).

[13] Borch (n 3) 238.

[14] *Ibid* 226.

[15] Borch (n 3) 226. While Borch unfortunately provides no direct citation to Blackstone's work on this particular point, see the latter's reference to Case 15—Anonymous (1722), *Peere Williams* 2: 75–6, 24 ER 646: *Commentaries* vol 1, p 105.

[16] *Commentaries* vol 1, p 105.

[17] *Ibid* vol 2, p 51.

[18] On the relationship between the assertion of curial jurisdiction and sovereignty, see L Ford, 'Empire and Order on the Colonial Frontiers of Georgia and New South Wales' (2006) 30 *Itinerario: Geographies of Empire* 96, 107.

[19] *Ibid* 96.

subjecthood or nationality and the class of the people involved'.[20] Chief Justice Forbes assumed this retrospective sovereignty by a skewed interpretation of Blackstone. For example, ignoring the fact that Australia was inhabited by Indigenous people at the time of colonisation, Forbes cited Blackstone as authority for the proposition that laws passed in England prior to the statute were immediately in force in the uninhabited New South Wales:

> The New South Wales Act [9 Geo IV, c 84] does not introduce a new principle. It is recognised in the old common law of the Colonies, and is laid down in Blackstone, vol. 1, 107, that, 'if an uninhabited country be discovered and planted by English subjects, all the English laws then in being, which are the birth-right of every subject, are immediately there in force,' with the restrictions therein set forth. The laws of England are declared by the Act for settling the succession to the throne, to be the birth-right of the subject. Let an Englishman go where he will, and settle a new country, he carries with him all the laws which are applicable to his condition. What laws do or do not apply, must necessarily be left to the local authorities to determine, always subject to an appeal to the King in Council.[21]

Blackstone's *Commentaries* were the bible of colonial lawyers. Lawyers who referred to Blackstone's doctrines at length in their submissions included William Charles Wentworth in *R v Steele* (1834).[22] Consequent to Wentworth citing Blackstone, the Supreme Court held that the English 'doctrine of tenures' applied to Australia:

> By the laws of England, the King, in virtue of his crown, is the possessor of all the unappropriated lands of the kingdom; and all his subjects are presumed to hold their lands, by original grant from the crown. The same law applies to this colony. It is a matter of history that New South Wales was taken possession of, in the name of the King of Great Britain, about fifty-five years ago.[23]

In the case of *R v Steele*, it was found that the Crown appropriated New South Wales between 1788 and the formation of Parliament and the courts in 1823, not through legal means but as a 'matter of history'.[24] Although the court referred to Blackstone's *Commentaries* for authority, the assumption of sovereignty was already founded. Blackstone was merely the justifying pretext for colonisation in a process that had already been undertaken under an assumption that had already been made: Australia was a settled colony.

[20] Ford (n 18) 96.

[21] *R v Farrell, Dingle and Woodward* (1831) *In Banco* (23 July 1831): www.austlii.edu.au/au/other/NSWSupC/1831/44.html.

[22] *R v Steele* (1834) (Forbes CJ) www.law.mq.edu.au/scnsw/Cases1834/html/r_v_steele__1834.htm.

[23] *Ibid.*

[24] *Ibid.*

However, the colonial court recognised that colonisation was not a blank cheque for the application of English laws. Conveniently for the authority of New South Wales judges, Blackstone was cited to support the proposition that colonial courts had discretion to develop legal principles. They referred to Blackstone to highlight the restrictive application of English laws. Thus in *R v Broadbear and Broadbear*, Chief Justice Forbes stated

> a general proposition, it is laid down by text writers on the subject, that if a new country be settled by English subjects, all the laws then in being are transported there as the birth-right of every subject. 'But this,' says Judge Blackstone, 'must be understood with very many and very great restrictions; such Colonists carry with them only as much of the English law as is applicable to the condition of an infant Colony.'[25]

The case of *MacDonald v Levy*[26] dealt with the reception of English laws into colonial New South Wales. In his judgment, Chief Justice Forbes sought to retain some autonomy for the colonial courts. Accordingly he cited Blackstone, who was said to have expounded the 'reception' issue in 'clear and comprehensive terms' and to be supported by the 'most eminent lawyers'.[27] His Honour quoted Blackstone's second edition, where it was laid down of English laws that

> What shall be admitted, and what rejected, at what time, and under what restrictions, must, in case of dispute, be decided in the first instance by their own provisional judicature.[28]

Forbes's admission was limited to the substantive laws which applied in the colony, and did not threaten the premise of British sovereignty. According to Forbes, the English law of marriage, poor laws and excise laws had never been used in the colony and were therefore inapplicable. However the New South Wales Supreme Court quoted Blackstone to the effect that the English laws of police, penalties, punishments and property are highly relevant to a colony. These were the laws of control and sovereignty, which judges perceived as necessary for colonial command. Even more importantly, the laws of 'general regulation of property [are] equally applicable to any country in which property is governed by English law'.[29] The invocation of Blackstone to support the English land tenure system will now be discussed.

[25] *R v Broadbear and Broadbear* (1826) NSWSupC 34 www.austlii.edu.au/au/other/NSWSupC/1826/34.

[26] *MacDonald v Levy* (1833) NSWSupC 47 (Forbes CJ) www.austlii.edu.au/au/other/NSWSupC/1833/47.html.

[27] *Ibid*, Forbes CJ citing *Commentaries*, vol 1, p 107 (2nd edn, 1766).

[28] *Ibid.*

[29] Blackstone is citing the Master of the Rolls denying the application of the statute of Mortmain to the island of Grenada, in *Anonymous* (1722) 24 ER 646.

Early colonial judges relied and expanded upon Blackstone's *Commentaries* not only to validate colonial acts, the courts' jurisdiction and British sovereignty, but also to stipulate the terms of land tenure and Crown title. Originally judgments arose where colonisers called on the courts to adjudicate intra-colonial land disputes, that is, settlers challenging Crown land claims. However, the judicial use of Blackstone to enforce Crown title became particularly pronounced when Indigenous claimants finally took the opportunity to bring a native title case in 1971. This section discusses the reliance on Blackstone in colonial land disputes, and subsequently disputes involving Indigenous native title claimants in the latter part of the twentieth century.

One of the first major challenges to Crown title to land was in *Attorney-General v Brown*, adjudicated by the New South Wales Supreme Court in 1847. This case involved the Crown's complaint that the defendant had intruded on Crown mineral rights by mining coal on his leasehold land near Newcastle. The defendant argued that he had a right to make such an entry and 'dig for and carry away the coals, as he might think fit'.[30] He further submitted that 'the Crown has not and never had any property in the waste lands of the Colony—that is, any beneficial ownership or right to grant any of them without authority of Parliament'.[31]

Chief Justice Stephen's judgment dismissed this claim. In explaining sovereignty and the colonisation of New South Wales lands (that now 'belong[ed]' to the British Crown), Stephen pointed to the fact that Britain found Australia as a 'newly-discovered country'.[32] This meant that the settlement of British subjects rendered valid the Crown's 'occupancy' and 'executive authority'.[33] The Crown is '[the] moral personality … by whom the nation acts, and in whom for such purposes its power resides'.[34]

Chief Justice Stephen stated that the Crown's power emanates from settlement itself. To support the claim that 'at the moment of settlement the colonists brought the common law of England with them', he cited Blackstone's statement that the rules of inheritance are received in a settled colony.[35] The Chief Justice then extended Blackstone's reference to all common law and statute law. He concluded that the 'feudal principle' of Crown land possession and grants 'is as much in force in the colonies as the law which provides for the succession of the eldest son'.[36]

30 *Attorney-General v Brown* (1847) 1 Legge 312, 313 (Stephen CJ).
31 Defence argument summarised by Stephen, *ibid.*
32 *Attorney-General v Brown* (n 30) 317.
33 *Ibid* 318.
34 *Ibid.*
35 *Ibid.*
36 *Ibid.*

The reasoning of Chief Justice Stephen, as analysed by Justice Brennan in *Mabo*,[37] was that if the land were desert and uninhabited, the Crown would take an absolute beneficial title to the land because there would be no other proprietor. But if the land were occupied by the Indigenous inhabitants and their rights and interests in the land are recognised by the common law, the radical title acquired with the acquisition of sovereignty cannot itself be taken to confer an absolute beneficial title to the occupied land. Stephen asserted that there was no other proprietor and so the Crown gained beneficial title 'from the first time of its first settlement in 1788'.[38]

However, the Chief Justice's position that all title to land must emanate from the Crown was not a departure from New South Wales orthodoxy at the time, nor exclusively reliant on Blackstone's doctrine. It echoed Chief Justice Forbes's Memorandum in July 1834:

> In considering the rights of the Crown, with reference to the Colonies, it is important to bear in mind the distinction between conquered or ceded foreign possessions, and such as have been peacefully acquired and settled by His Majesty's subjects ...Where British subjects settle an uninhabited country, they carry the laws of the parent country with them—and among other parts of the law, the prerogatives of the Crown, become in force. By the laws of England the King is the *ultimus heres*, and becomes entitled to all the waste lands of the Colony. These lands form the demesne lands of the Crown, and are part of the Royal revenue. His Majesty may grant them upon such reserved rents as may be deemed proper. ... The Colony of New South Wales is a settled Colony—on a possession acquired by the act of His Majesty's subjects settling an uninhabited country.[39]

Towards the end of the nineteenth century, the Privy Council, on appeal from the Supreme Court of New South Wales, visited the issue of whether an 1823 Crown grant of lands in fee simple (freehold) was valid. The appellant was the successor in title. The year of the grant to the successor is significant because it was before the Australia Courts Act (1828), when the reception of English laws (and in particular, Crown radical title to all land) was given statutory backing by the British Parliament.

In 1882 the government of New South Wales, in pursuance of a reservation on the land, resumed and took possession of a parcel of land 10 acres in extent, and excluded the appellant from it. In the case of *Cooper v Stuart* (1889) the appellant sought a declaration that the

[37] *Mabo v Queensland (No. 2)* (1992) 175 CLR 1, 26 (Brennan J).

[38] *Attorney-General v Brown* (1847) 1 Legge 316.

[39] F Forbes, 'Memorandum', [July 1834], in Sir Richard Bourke Papers, vol 11, Mitchell Library, MS A1738; Sir Francis Forbes Papers, National Library of Australia, MS 1293, in JM Bennett (ed), *Some Papers of Sir Francis Forbes* (Sydney, 1998) 227–8.

reservation was void, contending that it violated the rule against perpetuities (that prohibits vesting a grant in land after a certain period), to which the Crown was also subject in 1823. The issue was whether the Crown's radical title prevailed.

The appellant failed on the basis that the rule against perpetuities was inapplicable to Crown grants in the settled colony of New South Wales. In the Privy Council Lord Watson held that New South Wales belonged to a class of settled colonies; it was 'a Colony which consisted of a tract of territory practically unoccupied, without settled inhabitants or settled law, at the time when it was peacefully annexed to the British dominions'.[40] Lord Watson cited Blackstone to invoke a notion of *terra nullius* where the people first occupying colonised lands were 'primitive', making the land 'practically' uninhabited,[41] and hence capable of British settlement.[42] Therefore upon settlement the Crown immediately held radical title to all land. In 1823 the reception of English law, according to the Privy Council, was governed not 'by any statutory provision, but entirely by the silent operation of constitutional principles'[43] as enunciated by Blackstone.[44]

Lord Watson stated that 'the often quoted observations of Sir William Blackstone (1 Comm 107) appear to their Lordships to have a direct bearing on the present case'. New South Wales, for the Privy Council, was indeed uninhabited land.[45] Lord Watson then quoted Blackstone verbatim: 'It hath been held that, if an uninhabited country be discovered and planted by English subjects, all the English laws then in being, which are the birthright of every English subject, are immediately there in force (Salk. 411, 666)'.[46] Ultimately the rule against perpetuities did not apply to Crown grants of land in the colony of New South Wales because in a colony it is impossible to foresee what land will ultimately be required for public uses, so that a reservation was the only feasible way of protecting the future needs of the colony. Here the Privy Council developed these retrospective principles to legitimise the needs of Crown control. Blackstone became a pawn in *ex post facto* law.

Blackstone would serve to justify not only the colonisation of Australian land, but also the form of colonial land tenure. Australia's land system was not established in the mould of a modern market-capitalist system, in which allodial (individual) title prevails. This was despite the industrial revolution and principles of individual land ownership taking hold in

40 *Cooper v Stuart* (1889) 14 App Cas 286 at 291.
41 *Ibid* 291.
42 *Cooper v Stuart* (n 40) 294.
43 *Ibid* 293.
44 See RS O'Regan, 'The Common Law Overseas: A Problem in Applying the Test of Applicability' (1971) 20 *The International and Comparative Law Quarterly* 342, 342–3.
45 *Ibid.*
46 *Ibid.*

England at the time of Australian colonisation.[47] Rather, colonial land was feudal in the sense that, firstly, the Crown ultimately owned all land, and secondly, the possession of land was granted in return for paying rent and meeting certain conditions.

Although not adjudicated at the time of colonisation, by the mid nineteenth century there was a prevailing legal view that the Crown acquired ultimate title of New South Wales in 1788.[48] The reception of feudal laws was formalised by the *Australia Courts Act* 1828 and upheld (retrospectively) in the 1847 New South Wales Supreme Court decision of *Attorney-General v Brown*. Chief Justice Stephen there stated explicitly that colonial lands were in the 'Sovereign's possession; and that, as his or her property, they have been and may now be effectually granted to subjects of the Crown'.[49] This represented, according to the Chief Justice, the 'adoption of the feudal system', in New South Wales.[50]

Classical feudal law notions[51] identified feudal relations based on the legal existence of the fief. The fief is a unit of land that is ultimately held by the Crown and granted to a liege lord in return for service and homage. While a stratified land system may develop (with several layers of possession with attendant legal rights and obligations to the superior lord), all land titles originate with the Crown.[52] The Crown grants land in exchange for obligations.

Blackstone expounded the legal constitution of feudalism. He identified the 'constitution of feuds' as originating from military obligations, where in the northern or Celtic nations, 'parcels of land were allotted by the conquering general to the superior officers of the army, and by them dealt out again in smaller parcels or allotments to the inferior officers and most deserving soldiers'.[53] Since English feudal tenure was predicated on the Crown as the paramount lord over all conquered land, the Crown has the power to issue land titles.[54] So Blackstone wrote,

> it became a fundamental maxim and necessary principle (though in reality a mere fiction) of our English tenures, that the king is the universal lord and original proprietor of all the lands in his kingdom; and that no man doth or can possess any part of it, but what has, mediately or immediately, been derived as a gift from him, to be held upon feodal [sic] services.[55]

[47] CB Macpherson, 'Capitalism and the Changing Concept of Property' in E Kamenka and RS Neale (ed), *Feudalism, capitalism and beyond* (Canberra, 1975) 105.

[48] *Attorney-General v Brown* (1847) 1 Legge 316 (Stephen CJ).

[49] *Ibid.*

[50] *Attorney-General v Brown* (n 48) 318.

[51] See eg T Craig, *Jus Feudale* (tr) JA Clyde (Edinburgh, 1934).

[52] Cited in EAR Brown, 'The Tyranny of a Construct: feudalism and historians of Medieval Europe' (1974) 79 *American Historical Review* 1064.

[53] *Commentaries* vol 2, p 45.

[54] *Ibid*, p 51.

[55] *Ibid.*

Feudal tenure was an imperial device in the Norman Conquest of 1066 to assert the rule of King William I. There, the feudal legal relations were fictitious because the land claims of the lords preceded the reign of King William I, and did not flow immediately from the king.[56] Blackstone nonetheless explains the doctrinal significance in terms of homage owed to the conquering general. He points to treason against the sovereign as representing a breach of a condition of the feudal 'contractual' relationship

> the condition annexed to them [the fiefs] was, that the possessor should do service faithfully, both at home and in the wars, to him by whom they were given; for which purpose he took the *juramentum fidelitatis*, or oath of fealty: and in case of the breach of this condition and oath, by not performing the stipulated service, or by deserting the lord in battle, the lands were again to revert to him who granted them.[57]

These feudal property principles are two-fold. First, the 'Doctrine of Tenures and Estates' provides for a 'single devolving chain of title' by ensuring that 'no land in which the Crown has granted an interest is ever without a legal owner'.[58] Second, the 'Doctrine of Estates' articulates the interests of those who hold land from the Crown to further grant their estate to a lessee or a tenant.[59] This system of top-down accountability among landowners guaranteed adherence to colonial objectives and established 'order' among the various landed interests. For Blackstone, in the 'more di[s]tant plantations'[60] Crown ownership of land would be the 'fundamental maxim' of tenure.[61]

Attached to the Crown's acquisition of land also came the right to exercise laws. The courts have treated British sovereignty and Crown land title as inexorable.[62] From the early 1800s, Indigenous litigants have challenged the application of these laws to themselves and their communities. The most notable examples are where an Indigenous defendant is alleged to have committed an offence against another Indigenous person. These litigants argued that colonial laws should not apply where both the

[56] Allodial estates were surrendered to the king's hands and were granted back as feuds. Nonetheless, the King claimed to have produced co-existing interests in land by granting possession to landlords. The granting of land maintained homage from landlords to the Crown: see AWB Simpson, *An Introduction to the History of Land Law* (Oxford, 1961) 47–8.

[57] *Commentaries* vol 2, p 45.

[58] *The Wik Peoples v Queensland* (1996) 187 CLR 1, 90 (Brennan CJ).

[59] *Ibid* 128 (Toohey J).

[60] *Commentaries* vol 1, p 104.

[61] *Ibid* vol 2, p 51.

[62] See *Milirrpum v Nabalco and the Commonwealth* (1971) 17 FLR 141, 247 (Blackburn J).

perpetrator and the victim were Indigenous. Once again, the courts referred to Blackstone for authority on the supremacy of British laws to the exclusion of Indigenous laws.

One of the earliest cases on this point was *R v Murrell and Bummaree* (1836), involving the trial of an Aboriginal man, Murrell, for the wilful murder of another Aboriginal man, Jabbingee, in Windsor, New South Wales (a white settlement with predominantly Aboriginal people). At trial, Murrell pleaded not guilty, but nevertheless argued that if he were to be tried the applicable law was his customary law. He claimed that New South Wales was occupied by his own people before it was occupied by the King of England. Murrell's defence lawyer, Mr Sydney Stephen, invoked Blackstone to suggest that Australia was not uninhabited, conquered nor ceded, and thus Indigenous laws should be recognised:

> It was laid down in 1st Blackstone, 102, and in fact in every other work upon the subject, that land obtained like the present, were not desart [sic] or uncultivated, or peopled from the mother country, they having originally a population of the own more numerous than those who have since arrived from the mother country. Neither could this territory be called a conquered country, as Great Britain never was at war with the natives; it was not a ceded country either; it, in fact, came within neither of these, but was a country which had a population having manners and customs of their own, and we had come to reside among them, therefore in point of strictness and analogy to our law, we were bound to obey their laws, not they to obey ours.[63]

At trial, Chief Justice Forbes took a seemingly radical stance by describing Mr Stephen's plea to have 'any acts of violence committed by the natives against each other … subject to the custom of their own laws' as 'perfectly just'.[64] The Chief Justice regarded the issue as one to be decided by the legislature, but in the interim allowed the matter to be heard by the Full Court.

(A similar reading of Blackstone to that put by Murrell's defence counsel was adopted a few years later in the case of *R v Bonjon*.[65] In 1841 Justice Willis of the New South Wales Supreme Court, trying the murder of an Aboriginal man allegedly perpetrated by another Aboriginal man, stated that New South Wales was not 'unoccupied' in 1788 because 'a body of aborigines appeared on the shore, armed with spears'. His Honour applauded the English settlers who entered treaties with the United States Indians.)

[63] *R v Murrell and Bummaree* (1836) www.law.mq.edu.au/scnsw/cases1835–36/html/r_v_murrell_and_bummaree__1836.htm.

[64] *Ibid.*

[65] *R v Bonjon* (1841). www.law.mq.edu.au/scnsw/cases1840–41/cases1841/R%20v%20Bonjon,%201841.htm. See also, *R v Ballard* (1829). http://www.austlii.edu.au/au/other/NSWSupC/1829/26.html.

Notwithstanding the decision in *R v Bonjon* that allowed the recognition of Indigenous law with reference to Blackstone's *Commentaries*, the Full Court decision of *R v Murrell* (21 December 1836) remains legal authority. The leading judgment was handed down by Justice Burton who held that the jurisdiction of the New South Wales Supreme Court was exclusive, and included Indigenous people. This was because New South Wales was not inhabited by people who had 'attained the numbers and civilization to form government and laws of sovereign states'. Accordingly, Britain held New South Wales by occupation, and so the Crown's laws applied immediately: 'That a tract of country before unappropriated by any one has been taken into actual possession by the King of England'.[66] Murrell was therefore tried for the murder of Jabbingee under the common law.

Moving now to the twentieth century, following federation of the six original colonies to form the Commonwealth of Australia in 1901, the first Indigenous land claim was made by the Yolngu people at Yirrkala in the Northern Territory. The initial legal issue at trial in 1971 was whether the Indigenous people had maintained ongoing connections to their land. Justice Blackburn who presided over the case in the Federal Court found that the Yolngu people exercised laws and customs over the land. The second issue was whether the Australian law could recognise Indigenous connections to land. To decide the latter issue, Justice Blackburn assessed the legal foundations for colonisation and Crown title to land with reference to Blackstone:

> In my opinion the authorities show that the law relating to the application of English law to the overseas possessions of the Crown was, in principle, well settled by 1788: indeed, it had been so ... since the publication of Blackstone's *Commentaries* (1765). ... Blackstone (*Commentaries* I. 107) stated ... There is a distinction between settled colonies, where the land, being desert and uncultivated, is claimed by right of occupancy, and conquered or ceded colonies. The words 'desert and uncultivated' are Blackstone's own; they have always been taken to include territory in which live uncivilized inhabitants in a primitive state of society. The difference between the laws of the two kinds of colony is that in those of the former kind all the English laws which are applicable to the colony are immediately in force there upon its foundation. In those of the latter kind, the colony already having law of its own, that law remains in force until altered.[67]

[66] *R v Murrell and Bummaree* (1841), Forbes C.J., Dowling and Burton JJ, in *Banco* (11 April 1836): Supreme Court, Miscellaneous Correspondence relating to Aborigines, State Records of New South Wales, 5/1161, 211.

[67] *Milirrpum v Nabalco and the Commonwealth* (1971) 17 FLR 201.

His Honour admitted that these were not 'matters of plain fact' or 'an express pronouncement either by the government at home or by the authorities in the colony, making clear what the basis of law in the colony was'.[68] He added that:

> it was sometimes a matter of debate to which class a particular colony belonged. Thus Blackstone, referring to the class of conquered or ceded colonies, says roundly (I. 108): 'Our American plantations are principally of this latter sort, being obtained in the last century either by right of conquest in driving out the natives (with what natural justice I shall not at present inquire) or by treaties.'[69]

Blackstone obviously provides no specific direction with regard to the Australian colonies. Nonetheless, Justice Blackburn concluded that Blackstone's legal distinction has been established: 'attribution of a colony to a particular class is a matter of law, which becomes settled and is not to be questioned upon a reconsideration of the historical facts'.[70] Therefore, these issues of native title and colonisation were not 'reopened'. All Australian land must be traced to a Crown grant. Furthermore, there was no doctrine of communal native title in Blackstone's *Commentaries* that would warrant its recognition in the common law.[71] Blackstone's omission was indeed taken to imply that 'the doctrine of communal native title does not apply in any territory *as a doctrine of the common law*. It does not apply in a settled colony because ex hypothesi it is not part of the law of England.[72]

II THE REALITY OF BLACKSTONE'S *COMMENTARIES* IN AUSTRALIAN COLONIES

The spectre of Blackstone in the colonial courts was not merely doctrinal. Rather, his *Commentaries* on feudal tenure resonated with the Australian land system even more clearly than in England. This was the position of Chief Justice Stephen in *Attorney-General v Brown* when he stated that feudal tenure had greater potency in colonies than its original articulation in the Norman Conquest, which was based on a fiction. His Honour held, '[I]n a newly-discovered country … the occupancy of the Crown with respect to the waste lands of that country, is no fiction'.[73] This was because all land *can* be traced to the Crown. In concurrence with Chief Justice

[68] *Ibid* 202.
[69] *Milirrpum v Nabalco* (n 67).
[70] *Ibid*.
[71] *Ibid* 206–7, 245, 247.
[72] *Ibid* 207 (emphasis in original). His Honour went on, 'It would also be surprising if Blackstone allowed such an omission [ie of a doctrine of communal native title] to pass, whether advertently or not'.
[73] *Attorney-General v Brown* (1847) 1 Legge 312, 316.

Stephen, the majority in *Mabo* recognised the persuasive force of the feudal doctrinal myths for the colonial project. '[W]hatever the fact, it is the fiction of royal grants that underlies the English rule.'[74] These royal grants were, according to the High Court, informed by the writings of Blackstone.[75]

In recent years, Australian historians have tended to downplay the role of Blackstone and feudal laws in Australia. Studies by an innovative team of legal historians—including Brendan Edgeworth, Andrew Buck and Bruce Kercher—highlight the uniqueness of Australian land law.[76] They particularly point to the South Australian invention of 'Torrens title' registration, which does not require that land be traced to a Crown grant.[77] This system, Buck claims, represents the parochial nature of Australian land law.[78] For Kercher, it reveals that Australia is 'an unruly child' of the 'mother country'. However, these historians tend to focus on the allodial regime in south-eastern Australia, paying little attention to leasehold in northern Australian, where feudal tenure is an ongoing reality.

Blackstone's explication of the feudal land tenure system was appropriated as a source of legitimacy for not only the colonisation of land, but also for the feudal form of Australia's land system. This system existed in south-eastern Australia for eighty years—until the introduction of individual registered title under the Torrens system in the mid nineteenth century, although that system did not preclude land being held by the Crown in the form of radical title. However, in the largest area of the Australian landmass, which remains under leasehold, the feudal system perseveres. My archival research reveals that pastoral lessees in northern Australia were cognisant of their obligations to the Crown. The Crown also had an interest in maintaining this system in order to maximise the productivity of land by keeping lessees accountable.

English Crown land grants and the ensuing leasehold system were the principal means by which the Crown alienated land in colonial New South Wales.[79] Peter Butt notes that this occurred for the first '40 years or so after 1788'.[80] Land holders in colonial New South Wales held their land conditionally, via leasehold. Their leases generally required that the land

[74] *Mabo v Queensland (No. 2)* (1992) 175 CLR 1, 47 (Brennan J).

[75] *Ibid.*

[76] A Buck, '*Attorney-General v Brown* and the Development of Property Law in Australia' (1994) 2 *Australian Property Law Journal* 128; B Kercher, *An Unruly Child: A History of Law in Australia* (Sydney, 1995).

[77] N Bhuta, '*Mabo*, *Wik* and the Art of Paradigm Management', (1998) 22 *Melbourne University Law Review* 29.

[78] Buck (n 76) 128. See also B Edgeworth, 'Tenure, Allodialism and Indigenous Rights at Common Law: English, United States and Australian Land Law Compared after *Mabo v Queensland*' (1994) 23 *Anglo-American Law Review* 397.

[79] P Butt, *Land Law* (Sydney, 1996) 839–40.

[80] *Ibid* 839.

was fenced, irrigated and put to productive use (such as pastoralism or agriculture). These obligations to the Crown created a feudal proprietary relationship where the landlord and Crown were mutually dependent. This was conducive to colonial development as it allowed the Crown to distribute land according to its prerogative and discourage speculators from taking large areas of land for capital gain rather than productive use.

A colonial commentator, James Collier, noted the differences in feudal tenure between the time of the Norman Conquest and colonial New South Wales until the late 1820s. In the case of New South Wales, the Crown took absolute property rights and conferred rights on its subjects who would fulfill obligations. This was a true expression of feudal tenure, which contrasted the manufactured expression in England

> This first stage of colonial land-ownership did not repeat that stage in European history, when a conquering Power possessed itself of all the rights which the overlords already had. When Norman William conquered England, he did not take from the English farmers or landholders all their land. He simply took from their overlords all the rights that inhered in those who were afterwards called *seigneurs*. It was consequently these that he granted. In New South Wales, on the contrary, the English conquerors acquired, of course, by force, the absolute possession of the soil, and it was this kind of possession—with necessary reservations on the part of the Crown—that was now conceded to the grantees.[81]

From the mid to late nineteenth century, while the certainty and simplicity of Torrens title made economic sense in the industrialising cities across south-eastern Australia, northern Australia continued to rely on the lease system.[82] In northern Australia (the Northern Territory, the Kimberley and northern Queensland) the predominant pastoral economy necessitated a system of Crown control to prevent land speculation. The Crown attached obligations to the land it leased in northern Australia. Leases also had resumption clauses to ensure that the Crown could re-acquire land that was unproductive, or where lessees did not meet conditions or pay rents. It was in northern Australia that Blackstone's feudal doctrine materialised and continues to manifest itself.

Leases were issued mainly to British settlers, and certainly to non-Indigenous people, who could make the land 'productive' and afford to pay rents to the colonial state.[83] Lease rents were a primary source of taxation and state revenue in northern Australia. The conditional nature of

[81] J Collier, *The Pastoral Age in Australasia* (London, 1911) 60.

[82] C Brazenor, C Ogleby and I Williamson, 'The Spatial Dimension of Aboriginal Land Tenure', Presented to 6th SE Asian Surveyors Congress, Fremantle, 1–6 November 1999, 4: www.sli.unimelb.edu.au/research/publications/IPW/ipw_paper35.pdf.

[83] The Crown's right to revenue collection was treated as the natural right of a feudal governing power: see JP Stow, *South Australia: Its History, Productions, and Natural Resources* (Adelaide, 1883) 67–8.

leasehold was evident in the terms of Northern Territory leases. Under the *Northern Territory Act* (1863), five per cent of the payments for the lease had to be put towards improvements of Crown property (such as land fixtures).[84] In later enactments, lessees had to be able to meet conditions required under the *Crown Lands Ordinance* (Cth) 1912. This involved substantial investments in the property, such as fencing, stocking and irrigation. Pastoral lands, according to an 1883 government report, 'must be declared stocked within three years from the date of application'.[85]

Consequently, leases in Australia were substantially taken up by wealthy British immigrants, absentee lessees (often British aristocratic farmers) or corporations. They had the capacity to pay the rent and the ability to meet Crown conditions.[86] Vestey Bros, a transnational British family company, held much of northern Australian land as cattle property.[87] Pastoral lessees regarded themselves as feudal lords.

The Crown had inviolable resumption rights to the colonial lands. In northern Australia, pastoral leaseholders were constantly vulnerable to resumption, as the Crown regularly exercised its rights to resume land for failure to comply with lease terms such as fencing, stocking and irrigating.[88] The first pastoral leases issued under the *Northern Territory Crown Lands Act* 1890 contained a clause that at the expiration of the lease all improvements thereon would revert to the Crown without compensation.[89]

Resumption rights were also stipulated under the Commonwealth's *Crown Lands Ordinance* 1912 s2 (3) and enforced when lease conditions were unmet or rents unpaid.[90] The Crown's right could be exercised during the currency of a lease.[91] Lessees could not appeal against the exercise of these rights to 'an independent land tribunal'.[92]

The feudal land relationship—with obligations to the Crown and high rents—meant that land holders perceived themselves as feudal lords. In colonial northern Australia pastoralists referred to themselves as 'Cattle

[84] Department of Lands and Surveys, 'Notice of Provisions of Pastoral Leases to be Allotted by the Pastoral Board' (1922) in Crawford Family: Summary Record, State Library of South Australia, PRG 1148/16. This was also a condition in NSW: Collier (n 81) 61–2.

[85] Stow (n 83) 176.

[86] T Anthony, 'Postcolonial Feudal Hauntings of Northern Australian Cattle Stations' (2003) 7 *Law Text Culture* 277, 281.

[87] P Knightley, *The Vestey Affair* (London, 1981) 143.

[88] See: FP Shepherd, *General Report on the investigation of pastoral leases in the Northern Territory 1933–1935* (Schedule F: conditions of leases), presented to the Federal Department of the Interior, Canberra (1935): National Archives (Darwin), Record NN F987, p. 2.

[89] JP Woods, *The Province of South Australia* (Adelaide, 1894) 425.

[90] DD Daly, *Digging, Squatting and Pioneering life in the Northern Territory of South Australia* (London, 1887) 221–2.

[91] Woods (n 89) 425.

[92] [Anonymous], '"We must face the facts"', *Brisbane Courier Mail* (9 December 1937): National Archives (Adelaide), Record B300/2, 7751/1.

Kings' or 'Cattle Barons'.[93] These landlords were willing and able to meet stringent lease conditions. The Queensland colonial commentator Walter Tyrwhitt stated that pastoralists were the 'natural aristocracy' in the social hierarchy due to their land claims.[94]

Feudal power relations are characterised by the stratification of rulership, which corresponds with the stratification of land possession. This system protects the overall Crown land interests as well as the lords' local proprietorships.[95] Pastoralist Billy Cox who 'ruled' the 'vast' Louisa Downs Station in the Kimberley, Western Australia for fifty years, and passed it on to his son and grandson, was attached to the idea that the 'station was theirs by right'.[96] Their land holding meant they were self-styled 'natural rulers'.[97]

Many pastoralists conceived of themselves as lords who bestowed rights over their land to dependent workers. In northern Australia, it was the pastoral lessees who initially dispossessed Indigenous people of their land, quelled their resistance and then forced Indigenous people to work on their cattle stations. Their choices, according to pastoralist Albert Wright, were 'to die, or to serve'.[98] Governments recognised pastoralists' rights over their Indigenous workers. In the Northern Territory, Regulation 14 under the *Aboriginals Ordinance* 1918 gave pastoralists responsibility for Aboriginal workers, their relatives and dependants.[99] Consequently, land holders overwhelmingly employed unpaid Indigenous workers in the northern Australian cattle industry.

Thousands of Indigenous workers took on roles as stock workers, domestic servants, gardeners and track and fence builders. These non-waged employees who lived on cattle stations with their families and communities were dependant on the landlord to stay on their ancestral 'homelands'.[100] Indigenous workers depended on the landlord for sustenance (provided by food rations and their own hunting and gathering on the lord's lease) and retaining their connections to country.[101]

[93] M Durack, *Kings in Grass Castles; Sons in the Saddle* (Sydney, 2000) iii; LA Schubert, *Kimberley Dreaming: the Century of Freddie Cox* (Mundurah, 1992) 40.

[94] WSS Tyrwhitt, *The New Chum in the Queensland Bush* (London, 1888) 78.

[95] S Reynolds, *Fiefs Versus Vassals: the Medieval Evidence Reinterpreted* (Oxford, 1994) 476, 481.

[96] Schubert (n 93) 150.

[97] Collier (n 81) 316.

[98] J Wright, *The Generations of Men* (London, 1960) 155.

[99] B Thorpe, 'Aboriginal Employment and Unemployment: colonised labour' in C Williams and W Thorpe (ed), *Beyond Industrial Sociology: the Work of Men and Women* (Sydney, 1992) 91.

[100] T Rowse, '"Were You Ever Savages?" Aboriginal Insiders and Pastoralists' Patronage' (1987) 58 *Oceania* 84.

[101] T Anthony, 'Labour Relations on Northern Cattle Stations: Feudal Exploitation and Accommodation' (2004) 4 *The Drawing Board: An Australian Review of Public Affairs* 128–9.

Paul Hasluck, a former Federal Minister for Territories (1951–63), wrote that managers of Kimberley stations in the 1930s acted as feudal 'overlords' over Indigenous 'serfs'.[102] One aspect of the lords' feudal obligations was to 'protect' their workers.[103] Thus, Blackstone's feudal mantra went beyond the relationship between the Crown and lord, and extended down to the feudal workers. Landlords' power over their Indigenous workforce emanated from Crown-granted rights to land. Although Blackstone's feudal doctrine was premised on the interests of the Crown, it was the interests of the local landholders that ensured the feudal reality of northern Australian landholding.

III BLACKSTONE'S *COMMENTARIES* IN A POST-*MABO* AUSTRALIAN LANDSCAPE

William Blackstone identified the means by which nations can be lawfully colonised and was often cited in New South Wales colonial judgments to justify colonisation retrospectively. However, the supposed legal basis for colonisation—occupation of an uninhabited territory—was not founded in fact. Blackstone himself pointed out that the factual basis for sovereignty tends to go uninterrogated:

> Pleased as we are with the possession, we seem afraid to look back to the means by which it was acquired, as if fearful of some defect in our title; or at best we rest satisfied with the decision of the laws in our favour, without examining the reason or authority upon which those laws have been built.[104]

The historical classification of pre-1788 Australia as uninhabited was unravelled by the High Court of Australia in the *Mabo* case. Justice Brennan referred to Blackstone to elucidate the fiction that Australia was *terra nullius*:

> The general rule of the common law was that ownership could not be acquired by occupying land that was already occupied by another. As Blackstone pointed out: 'Occupancy is the thing by which title was in fact originally gained; every man seizing such spots of ground as he found most agreeable to his own convenience, *provided he found them unoccupied by any one else*.'[105]

Justice Brennan further cited Blackstone's caution that 'sending colonies' of settlers should be

> kept strictly within the limits of the law of nature. But how far the seising on countries already peopled, and driving out or massacring the innocent and

[102] P Hasluck, *Shades of Darkness: Aboriginal affairs 1925–1965* (Melbourne, 1988) 54.
[103] A McGrath, *'Born in the cattle': Aborigines in Cattle Country* (Sydney 1987) 13.
[104] *Commentaries* vol 2, p 2.
[105] *Mabo v Queensland (No. 2)* (1992) 175 CLR 1, 45 (Brennan J).

defenceless natives, merely because they differed from their invaders in language, in religion, in customs, in government, or in colour; how far such a conduct was consonant to nature, to reason, or to Christianity, deserved well to be considered by those, who have rendered their names immortal by thus civilizing mankind.[106]

Brennan added that Blackstone was 'unable to declare any rule by which the laws of England became the laws of a territory which was not a "desert uninhabited" country when the Crown acquired sovereignty over that territory by discovery and occupation as terra nullius'.[107]

The High Court established that colonisation did not vest in the Crown exclusive legal possession ('beneficial title') of all Australian land, but only ultimate land ownership ('radical title').[108] There were tracts of land where the Crown had not acquired exclusive legal possession, including Eddie Mabo's land on the island of Mer in the Torres Strait. This land could be claimed by Indigenous people who possessed the land before colonisation and have retained ongoing connections to and continuous use of the land.

Not only was Australia inhabited, but on Mer, Indigenous people also cultivated the land. Nonetheless, Justice Brennan adopts the phrase 'desert uninhabited' to mean that cultivation is not intrinsic to a definition of *terra nullius*.[109] Arguably, this was Blackstone's original intention.[110] For the High Court in 1992, Australian land fell within Blackstone's concept of an inhabited territory.

However, the High Court did not address how Australia was colonised if it does not conform to 'Blackstone's criteria' of an occupied, conquered or ceded land.[111] Justice Brennan merely noted that,

> It was only on the hypothesis that there was nobody in occupation that it could be said that the Crown was the owner because there was no other. If that hypothesis be rejected, the notion that sovereignty carried ownership in its wake must be rejected too.[112]

Both in the *Mabo* judgment and since *Mabo*, the courts have refused to reopen the foundations of Crown sovereignty.[113]

[106] *Commentaries* vol 2, p 7 cited in *Mabo v Queensland (No. 2)* (1992) 175 CLR 1, 33 (Brennan J).

[107] *Mabo v Queensland* (n 106) 34.

[108] *Mabo v Queensland* (n 106) 63, 110, 184.

[109] U Secher, 'The *Mabo* Decision- Preserving the Distinction between Settled and Conquered or Ceded Territories' (2005) 24 *University of Queensland Law Journal* 35.

[110] Borch (n 3) 238.

[111] This issue was raised by R O'Grady, 'The Kimberley Land Claim Case' (1991) 2 *Aboriginal Law Bulletin* 14.

[112] *Mabo v Queensland (No. 2)* (1992) 175 CLR 1, 45 (Brennan J).

[113] Post-*Mabo* judgments include *Coe v Commonwealth* (1993) 118 ALR 193 and *Walker v New South Wales* (1994) 182 CLR 45.

There were two reasons which the judges in *Mabo* gave for refusing to reopen the sovereignty issue: firstly because it is an Act of state and thus unable to be challenged by a court of law, and secondly because it would fracture the feudal skeleton of Australia's legal system. According to Justice Brennan, the feudal skeleton shapes Crown leasehold which underpins the Australian land system:

> Though the rejection of the notion of terra nullius clears away the fictional impediment to the recognition of indigenous rights and interests in colonial land, it would be impossible for the common law to recognize such rights and interests if the basic doctrines of the common law are inconsistent with their recognition ... A basic doctrine of the land law is the doctrine of tenure, to which Stephen C.J. referred in *Attorney-General v. Brown*, and it is a doctrine which could not be overturned without *fracturing the skeleton* which gives our land law its shape and consistency. It is derived from feudal origins ... *of absolute Crown ownership*. (emphasis added)[114]

This chapter has shown that Crown ownership and the leasehold system was an instrument of power for landholders (especially in northern Australia). Lessees continue to defend vehemently their rights to land. The High Court overlooks the fact that the feudal skeleton is an incident of Australian *realpolitik*, rather than a doctrine that Blackstone laid down in perpetuity. Accordingly, it is doubted whether the second premise of fracturing the 'feudal skeleton' is anything more than a continuation of the conservative authority of the courts. Commentators encourage courts to provide a workable system of Indigenous customary law recognition without undermining Australian sovereignty.[115] Given widespread agreement that Indigenous laws pre-dated colonisation,[116] and in some instances currently co-exist with Anglo-Australian legal rights, there should be greater capacity for recognition of Indigenous laws beyond native title. Blackstone wrote that the application of English law is qualified by the 'condition of the infant colony'.[117] Where Indigenous laws still operate as a

[114] *Mabo v Queensland (No. 2)* (1992) 175 CLR 1, 45 (Brennan J).

[115] See H Reynolds, 'After *Mabo*, What About Aboriginal Sovereignty?', *Australian Humanities Review* (1996) www.australianhumanitiesreview.org/archive/Issue-April-1996/Reynolds.html; Garth Nettheim, 'A Response to Henry Reynolds', *Australian Humanities Review* (1996) www.australianhumanitiesreview.org/emuse/Mabo/Nettheim.html.

[116] Indigenous societies exercise authority consistent with Blackstone's notion of a legal system that entailed 'commands and decisions all the members are bound to obey' (*Commentaries* vol 1, p 48). These strict laws were recognised by explorers, commentators and missionaries in early colonial society; it was noted that such customs 'forged the chain that binds in iron fetters': E Eyre, *Journals of Expeditions of Discovery* (London 1845) vol 1, p 351. Indigenous laws were also identified by Justice Blackburn as a system of obligations in *Milirrpum v Nabalco* (1971) (n 12) 267. Recently, the ongoing exercise of customary law was recognised in Western Australian Indigenous communities: Law Reform Commission of Western Australia, *Aboriginal Customary Laws: The Interaction of Western Australian Law with Aboriginal Law and Culture*, Final Report, Project 94 (Perth, 2006) 80.

[117] *Commentaries* vol 1, p 105 (2nd edn).

surviving aspect of the 'condition of the infant colony', Blackstone's qualification challenges the Parliament (if not the courts) to provide a workable coexistence of Indigenous laws and Anglo-Australian law.

It is also opportune to address the broader question of Australian sovereignty. In 1992 the High Court of Australia scrutinised the interpretation of Blackstone by colonial and subsequently federal Australian courts. The Court brought to light their skewed reading of Blackstone's *Commentaries*. In doing so, the Court also undermined the notion that Australian colonisation was merely occupation of an uninhabited land. The *Commentaries* explain that the lawful vehicle for colonising inhabited lands is by treaty or conquest. Given that there was an absence of authoritative sources of law in 1788—in terms of British policy or court decisions—and if Blackstone is to continue to be accepted as a valid source of law at that time,[118] the legitimacy of colonisation depends on a treaty with Aboriginal and Torres Strait Islander peoples. While this may be an *ex post facto* initiative, it would provide a legitimate base for the Australian nation to assert sovereignty into the future.

[118] This accords with the High Court of Australia's treatment of Blackstone in *Mabo v Queensland (No. 2)* (1992) 175 CLR 1.

10

Restoring the 'Real' to Real Property Law

A Return to Blackstone?

NICOLE GRAHAM

JEREMY BENTHAM REGARDED William Blackstone's work as a 'striking example of the inability of the common law to provide adequate definitions of property'.[1] He attributed this in part to the bifurcated categories of 'real' and 'personal' property that Blackstone embraced—and which Bentham dismissed as an obsolete structure, inherited from and particular to the feudal context. For Blackstone, property was a relation between a 'person' and a 'thing'. For Bentham, property was an abstract relation between persons—it was thus 'metaphysical … a mere conception of the mind'.[2] The loss of the 'thing' in the property equation, known as the dephysicalisation of property,[3] has served and facilitated a market economy in which 'things' are regarded and traded not for their 'thingness' but for their value as commodities. The dephysicalisation of property was the most important development in the modern history of property law and indeed, is central to the current market economy it facilitates and protects.

However, the dephysicalisation of property has also created problems of an urgent and serious nature. These problems are particularly well-recognised in contemporary Australia; where vastly different geographical and climatic conditions present a materiality at odds with the practices that accompanied the dephysicalisation of property in Old England. The

[1] M Sokol, 'Bentham and Blackstone on Incorporeal Hereditaments' (1994) 15 *Journal of Legal History* 287.

[2] J Bentham, *A Theory of Legislation*, ch 8 'Of Property' in CB Macpherson (ed), *Property: Mainstream and Critical Positions* (Toronto, 1978) 41.

[3] K Vandervelde, 'The New Property of the Nineteenth Century: The Development of the Modern Concept of Property' (1980) 29 *Buffalo Law Review* 325.

problem with a metaphysical definition of property is that it detaches land use practices from the physical capacities of the property itself. Bentham's rejection of Blackstone's division of real and personal property led the way for our contemporary perceptions of and legal engagement with land not as a physical 'thing' with particular physical attributes but as a commodity that is infinitely available for exploitation and trade. Faced with ongoing and escalating concerns regarding the regulation of land and water ownership and use, it is time to re-evaluate the dephysicalisation of property. Blackstone's legacy, amongst other things, is (admittedly an idiosyncratic rather than systematic) record of a kind of property relation from which we might retrieve an understanding of the role of 'things' that preceded dephysicalisation. Such an understanding may render it thinkable to review and reform an unsustainable system of property law that is based, as Bentham says, on metaphysics rather than the world itself.

Blackstone wrote in the midst of the most recent paradigmatic shift in property relations in the Anglo-European world. Although the distinction between 'person' and 'thing' and the categories of real and personal property that Blackstone embraced were not unique to common-law jurisdictions, this chapter does not deal directly with the recognition of the distinction in civil law jurisdictions. Blackstone's work offers both a record of the old 'physical' paradigm into which he was born and a signal of the new 'dephysicalised' paradigm that he saw develop. This paper will evaluate the possibilities and limitations of Blackstone's model of property by situating it, both chronologically and intellectually, within the context of the shift from the person–thing model of property that he wrote about to the person–person model advanced by Bentham. The paper opens with a discussion of the role of the 'thing' in property relations in the work of John Locke and Blackstone. The following section then discusses the concept of dephysicalised property or the person–person model by Blackstone's former student, Jeremy Bentham and its elevation by an American disseminator of his ideas, Wesley Hohfeld. The paper concludes that the concept of dephysicalised property is no longer useful nor appropriate—literally, the concept of is *out of place*. However, in arguing for a return to a property relation that contains 'things', the paper cautions against the hierarchical dynamic of Blackstone's model, being as it was, part of an Enlightenment philosophy of nature that privileged the 'person' over the 'thing' in the relation.

I THE PERSON–THING MODEL OF PROPERTY

John Locke (1632–1704) published his theory of property anonymously in 1689[4] at a time when land in England was regarded as a symbol of power and the main source of food, fuel and shelter more than a form of capital. The power to enjoy land and its direct connection to political participation were more important at that time than financial gain. The developments of the property law creations of primogeniture and the equity of redemption[5] for example indicate that despite the gradually increasing value of land as a source of wealth, it remained predominantly socially, politically and agriculturally valuable. However, with the secularisation of land in the Protestant Reformation[6] and the appropriation of foreign lands through colonisation[7], land became part of the growing capitalist market economy and property law facilitated the market in land and natural resources.

Locke's argument was that property was not a natural inheritance to which all people are entitled but something earned through a particular kind of land use. His ideal of labour-intensive agricultural land use was intended to provide the maximum quantity of resources available from the land. Locke's philosophy conceived of the natural world as a collection of resources that were designed entirely for human consumption and enjoyment rather than as part of an intrinsically valuable realm independent of human need or desire. Locke's philosophy arises from a belief that people are somehow separate or separable from the natural world and therefore capable of transcending it. Locke's theory of property was part of the broader philosophy of the time that was concerned with such notions as 'progress' and 'improvement', according to which people could and should transcend the limitations of nature as it already is and transform it and themselves into 'more developed' products and societies.[8] Such transcendence was imagined to be possible only after first possessing and dominating the natural world.

Locke's work attempted to influence, rationalise and defend the two biggest changes to property law at the time: enclosure (the privatisation of

[4] J Locke, *Two Treatises on Government*, ed P Laslett (Cambridge, 1970; 1689).

[5] See especially, R Warrington and D Sugarman, 'Land Law, Citizenship and the Invention of "Englishness": The Strange World of the Equity of Redemption' in J Brewer and S Staves (ed), *Early Modern Conceptions of Property* (London, 1995).

[6] Between 1536 and 1603, a quarter of the land of England changed hands as a consequence of the expropriation of monastic and other church lands: GR Elton, *The Tudor Constitution: Documents and Commentary* (Cambridge, 1982) 378–94.

[7] From the earliest days of European colonisation of 'New Worlds' the lands, waters and natural resources of many nations and peoples around the world were appropriated with minimal or no compensation, with limited or no consent and most often, against the express interests, views and actions of those nations and peoples.

[8] See eg, L Brace *The Idea of Property in Seventeenth-Century England* (Manchester University Press, 1998) and M Leslie and T Raylor (ed) *Culture and Cultivation in Early Modern England: Writing and the Land* (London: Leicester University Press, 1992).

the common lands of England, Wales and Scotland) and British colonialism.[9] His theory of property is that one owns one's body, its efforts and thus the fruits of those efforts. Locke's contribution to the concept of dephysicalised property is that he considers land not the source of sustenance through food, fuel and water resources, but the source of profit in excess of the necessities of life. For Locke, land is interchangeable with money, a non-perishable form of wealth, and land is detachable from historically adapted cultural practices (customs) particular to the geographical capacities and limits of a given place.

William Blackstone, like Locke, opens his account of property law with a landscape in which natural resources are plentiful and conflict over them was as unnecessary as it was non-existent: '[W]hile the earth continued bare of inhabitants, it is reasonable to suppose, that all was in common among them, and that every one took from the public stock to his own use such things as his immediate necessities required.'[10]

And, like Locke, Blackstone tells us that as the population increased and demand for natural resources increased with it, the resources became more scarce and competition for and dispute over natural resources arose. According to Carol Rose, both Locke and Blackstone's accounts provide a

> natural history (which) presents property rights as an emergent response to scarcity, inducing individuals to invest in and trade resources instead of dissipating their time and effort—and the resources themselves—in unproductive disputes and wasteful attempts to be the first to grab the most.[11]

What Rose means by 'natural history' is that the story of property is bound to a teleological or quasi-evolutionary story about the necessarily physical relation between people and natural resources. In other words, it is a story of physical necessity that Locke and Blackstone use to rationalise the shift from common property to individual or private property. The use of the physical or a 'natural history' is not only intellectually convenient, it is intellectually strategic. Why? Because at the time of their writing it is not simply an idea or theory of property that is changing, but an entire system of practices relating to the distribution and use of natural resources. We might think of Blackstone as a 'transition man'. Enclosure and private property in his time were by no means novel but nor were they universal. Blackstone was more or less a witness to a transformation of one property regime into another quite different property regime. His *Commentaries* on the one hand record the passing regime and on the other hand, rationalise and facilitate that change (perhaps more than he knew or intended).

[9] See esp B Arneil, 'Trade, Plantations and Property: John Locke and the Economic Defence of Colonialism' (1994) 55 *Journal of the History of Ideas* 591.

[10] *Commentaries* vol 2, p 3.

[11] C Rose, 'Energy and Efficiency in the Realignment of Common-Law Water Rights' (1990) 19(2) *Journal of Legal Studies* 261–96.

Attention to property law and to cataloguing its intricacies and connection to the complexity of land use practices was perceived by Blackstone as necessary. As Mary Sokol points out in her study of the treatment of property by Blackstone and Bentham, the period in which they wrote was one of great change. Questions about the meaning and extent of property were important and urgent because

> of the continuing enclosure of open fields, common land and waste land by private and public acts of parliament during this period. The enclosure movement made precarious many traditional rights in common land, for example, the grazing of animals.[12]

Blackstone presents a model of property that is firmly physical because it was the context in which he lived. Blackstone was born and grew up in a time when industrial-scale production of food transported from distant regions and countries was far from the norm. For Blackstone, the link between land and property (be it common or private property) was not simply ideological, it had been a fact of his own life. Blackstone wrote during a time of great change not only to the ownership of land brought about by the enclosure movement but of change to the uses of land. Some historians have seen resistance to and critiques of enclosure as being fundamentally a form of resistance to the Enlightenment's philosophy of Progress and an expression of nostalgia for the past.[13] It is in this vein that the Law and Economics scholar Richard Posner attributes a sense of nostalgia to Blackstone. Posner writes:

> The role of fictions in modernising English law is lovingly chronicled in Book II of the *Commentaries*, which deals with real property. The English law of real property in Blackstone's time had been shaped by the feudal system introduced by the Normans, and many provisions of the medieval law, while functional in the context of a feudal society, had become dysfunctional, and indeed an intolerable impediment to the creation of a free market in real estate.[14]

The supposed dysfunctionality of the property laws emerged precisely when the desire for a 'free market in real estate' (which was linked directly to the enclosure of the commons) took hold. Blackstone's detailed attention to the customs of such practices as gleaning for example is regarded by Posner as a sign of Blackstone's 'faint'[15] thinking and a kind of semi-senile romanticism for a decaying way of life. 'Blackstone's pre-Norman England is to be understood not as historical reality' Posner says, 'but as an ideal of justice and legality, and thus as a criterion for the appraisal and reform of

[12] Sokol, (n 1) 290.

[13] See J Neeson, *Commoners: Common Right, Enclosure Sand Social Change in England 1700–1820* (Cambridge, 1993).

[14] R Posner, 'Blackstone and Bentham' (1976) 19 *Journal of Law and Economics* 584.

[15] *Ibid* 570.

real-world institutions.'[16] AWB Simpson compounds Posner's charge of nostalgia with an accusation of class-biased romanticism:

> [Blackstone's] whole account of personal property, with its discussions of the problems of the beekeeper and the legal position of partridges in mew, smells of the countryside; the law is the law of the country gentry, not Cheapside.[17]

In essence, Posner and Simpson paint Blackstone as anti-progress and anti-reform. This was certainly Bentham's view. While Blackstone was interested in recording the customs of English property law that had endured until his own life time, Bentham was not. As Mary Sokol has pointed out: 'Bentham was not interested in perpetuating the "wisdom of our ancestors" when it came to proposals for reform.'[18]

The portrait of Blackstone painted by legal scholars in regard to his writing on property is hardly flattering. It is one of a man who merely repeated an intellectually strategic 'natural history' account of the shift or 'evolution' from common property to private property.[19] It is one of a man who was irrationally attached to and simultaneously unreflective and idealistic about the customs and privileges of the property regime into which he had been born and raised.[20] Finally, and more famously, it is one of a man who spoke of property as exclusive dominion. But the portrait is inaccurate and disingenuous. Many criticisms of Blackstone's approach to property relate to the fact that his model of property included the very 'thing' or physical realm that the proponents of the 'dephysicalised' model preferred to erase.

Blackstone may have repeated the 'natural history' account of the shift from common property to private property and it is fair to say he did not wish to buy into the debate around that. It is clear then that Blackstone could not be regarded as an ideologue and nor was that his claim or intention. The narrative of property in the *Commentaries* arises only briefly and is certainly not a place in which Blackstone is comfortable. As with many introductory chapters of property law textbooks across the world, historical narrative seems to perform a legitimising function more than an intellectual one. Perhaps this is a property law textbook convention that Blackstone himself began. It would be unreasonable to criticise a mainstream contemporary property law textbook writer for failing to discuss to a scholarly standard the various historiographical issues related to the normative aspects of property law. It would be fairer and more accurate to credit Blackstone with simply attempting to record, albeit

16 Posner (n 14) 583.

17 AWB Simpson quoted in Sokol (n 1) 295.

18 Sokol (n 1) 301.

19 See Rose (n 11).

20 See Posner (n 14); and Simpson, quoted n 17 above.

idiosyncratically and selectively, some of the laws as they were practised during his life time. The historical value of the *Commentaries* is not that they are in themselves, dedicated and complete historical records. Rather, it is that they were written during a time so different to our own that they can't but offer striking examples of historical change, particularly book II: Of the Rights of Things, which used the word 'thing' as an entirely appropriate and central concept in a textbook on property law.

The basis of Posner's critique of Blackstone is identical to Bentham's, in that both Bentham and Posner subscribe to a particular theory of law and economy, irrespective of the actual availability (abundance or scarcity) of the natural resources which necessarily facilitate or prohibit the existence of that specific form of economy. Posner is renowned for his leading work in the field of Law and Economics, a field that takes as its starting point the proposition that markets govern better than governments. Posner could not but object to Blackstone's approach to property law, because of the latter's insistence on the physical thing in the property equation and because of Blackstone's establishment of a catalogue of pre-enclosure common-law doctrines derived from the complexity of a land-based property system. Finally, the countless critiques of Blackstone's statement about property as exclusive dominion evidence not the absolutist property they endeavour to attribute to Blackstone but their own failure to finish reading the page from which the quote is taken—which elaborates a doubt about the move from an ideal absolutist property right to an actual relative property right. As Carol Rose has shown, 'the exclusivity axiom was in a sense a trope, a rhetorical figure describing an extreme or ideal type rather than reality'.[21]

Whatever the reasons for Blackstone's efforts to record in some detail the customs of English law related to land use and ownership, the fact remains that the model of property he offered was fundamentally attached to the physical world. 'Blackstone was emphatic that property related to external things apart from one's self, be they corporeal or incorporeal.'[22]

> In his whole discussion "Of The Rights Of Things" *land* clearly takes the predominant role. There were undoubtedly good reasons for this: Land had been and continued to be a major source of wealth in Blackstone's time … Land is fixed, enduring, stable.[23]

Carol Rose makes an interesting point about the importance of land to the doctrinalist approach that Blackstone takes in the third and largest part of his account of property law. According to Rose, it is precisely the

[21] C Rose, 'Canons of Property Talk, or, Blackstone's Anxiety' (1998) 108 *Yale Law Journal* 604.

[22] S Zellmer and J Harder, 'Unbundling Property in Water' (2008) 59 *Alabama Law Review* 679–745.

[23] Rose (n 21) 611.

undeniable physicality of land that necessitates a level of complexity to deal with the myriad of interests in land and its resources across time.

> Land … sticks around indefinitely, while claims against land can go on and on, in layer after layer, to be lost, found, banished, restored, relished, then lost again to longstanding practice and prescription. This enduring quality is one reason why claim-clearing doctrines like 'adverse possession' and prescription are essential with respect to land. But land's durability is also the reason why land is so central to doctrinalism: Land offers a goldmine of doctrinal variation, a subject on which taxonomic exactitude—rather like Blackstone's is the central effort.[24]

It is not necessary or desirable to attribute to Blackstone a greater interest in land use management than he may have had. However, it is important to acknowledge that the sheer density of property law that continues to this day may in part be attributed to the fact that, originally, if not enduringly, property law in England was about land. It was of course precisely such density and complexity that Bentham sought to collapse into a simpler, neater, positivist system of law in which property was not about land at all but about legal rights. Blackstone was the transitional figure in the paradigm shift, whose work described property as the law of things and reflected the development of an elaborate system of land use and ownership over a long period of time even as that very structure was on the point of being questioned and eclipsed by a deceptively simple system that took no account of the physical realm. Rights to property for Blackstone were rights *in rem*. The following section traces the emergence and eventual domination of a system of property based on rights that are essentially 'a multiplicity of *in personam* rights'.[25]

II THE PERSON–PERSON MODEL OF PROPERTY

Kenneth Vandevelde juxtaposes the 'Old' and physical model of property with the 'New' dephysicalised property model and relies heavily on the work of the early twentieth-century legal scholar Wesley Hohfeld to do so. But the dephysicalisation of property began much earlier than Hohfeld and in fact, the person–person model of property that has come to dominate contemporary definitions of property law was most strongly advocated by Jeremy Bentham in the late eighteenth century. The theoretical movement from the model of person–thing property relations to the model of person–person property relations was not peculiar to legal theory. It was part of broader paradigmatic process that expressed radically different

[24] Rose (n 21) 614.

[25] A Bell and G Parchomovsky, 'A Theory of Property' (2005) 90 *Cornell Law Review* 531–615, 579.

economic dynamics and demands. Bentham did not invent the idea of dephysicalisation, he merely crystallised it and berated those who either did not understand or agree with it.

Bentham thought of property as a creation of law, rather than as a material thing: 'It is metaphysical, it is a mere conception of the mind.'[26] Bentham rejected the natural rights theory of John Locke and William Blackstone, for whom property relations were relations between persons and things. The problem with Locke's idea of property in specific terms, Bentham argues, is that it 'overlooks so many other valuable subject matters of possession, namely power, reputation and condition in life'.[27] Blackstone on the other hand had to a limited degree 'widened the range of property discussed at a time when most discussions of property were restricted to land, interests in land and money in so far as it was to be regarded as a debt that could be charged against the debtor's land'.[28]

The problem with Blackstone's person–thing model of property, as Bentham saw it, was that such an historically developed definition of property constrained its ability to adapt to and serve the changing demands of the economy, in which land no longer functioned as the sole source of wealth and power as it was in feudal times, and was thus anachronistic and irrational. Blackstone had not only upheld this 'irrational' division of real and personal property, he had also hierarchised it by privileging real property.[29] And indeed the need to reform property law to account for growing forms of wealth holding was the basis of Bentham's submission to the 1828 Real Property Commission.[30]

In his submission, Bentham proposed a unified system of property law that would encompass 'newer proprietary rights such as shares in companies and copyright'[31] and that would ultimately 'take its place in the civil law, forming part of a code of law coherent in all its part and comprehensible to all'.[32] Significantly, the agenda of the Commission itself was to promote efficient management and security of land title, following the enclosure movement which had 'made precarious many traditional rights in common land'[33] and which was challenging the adequacy of the common law to enforce this programme of privatised and positivised property.[34] Responsive to the 'needs' of law at the time, this Commission

[26] Bentham (n 2).
[27] GJ Postema, *Bentham and the Common Law Tradition* (Oxford, 1986) 174.
[28] Sokol (n 1) 297.
[29] *Ibid* 294.
[30] *Ibid* 287.
[31] *Ibid* 287.
[32] *Ibid* 300.
[33] *Ibid* 290.
[34] See D Brown and F Sharman, 'Enclosure: Agreement and Acts' (1994) 15 *The Journal of Legal History* 267.

heralded a changing operation of law as a 'scientific administration' of positive principles. The reforms of the Commission, Bentham hoped, formed 'a universal jurisprudence that would provide the necessary concepts of rights on which to base the rational utilitarian system of property law'.[35] Bentham had criticised the inadequacy of the common law for its inconsistency and confusion of real and personal property in his critiques of Blackstone.[36] But the common-law property regime was unsatisfactory to Bentham not merely because it was outdated, but because it vested law's legitimacy in Nature and an existent 'natural order.'

Bentham's critique of natural rights in property was part of his broader radical philosophy of legal positivism and utilitarianism. 'Bentham, conceiving himself as the Newton of the moral world, combined law's completeness with its limitless sovereignty in the prospect of an eventual attainment of total and "certain order"'.[37] The impact of Bentham's philosophy on the development of modern property was twofold. His rejection of the person–thing relation in Blackstone's natural rights theory of property produced the notion of property as a person–person relation. Secondly, the proposed integration of the distinct bodies of personal property and real property into one broad system of property rights, according to the person–person model of property, transformed the locus of social wealth from land (the physical realm) to law (the metaphysical realm).

In effect what Bentham's theory of property achieved was the separation of land from the idea of property and from the body of law itself, by 'elevating' the entire basis of property from natural rights to cultural rights. 'Bentham anticipates the modern tendency to regard all rights secured to an individual by law as "a species of normative property belonging to the right of the holder"'.[38] To Bentham, the function of law was to protect the security of the individual citizen and the government by protecting the institution of property rights.[39] The integration and codification of real and personal property into a positive scheme of private property rights, Bentham argued, was the means by which to achieve a 'civilised society'. The expansiveness of Bentham's idea of property proposed that 'all forms of social interaction available to human beings except political relationships and institutions fall under the concept of property.'[40] The movement from property in 'things' to rights between persons was 'contemporaneous with the consolidation of the corporate form, which

[35] Sokol (n 1) 300.
[36] *Ibid* 292.
[37] P Fitzpatrick, *The Mythology of Modern Law* (London, 1992) 57.
[38] Postema, quoting HLA Hart (n 27) 174.
[39] *Ibid* 175.
[40] *Ibid* 174.

rendered the traditional notion of property (still overwhelmingly 'derived from ideas about landed property') insufficient for a vast array of new kinds of ownership'.[41]

In Bentham's time, the economic and legal primacy of the category of real property was diminishing and so law could no longer be conceptually dependent on 'any exterior reality'[42] for its authority. The particularities of reality had to be rejected or incorporated into a universal model of law that would transcend the particularities of place.[43] Bentham's property was law and the law was property. 'Property and law are born together, and die together. Before laws were made there was no property; take away laws, and property ceases.'[44] Both law and property were dephysicalised, Bentham argued, they existed only as abstract logical forms.

Bentham's claim that 'there is no such thing as natural property'[45] (property in and through nature) is not entirely radical however. While it removed 'things' from the property equation and replaced them with 'persons', the dynamic of his model of property maintained the anthropocentric logic of Locke and Blackstone's models. Locke and Blackstone wrote about property in a way that was consistent with the broader ontology of the Enlightenment. Specifically, Locke and Blackstone had no doubt that the person–thing model of property took place in a 'natural world' in which Nature was subordinate to Culture. Both Locke and Blackstone approach the 'thing' of property with a view to owning and controlling that thing. In their work, the person is the agent of the person–thing relationship.

For Locke and Blackstone, Nature had replaced God, and natural rights replaced divine rights. Bentham's idea of positive law replaced the notion of transcendent authority altogether and using the idea of rational immanence. Bentham's theory of law did not need to appeal to either God or Nature, because it was self-legitimating and guaranteed by positive institutions and processes. Nevertheless, the instrumentalist view of nature was common to all three theorists. Bentham, like Locke and Blackstone, conceived of nature as something to be altered and improved by human action. 'Who has renewed the surface of the earth? Who has given to man this domain over nature – embellished, fertilised, and perfected?' The answer of course is the 'beneficent genius' and security of law.[46] The key difference between Locke, Blackstone and Bentham's instrumentalist view

[41] B Maurer, 'Forget Locke? From Proprietor to Risk-Bearer in New Logics of Finance' (1999) 11 *Public Culture* 365, 370.

[42] Fitzpatrick (n 37) 56.

[43] *Ibid*.

[44] Bentham (n 2).

[45] *Ibid*.

[46] *Ibid* ch x: 'Analysis of the Evils which result from Attacks upon Property'.

of nature is that Locke and Blackstone defended it whereas Bentham simply assumed it as an already accepted and practiced truth.

A consequence of the dephysicalisation of property was that the concept of property itself 'became infinitely expandable. The result was that during the 1880s and 1890s a variety of new property interests for the first time received recognition by American courts.'[47] One American legal scholar whose work in the area of property is renowned for repeating the concept of dephysicalised property was Wesley Newcomb Hohfeld. Hohfeld contributed two essays to the growing controversy over the definition of property law in 1913 and 1917.[48] He was concerned to clarify and reduce the concept of property relating to contemporaneous changes in the courts. Courts 'began to define property as the right to value rather than to some thing.'[49] The subsequently augmented body of property rights had been relativised according to liberal and utilitarian ideals of social organisation, and since the distinction between real and personal property rights was eroding, determinations of what constituted a legitimate property right varied from case to case. Such indeterminacy of property was the reason for, as well as the context of the property theory of Wesley Hohfeld.[50]

Hohfeld's main point is that property law weighs the aggregate of abstract legal relations' rather than deferring to 'figurative or fictional' categories of property according to distinctions between physical things.[51] Property was no longer defined by categories of 'real' or 'personal' things, because these 'things' were now, as 'things', meaningless. Instead, property was defined as relative, that is, by relating the rights of persons to each other. Hohfeld unequivocally buried the significance of the physical to the meaning of property. Land was pronounced irrelevant.

More recently Kenneth Vandevelde structures his thesis on the dephysicalisation of property by juxtaposing the 'Old Property' of Blackstone and the 'New Property' of Hohfeld. He draws from this contrast his central point, that the shift from natural rights in property (person–thing) to dephysicalised rights in property (person–person) is a movement toward an unbridled politicisation of property and, subsequently, toward the destruction of law itself. Vandevelde argues that because property was no longer finite and absolute, it was indeterminable. 'This century long evolution resulted in an inability of property concepts to settle controversies and legitimate the results.'[52] The 'explosion of the concept of property' meant

[47] Maurer (n 41) 370

[48] WN Hohfeld, 'Some Fundamental Legal Conceptions as Applied in Legal Reasoning' (1913) 23 *Yale Law Journal* 16–59 and his 'Fundamental Legal Conceptions as Applied to Judicial Reasoning' 26 *Yale Law Journal* (1917) 710–70.

[49] Vandevelde (n 3) 333.

[50] *Ibid*.

[51] Hohfeld (1913) (n 48) 189.

[52] Vandevelde (n 3) 330.

that property, as a distinct category of law, had become meaningless. The consequence of this development bears a profound impact on the legitimacy of law, Vandevelde argues that 'the destruction of meaning in the concept of property destroyed the concept's apparent power to decide cases.'[53] The courts' response to this crisis in meaning could no longer derive from any specific logic of property law, as it did not exist, but only from 'overt recourse to political goals.'[54] Property *as* law, he concludes, thus 'came at the price of the courts' legitimacy'.[55]

Drawing from American jurisprudence, Vandevelde concludes that, in this way, property was ultimately 'what the law said it was'.[56] It was precisely such indeterminacy and absence of an internally logical and coherent order of property relations that Blackstone resisted in his critique of the rise of Parliament in his own time. Blackstone contrasted the enacted law of Parliament, 'the visible evidence of a supreme exercise of power', with judicial decisions of the common law, 'merely reports of discoveries of an *already existing* prescriptive order'.[57] As Postema describes, the augmented status and altered notion of Parliament's role in creating law was by no means part of accepted legal culture in the seventeenth century and was certainly one of which common lawyers such as Coke and Blackstone remained unconvinced:

> Medieval jurisprudence held that statutes performed, in a more explicit and general way, the same task which occupied the judiciary: namely, declaring, expounding, and making known law which already existed in the traditional practices of the people. To regard a body of persons as capable of creating *new* law, through exercise of their own wills, was a radical departure. Law could be seen not merely as the formal and public expression of an existing (or even natural) order, but as an instrument with which that order could be altered or even recreated.[58]

Just as Blackstone had regarded the diminished role of common law with scepticism and hesitation, Vandevelde lived to understand Blackstone's reasons. Where Bentham had dismissed the value of history and the enduring viabilities of "ancient" customary traditions, Blackstone and Vandevelde point to the arbitrary and ultimately meaningless outcomes of a dephysicalised legal discourse.

[53] *Ibid* 363.
[54] *Ibid* 330.
[55] *Ibid* 366.
[56] *Ibid* 364.
[57] Postema (n 27) 16.
[58] *Ibid* 15.

III THE TROUBLE WITH DEPHYSICALISED PROPERTY LAW

The historical development of property law from Blackstone to Hohfeld via Bentham, according to the evolution of rationality and British empiricism,[59] indicates the shifting evaluation of nature and physicality from a subordinate in a person–thing model to an irrelevance in the person–person model. This itself might not matter but for the fact that the irrelevance of the physical realm to property law has serious and negative environmental consequences. Cultural discourses put the concept of dephysicalised property into practice. This is evident in the intensive (and sometimes exhaustive) use of much land in the Anglo-European world owned by people whose business interests begin and end with land ownership: miners, farmers, pastoralists and irrigators. For these people, the dominant value of land is its value as a *commodity*.

Dominant forms of land-use such as mining, industrial-scale and irrigated agriculture, and pastoralism put the concept of dephysicalised property into practice by detaching various forms of land use from the capacities and limits of the lands themselves. Such land-use practices are not marginal; they are well founded in the broader social economy and are utterly consistent with legal discourse. Farms are businesses and land is valued as a commercial resource. It is not simply a question of theory, law and ideology: miners' and farmers' businesses (and some would add broader national economic interests) depend on the reproduction of the dephysicalised concept of property.

The normative import of property law is minimal in the context of contemporary Australian land and natural resource ownership and allocation. 'Property rights are simply an instrument to a transaction.'[60] In this situation, where on the one hand, property law is said to be a 'mere conception of the mind' but where on the other hand it is used for the provision of physical outcomes, it is important to measure those outcomes within the legal discourse itself. Current legal practice insists that property is about abstract rights between persons, when in fact it facilitates physical processes and outcomes. The danger is that with such disregard for the physical realm, property law is an inappropriate vehicle of environmental management. And yet, property law has been required to deliver solutions to natural resource management problems.

A current Australian example is in the area of water law, which has moved away from the riparian doctrine in which rights to water were 'tied intrinsically to the land, forming an indistinguishable nexus between the

[59] L Godden 'Preserving Natural Heritage: Nature as Other' (1998) 22 *Melbourne University Law Review* 725.

[60] A Dragun, 'Property Rights, "takings", and Environmental Management' (1999) 26 *International Journal of Social Economics* 1070.

land and the water'.[61] Water law reforms that have promoted the trading of water in the Murray-Darling Basin have divorced title to land from rights to water. Such reform compounds and exemplifies the trouble with a concept of dephysicalised property that

> does not leave room for the thing; instead, it is a one-dimensional depiction of various interests typically associated with property, with no prioritisation or acknowledgment of attributes that must invariably be present for a thing to be considered property. The bundle fails to assess either the character of the thing in question or the nature of human relationships with it, and it also overlooks the importance of that thing to related human and ecological communities.[62]

One of the most important aspects of the reforms is the emphasis on the government's ability to 'buy-back' water from the water market that it itself created as a solution to the over-use of the resource.[63] The idea of markets in water is not new—indeed environmental markets have been part of mainstream public policy discourse as important environmental management instruments for almost two decades. But environmental economists have observed that creating private property rights in natural resources is not always the most effective means to address environmental management issues. 'Jurisdictions that claim to recognize property rights in water, particularly those in the western United States, have not necessarily encouraged conservation but rather have created incentives for exploitation.'[64] Perhaps one main reason for the failure of markets to deliver environmental outcomes is that the concept on which they are hinged, property, remains a dephysicalised concept detached from the particularities of diverse local and entirely physical resource conditions.

The ultimate expression of dephysicalised property is the metaphor of the bundle of rights. The trouble with the use of this metaphor is that it either presumes or takes no account of the availability of the resources over which the rights exist. As other scholars of property have observed, 'the fundamental dilemmas of modern private property are firmly entrenched in the externality issues inherent in most environmental problems'.[65] In the case of the ownership and use of water resources in the Murray–Darling Basin, such a presumption is not only incorrect, it is dangerous. Contemporary property law, being based on the concept of dephysicalisation, treats land, water and natural resources as though they were incidental to

[61] J Tisdell, 'Equity and Social Justice in Water Doctrines' (2003) 16 *Social Justice Research* 405.

[62] Zellmer and Harder (n 21) 6.

[63] 'Water for Rivers' is a public company established by the governments of NSW, Victoria and the Commonwealth to meet 'environmental flow targets'; see further www.waterforrivers.org.au.

[64] Zellmer and Harder (n 22).

[65] Dragun (n 60) 1074.

property rather than the very condition of its existence. 'The seeds planted by Bentham struck root, and today… there is widespread agreement that the law orders property in response to societal needs, rather than in obeisance to a moral command or the natural order of the universe.'[66] Bentham eschewed traditional models of property law because of their attachment to land. Law and economics scholars have criticised Blackstone for mythologising Saxon land law and reverence for the past. But the fact remains that, fragmented and inaccurate as Blackstone's *Commentaries* are as historical records in themselves, they captured a notion of a land law based on practices sufficiently viable and enduring to have become traditions.

Dephysicalised property law is unsuited to regulate relations between land and water (which are nothing if not physical) and human societies. The fact that dephysicalised property has become orthodoxy should not prevent us from examining its original purpose and questioning whether 'the conditions that gave rise to it have changed'.[67] Until property law and environmental law are rationalised and realigned to approach matters of land use and ownership in an integrated manner, we cannot expect any part of current land and water policy, based firmly in markets for environmental products, to adequately regulate the resource distribution system that property law is designed to do. The model of property law that Bentham heralded and Richard Posner celebrated can only be sustained if we believe that the geographic and climatic conditions of a given land are irrelevant to the laws that govern its ownership and use. There is no indication that this is the case, and in fact the evidence points clearly in the other direction—that the most successful property regimes in human societies are the ones best adapted to the allocation and use of land, water and their many resources as available and confined within reality. It is appropriate to return to a model of property that includes the physical. And while Blackstone's model of person–thing was expressed in anthropocentric terms and for anthropocentric reasons, its merits need not be thrown out with the bathwater!

IV CONCLUSION

For Blackstone, the common law was a 'living body' of law that was the 'accumulation of judgments, decisions, refinements and adjustments of

[66] Bell and Parchamovsky (n 25) 546–7.
[67] Posner (n 14) 585.

immemorial custom'.[68] It existed primarily as the 'practice of the community' and was 'binding in virtue of that fact'.[69] Blackstone's view of law, unlike Bentham's—which was strongly universalistic and universalising—was that laws vary across societies depending on the climates, geographies and historical pasts of any given society at a given time: 'the development of which may be equally natural'.[70] Restoring the 'real' to property law cannot (and should not) involve an ingenuous nostalgia for a world far removed from contemporary life. A return to the real is exactly that—the re-inclusion of materiality into the legal framework that regulates the most fundamental relations between human society (persons) and their environment (things).

Blackstone's *Commentaries* were written at a time when real property was about land and when the notion of a 'thing' was one half of the property equation. Indeed, Blackstone's approach to property was so infused with 'thingness' that it motivated Jeremy Bentham to write against it. The concept of dephysicalised property was extremely useful to the grand projects of enclosure and colonisation, but those 'frontiers have long since vanished, while the frontier mentality remains'.[71] The idea of dephysicalised property operates in a real world and thus, however un-real property law is declared to be, it is very much actual. There are material consequences of the dephysicalised property and the most helpful thing we can do is examine its origins and its ongoing utility.

[68] Postema (n 27) 13.
[69] *Ibid* 14.
[70] R Willman, 'Blackstone and the "Theoretical Perfection" of English Law in the Reign of Charles II' (1983) 26 *Historical Journal* 50–1.
[71] Dragun (n 60) 1074.

III Influence

THE DISSEMINATION, reception and impact of Blackstone's *Commentaries*, both within and beyond England, and indeed outside the common-law world, is plainly a large topic. While there have been some studies of the educational, intellectual and jurisprudential influence of the *Commentaries*,[1] many geographical and thematic areas still remain unexplored. The following three chapters show that there are also various ways of undertaking the task.

It has long been known that Americans were avid purchasers and readers of Blackstone, both before and after the Declaration of Independence. However Michael Hoeflich here provides the first systematic bibliographical study of the various editions of the *Commentaries* on the US market in the nineteenth century and their respective readerships. In what might appear at first glance a somewhat quixotic enterprise, John Emerson then essays a preliminary survey of attitudes towards Blackstone and his work in France between the later eighteenth and early twentieth centuries. Overall he finds, notwithstanding a good deal of disdain and misunderstanding, considerable if often selective interest, and more recently growing appreciation, especially among legal and political scholars. Finally, Horst Dippel offers a very different perspective with his detailed account of Blackstone's changing reputation in the world of German scholarship from the 1760s to the early twenty-first century.

[1] eg, M Raeff, 'The Empress and the Vinerian Professor: Catherine II's Projects of Government Reforms and Blackstone's *Commentaries*' (1974) 7 ns *Oxford Slavonic Papers* 18–42; RA Ferguson, *Law and Letters in American Culture* (Cambridge MA, 1984); W Prest, 'Antipodean Blackstone: The *Commentaries* 'Down Under' (2003) 6 *Flinders Journal of Law Reform* 151–67.

11

American Blackstones

MICHAEL HOEFLICH

THERE ARE FEW more iconic figures in Anglo-American common law than Sir William Blackstone. His *Commentaries on the Laws of England* has remained in print for nearly two centuries and a half in both England and the United States. It has been estimated that the *Commentaries* have been cited more than 10,000 times in American judicial opinions and that the number continues to grow.[1] Here, however, I want to suggest something rather radical. In fact, there is not one *Commentaries*, but, on the contrary, multiple *Commentaries*. In the United States, particularly, there have been multiple textual traditions of Blackstone's *Commentaries*, many differing in significant ways from the text as it was produced by William and first published from 1765–69.

To make sense of my bald statement that there were multiple *Commentaries* it is necessary first to define what we mean when we speak of Blackstone's work. To a large extent, scholars who have studied the reception history of the *Commentaries* in the United States concern themselves with questions of impact. In his classic study Dennis Nolan looked at a sample of 471 citations to the *Commentaries* and, in so doing, assessed their impact on judicial decision making and legal education in the nineteenth century.[2] But nowhere in this otherwise admirable study did he attempt to understand the changes Blackstone's text underwent and the extent to which these differing books were actually utilised. Prof Alschuler, who extended Prof Nolan's study in 1996, took exactly the same approach.[3]

[1] See DR Nolan, 'Sir William Blackstone and the New American Republic: A Study of Intellectual Impact' (1976) 51 *New York University Law Review* (1976) 752 fn 138; C Klafter, *Reason over Precedents. Origins of American Legal Thought* (Westport CT, 1993) 31–3.

[2] Nolan (n 1) 753.

[3] AW Alschuler, 'Rediscovering Blackstone' (1996) 45 *University of Pennsylvania Law Review* 1–43.

When one looks at the printing and textual history of Blackstone's *Commentaries* in the United States it becomes clear that there were actually two traditions in play. The first tradition, what we might call 'literal reprinting', involved the reissue of English editions of Blackstone's work without changes from the original. The very first American printing of the *Commentaries* by the Philadelphia book seller John Bell was of this type.[4] Of course, English editions modified the text of Blackstone's original work over the course of its history. Many of the greatest English jurists, including Edward Christian, Charles Butler and Joseph Chitty produced editions of the *Commentaries* with notes designed to update the text to developments in English law. As new English editions were published in England they were also reprinted in the United States.

A second textual tradition began in 1803 when Birch & Small of Philadelphia published St George Tucker's edition of the *Commentaries*.[5] This edition, unlike Bell's and others of that ilk, was entitled *Blackstone's Commentaries: with notes of reference to the Constitution and laws of the federal government of the United States and of the Commonwealth of Virginia*. Tucker's version of Blackstone was crucially different from the literal reprints that preceded it in two ways. First, in addition to printing the original notes from the English edition upon which it was based, it also included notes written by Tucker specifically applicable to American and Virginian law, designed to increase the practical relevance of the book for American lawyers. Second, Tucker's version also included narrative appendices discussing certain aspects of federal and Virginia law where Tucker felt an extended treatment was warranted.

I would suggest that the addition of 'Americanising' notes and appendices is of crucial significance, both jurisprudentially and historically. In effect, what 'Americanising' authors like Tucker and his successors were doing was very much the same sort of thing that the medieval glossators on Roman, canon and Talmudic law did with their marginal annotations or glosses.[6] Such annotations show respect for the underlying text by not actually modifying it directly, but at the same time are able to modify–even

[4] See E Wolf, *The Book Culture of a Colonial American City: Philadelphia Books, Bookmen, and Booksellers* (Oxford, 1988) 156–60.

[5] St G Tucker, *Blackstone's Commentaries: with Notes of Reference, to the Constitution and Laws, of the Federal Government of the United States, and of the Commonwealth of Virginia; in Five Volumes. With an Appendix to each Volume, containing Short Tracts upon such Subjects as appeared necessary to form a Connected View of the Laws of Virginia as a Member of the Federal Union* (Philadelphia PA, 1803).

[6] On the importance of glossing in medieval law, see J Brundage, *Medieval Canon Law* (London, 1995); M Bellomo, *The Common Legal Past of Europe 100–1800* (Washington DC, 1995) 149–202; MH Hoeflich and J Grabher, 'The Establishment of Normative Legal Texts: The Beginnings of the *Ius Commune*' in K Pennington and W Hartmann (ed), *The History of Medieval Canon Law in the Classical Period, 1140–1234* (Washington DC, 2008) 1–21; B Holtz, *Back to the Sources. Reading Jewish Texts* (New York NY, 1984).

at times subvert– the text indirectly by adding commentary to it.[7] Annotations can both update as well as modify a base text. More importantly, the annotator of an 'iconic' text, like Justinian's *Digest*, Gratian's *Decretum* or the Babylonian *Talmud*, shares in the prestige of the underlying text and often will gain a far larger audience for his thoughts than he would by writing a separately published commentary. When an underlying iconic text is alien to the market in which it is being published, because of age, geographical, cultural or political differences, the annotations may be used to give new relevance to the underlying text. This is what 'Americanised' versions of Blackstone achieved. In England, annotations to Blackstone's original work were able to overcome the obsolescence that came from the passage of time and the great legal and political changes which occurred in the nineteenth century. They might well be characterised as constituting a new 'text' when their purpose was more than simply to update the original text. To some degree, texts, like Blackstone, when they are adapted (or 'Americanised'), really become two texts, the underlying original revered and of historical importance, and the new text which is to be found in the notes, appendices and other material.[8]

Tucker lays out the professional and jurisprudential reasons justifying his publication of an 'Americanised' edition in the 'Editor's Preface' of the 1803 edition. He begins by explaining the significance of the American Revolution for the *Commentaries:*

> Not many years after the reception of the *Commentaries* into the libraries of gentlemen of the profession, and the adoption of them as a guide to those who wished to acquire it, the revolution which separated the present United States of America from Great Britain took effect; this event produced a corresponding revolution not only in the principles of our government, but in the laws.[9]

Tucker was particularly concerned about the growing differences between English private law and American private law, differences which might not be so apparent to a law student or unlearned lawyer as would the differences in constitutional law:

> the almost total change in the system of laws relative to property, both real and personal, in Virginia, appeared more particularly to demand a strict scrutiny, and investigation; in the course of which it might not only be necessary to remark the more obvious, but the imperceptible and perhaps unintended, changes, wrought

[7] See S Reynolds, 'Inventing Authority: Glossing, Literacy and the Classical Text' in F Riddy (ed), *Prestige Authority and Power in Medieval Manuscripts and Texts* (York, 2000) 7–16.

[8] See a parallel argument for understanding the nature of Thomas Cooper's American edition of Harris's English edition of Justinian's *Institutes* a number of years ago in MH Hoeflich, 'Vinnius in the Anglo-American World' (1997) 114 *Zeitschrift der Savigny-Stiftung fur Rechtsgeschichte* 345–68.

[9] Tucker's *Blackstone's Commentaries* (n 5) iv–v.

> by a loose, or incautious phrase, or reference . . . Many parts of the laws of England are also either obsolete, or have been deemed inapplicable to our local circumstances and policy.[10]

Tucker's prefatory comments are interesting for several reasons. First, Tucker considered Blackstone's *Commentaries* primarily to be a 'student' book, one which would provide the would-be lawyer with a general overview of the law, not as an advanced text for regular research use by practitioners.[11] At the same time, by annotating portions of the *Commentaries* in detail and by citing Virginian and American cases, he not only increased the utility of the book as a source of general principles for elementary legal instruction, but also rendered it useful to practising lawyers. In effect, the original, untouched text of the volume would provide a discussion of the elementary principles of various areas of the law for the student, while the footnotes contained specific case references useful to the practising lawyer. This latter utility would have been lacking in the 'literal reprints', even those with current annotations to English cases, since a Virginian lawyer would have needed to cite Virginian cases and statutes. Indeed, Tucker was well aware that at the time he published his edition of the *Commentaries*, there were few specialist American treatises or even useful statutory compilations. Thus, his edition could also serve as a substitute of sorts for such absent texts.

The question arises, of course, as to why, given the severe limitations the use of a foreign text presented, Tucker did not simply write a new, American text. Tucker was blunt: it was far too much work.[12] Further, he may well have believed that there was neither a sufficient market for such a book nor that a text by a Virginian could succeed in dethroning Blackstone's *Commentaries* from its place in the libraries of American lawyers.[13]

Tucker's Blackstone was the first in what became a long tradition of 'Americanised' texts of the *Commentaries*. Throughout the nineteenth century, many leading American lawyers and jurists produced updated versions of Blackstone's work. Among the most notable of these editors were Judge George Sharswood of the Pennsylvania bar, best known for his *Essay on Professional Ethics*,[14] William Gardiner Hammond, the long-time

[10] Tucker (n 5) xi. For a different view of Tucker's approach to Blackstone, see Klafter (n 1) 40–7.

[11] *Ibid* v: 'the *Commentaries* have continued to be regarded as the *student's guide* in the United States'.

[12] *Ibid* vi. Tucker also stated that he retained Blackstone's text as the basis for his own work because it was 'a model of methodical elegance and legal perspicuity: a work in which the author has united the various talents of the philosopher, the antiquarian, the historian, the jurist, the logician, and the classic'.

[13] Tucker would have been fully aware that preceding American editions of the *Commentaries* had sold well; see Wolf (n 4).

[14] This work was published and republished throughout the nineteenth century with varying titles. It first appeared as G Sharswood, *A Compend of Lectures on the Aims and*

dean of the University of Iowa Law School and of the law school at Washington University in St. Louis, and Professor William Cooley of the University of Michigan Law School. In addition to the editions by named prominent lawyers, a number of publishers also produced editions by anonymous editors, often simply referred to as a 'gentleman of the Bar'.[15] Along with full editions, publishers also put out large numbers of abridgements, selections and even quiz books taken from the *Commentaries*.[16] These, too, were usually 'Americanised'. Further, the 'Americanised' editions also reflected the specific interests of the American editors. The additional material in Hammond's edition, for instance, reflected Hammond's interest in the civil law and its institutional writings.[17]

Of the later 'Americanised' Blackstones, George Sharswood's was one of the most popular and may be taken as representative of all of the various attempts to use notes and comments to maximise the utility and marketability of Blackstone's masterpiece in the United States.[18] This was not an easy task, since not only did American law grow to differ substantially from English law throughout the nineteenth century, but also because American governmental and professional institutions were, in many cases, not only different from but opposed to their English counterparts as described by Blackstone. Further, since lawyers would most commonly want to have not only an 'Americanised' version of the *Commentaries*, but also the most up-to -date English edition, Sharswood and other American editors found themselves with a finished work in which the footnotes and comments often equalled or exceeded Blackstone's original text in length. A few examples of the need for notes and comments in the American editions can be instructive.

By 1860, the date of publication of the first Sharswood edition, the American legal profession had very much developed its own institutions. Education for the bar in the United States was split between law schools and apprenticeship.[19] In England legal education for barristers still centred on the Inns of Court and for solicitors in the many offices scattered around

Duties of the Profession of Law (Philadelphia PA, 1854); the best known and most widely circulated edn was the second, under the title *An Essay on Professional Ethics* (Philadelphia PA, 1860).

[15] See, eg, W Blackstone, *Commentaries on the Laws of England* (New York NY, 1830), 'with Additional Notes and References by a Gentleman of the New York Bar'.

[16] One of the earliest and most famous of these was by Asa Kinne; see n 40 below.

[17] See MH Hoeflich, *Roman and Civil Law and the Development of Anglo-American Jurisprudence in the Nineteenth Century* (Athens GA, 1997) 91–7.

[18] W Blackstone, *Commentaries on the Laws of England*, ed G Sharswood (Philadelphia PA, 1860). This text included the notes of many English commentators and editors, among them E Christian, JF Archbold, J Chitty, J Stewart and RM Kerr, together with Baron Field's *Analysis of Blackstone's Commentaries … in a Series of Questions* and Sharswood's brief biography of Blackstone.

[19] See R Stevens, *Law School. Legal Education in America from the 1850s to the 1980s* (Chapel Hill NC, 1983) 3–19.

Britain.[20] Thus to Blackstone's advice on the study of the law, which was reprinted in virtually every American edition, the editor was forced to add an entirely separate footnote account of American methods of legal education for his American readers.[21] Three full pages of notes glossed a single sentence in the original text. Similarly, in a discussion of the rights and privileges of the clergy in England, Sharswood again had to draw attention to the fact that in England the law was premised upon the existence of an established church, while in the United States 'there is no established church', a difference which changed the law on clerical rights substantially.[22]

The two examples adduced above could be multiplied several hundred-fold. In effect, the reader who approaches Sharswood's and other 'Americanised' editions of the *Commentaries* is presented with not one, but multiple texts. There is the first and original text of Blackstone. Then there are notes by the English commentators. Finally, there are Sharswood's notes. A beginner reading Sharswood's edition would be able to choose which of these multiple texts he would read and the impression of the law which he gained would very much depend upon which he chose to study. The sophisticated American reader would, presumably, be able to read the original text for its historical value, the English commentators' notes to gain a knowledge of contemporary English usages,[23] and the American commentators' notes to gain a knowledge of American practice. It would not have been an easy read.

One should not assume, however, that the publication of 'Americanised' versions of the *Commentaries* immediately displaced literal reprints of English editions of the *Commentaries*. Indeed, editions 'after' the London editions continued to be published, sold and purchased throughout the first half of the nineteenth century and, in a few cases, even later. Why did these two textual traditions flourish side by side for so long?

One part of the answer to this question is to be found in American copyright law and the economics of the book trade in nineteenth-century America. Under the Copyright Act of 1790, foreign authors were not given

[20] For an excellent contemporary discussion of preparation for the bar in England, see S Warren, *A Popular and Practical Introduction to Law Studies and to Every Department of the Legal Profession* (London, 1836 and later edns). Interestingly, 'Americanised' versions of Warren's book were also popular in the US throughout the nineteenth century; eg S Warren, *A Popular and Practical Introduction . . .*(New York NY, 1856), with an American introduction and appendix by Thomas W Clerke.

[21] Blackstone ed Sharswood (n 18) vol 1, pp 37–9.

[22] *Ibid*, p 376 fn 1.

[23] Sharswood and his American contemporaries would also, on occasion, correct the English notes: Blackstone ed Sharswood, vol 1, p 61, fn 23. Of course, English commentators also felt free to correct Blackstone.

copyright protection in the United States.[24] Thus any American publisher who obtained a foreign text could reprint it without paying any royalties to the author, his estate, or his foreign publisher. All that an American publisher desirous of publishing a text of the *Commentaries* needed to do was send off to London for the newest English edition—or, better yet, a set of stereotype plates of the edition—and he could publish it royalty-free in the United States. Many of these American editions were produced cheaply, on rough paper with poor press work, simply to allow them maximum market saturation because of their low price.

On the other hand, if a publisher wished to produce a more expensive version and to be able to copyright his edition, the only way this could be done when the text was of foreign origin was to add material by an American author. Although the underlying foreign-authored text could not be copyrighted, those parts of the text originating in the United States would be protected under the 1790 Act. Thus, for the cost of an American editor (perhaps between $100–$200 per volume, an estimate based upon the account books of the Philadelphia firm Ticknor and Fields),[25] a publisher could ensure his edition of Blackstone was eligible for copyright protection. The use of a prominent editor only added to the marketability of the edition, making copyright protection all the more important.

One might still ask why any American would buy either a foreign printing of an 'un-Americanised' text of Blackstone's work. Certainly, for a practising lawyer an 'Americanised' edition would have been the more useful. However, as noted earlier, Blackstone's *Commentaries* were, quite properly viewed as primarily an introductory teaching text rather than a legal professional's practice manual. Many American lawyers criticised Blackstone's work precisely because it was written at such an elementary level, the level which was quite proper for its English, non-lawyer audience. In 1834 the *American Jurist*, the primary legal periodical in Boston, published an article on the 'Characters of Law Books and Judges'. This piece devoted seven pages to quotations on Blackstone's *Commentaries*.[26] The overall tenor of these comments is mildly positive, but only when viewing the work as a very basic textbook for beginners. Even Blackstone's

[24] Copyright Act of 1790, 1 *Statutes at Large* 124 (1790), s 5: 'nothing in this Act shall be construed to extend to prohibit the importation or vending, reprinting or publishing within the United States, of any map, chart, book, or books written, printed or published by any person not a citizen of the United States, in foreign parts or places without the jurisdiction of the United States' (in effect, a license to steal the works of any non-US citizen).

[25] D Kaser (ed), *The Cost Book of Carey & Lea 1825–1838* (Philadelphia PA, 1963) 21, noting that the 'gentleman of the Philadelphia bar' who edited the 6th US edition of Chitty on bills and notes was paid $150; see also MH Hoeflich, *Selling the Law in Antebellum America, 1780–1870* (Chapel Hill NC, 2009) ch 3.

[26] 'Characters of Law Books and Judges' (1834) 12 *The American Jurist* 9–16.

greatest American admirers recognised the limitations of his work.[27] In terms of the publishing traditions of the *Commentaries*, this view of them as a very basic elementary text is important, since at such a level the technical differences between American law and English law would have been of less significance. It is easy to imagine that a father might well purchase an inexpensive literal reprint for his son as an introduction to law study, but that when the son eventually came to practise law, if he purchased another copy, it would be one with American annotations.

Another factor which may well have maintained the viability of literal reprints in the American market was the use of the *Commentaries* by American lawyers as a sign of legal learning and erudition. Since the *Commentaries* were agreed to be characterised by an 'elegance of manners and language', many lawyers found a well-placed quotation from Blackstone a useful way of displaying their polished erudition.[28] For a lawyer without much learning and fewer books, the *Commentaries* could serve as a treasure trove of quotable phrases. Exact accuracy in the law would have been of little relevance to such usage. As the late A. Edward Newton, Philadelphia lawyer, raconteur and bibliophile put it:

> it is important to remember that there is something better than a knowledge of Blackstone, and that is the reputation for having it. If one enjoys such a reputation for learning and always takes the law seriously, one's fortune is probably made.[29]

Thus for many nineteenth-century American lawyers, having the four volumes of the *Commentaries* on their shelves, albeit unread, was much the same as having a copy of Justinian's *Institutes*, a nice piece of learned memorabilia, but rarely, if ever, consulted. This may well be the reason that in many early American portraits of lawyers, one sees a bookcase with copies of Blackstone and Justinian prominently displayed in the background.[30]

Having set out this historical framework of the two textual traditions of Blackstone's *Commentaries* in the US, it is also interesting to chart the availability and price of these books from American law-book sellers and publishers as well as the holdings of the work in the libraries of American lawyers. By the 1820s the law-book publishing and selling business in the United States was experiencing unprecedented growth.[31] Publishers like Little, Brown in Boston, Banks & Gould in New York, and Carey & Lee in

[27] The principal US competitor to Warren's introductory text includes an extensive and not uncritical review of the *Commentaries*: D Hoffman *A Course of Legal Study; Respectfully Addressed to the Students of Law in the United States* (Baltimore MD, 1817) 87–93.

[28] *Ibid* 87.

[29] AE Newton, *Newton on Blackstone* (Philadelphia PA, 1937) 22.

[30] See MH Hoeflich, 'Lawyers, Books & Paper' (2002) 5 *The Green Bag* 163–72.

[31] See my forthcoming book, n 25 above.

Philadelphia were producing dozens of volumes of reprinted English legal texts, of newly authored American works, and of American editions of foreign texts. By the 1830s a number of these houses had expanded their marketing reach across the settled continent by means of lavishly produced catalogues. These catalogues not only permit us today to learn what books were available to American lawyers of the period, but at what price.

In 1821 Stephen Gould, the patriarch of the Gould family law publishing and book selling empire, produced his *Bibliotheca Legum Americana,* a catalogue of forty-eight pages of available books.[32] He offered only a single, imported edition of Blackstone, the 1818 London printing with Edward Christian's notes. The price for the four volume set in octavo was $16 and $12 for the set in duodecimo. These high prices represented the cost of transatlantic shipping. The absence of Tucker's Blackstone from Gould's catalogue is most likely attributable to the difficulty of obtaining it nearly two decades after publication, given the small size of the original print run. It is also possible that Gould felt that a book primarily edited for Virginia lawyers would not sell well in New York.

By the time Little, Brown released its *Catalogue of Law Books* in 1844, the selection of Blackstone's *Commentaries* had increased substantially.[33] A lawyer perusing this catalogue had a choice of three editions. He could pay $7.50 for an 1825 Philadelphia literal reprint of the Christian/Archbold edition, four volumes in octavo, or $5 for a two volume, octavo 1842 New York literal reprint of the Chitty edition (incorporating the notes of Christian and Archbold) with Field's notes. Finally, he would have to pay $12 for an 1825 London edition with Coleridge's notes '*bound in old calf*'. One may well presume that the latter would have been bought by a lawyer of the type Newton described. The calf binding, of course, was a sign of wealth and high professional standing.

In 1849 a New York City bookseller, John S. Voorhies, offered two editions of Blackstone in his catalogue.[34] The literal reprint of the Chitty edition in four volumes, printed in New York in 1848, was available for the modest price of $4.50. He also had the New York edition of 1847 'with American notes, by Jno L. Wendell, Esq' for $7. Finally, Voorhies offered for $12 a copy of Serjeant Stephen's newly published successor volume, listed under Blackstone.[35]

[32] S Gould, *A New Bibliotheca Legum Americana* (New York NY, 1821) 4.

[33] C Little and J Brown, *A Catalogue of Law Books* (Boston MA, 1844).

[34] J S Voorhies, *A General Catalogue of the Best Editions of English and American Law Books* (New York NY, 1849) 36.

[35] ie H F Stephen, *New Commentaries on the Laws of England (partly founded on Blackstone)* (London, 1841–5)

By 1856, when Little, Brown produced a much expanded catalogue, its offerings of Blackstone's *Commentaries* had changed somewhat[36] It continued to offer the London 1825 Coleridge edition at $12. It also, however, sold a two-volume octavo of the nineteenth London edition by Chitty 'and others' but 'with references to American cases' printed at Philadelphia in 1855. This set cost only $4. Finally, Little, Brown had a one volume abridgement by William Curry printed at London in 1809 for a measly $1.50. Presumably this latter book was for the lawyer wanting a bit of prestige at a cut-rate price.

One might speculate as to the significance of these offerings. I would suggest that they confirm several points made earlier. First, both literal reprints and imported editions continued to be available for decades.[37] Second, as the United States matured and its legal system matured along with it, 'Americanised editions' also gained in popularity.

A quick survey of antebellum lawyer's library catalogues confirms these results.[38] Joseph Story, Associate Justice of the United States Supreme Court, Dane Professor of Law at Harvard, author of a series of *Commentaries* on various legal subjects, owned multiple editions of Blackstone. He had a set of the 1800 London edition with Christian's notes, an Oxford edition of 1785, and the 1825 edition with Coleridge's notes.[39] He also owned both the 1838 and the 1839 New York 'Americanised' editions of the selective abridgement of Blackstone by Asa Kinne.[40]

Rufus Choate, one of the greatest courtroom advocates of antebellum America, possessed five separate editions of the *Commentaries*. He owned the 1778 Oxford eighth edition and the 1796 Dublin literal reprint with Christian's notes. He also owned the 'Americanised' New York editions of 1854 and 1857 with John Wendell's notes, as well as the 1803 Philadelphia edition of Tucker's Americanised version.[41]

After the American Civil War many aspects of American society and politics changed, but the popularity of Blackstone's *Commentaries* endured. When one looks at the publication history of the work in the second half of the nineteenth century, it is clear that the market for it

[36] *General Catalogue of Law Books* (Boston MA, 1856) 15.

[37] There seem to have been quite a few copies of the 1825 London edition available in the United States for sale in the antebellum period. It is possible that this edition was dumped at some point by a London bookseller into the US market when a new edition became available in England. Such dumping of books into the colonial market was not uncommon.

[38] The catalogues used for this study are, for the most part, posthumous auction sale catalogues and, therefore, reflect the lawyers' book holdings at the end of their lives.

[39] *Catalogue of Law and Miscellaneous Books Belonging to the Library of the Late Mr. Justice Story* (Boston MA, 1846) 6, 8, 12, 15.

[40] For Edgar Allan Poe's review of this work 'which was originally prepared by Mr. Kinne (who is a citizen of Natchez) without any view to publication', see (1839) 5 *Burton's Gentleman's Magazine* 327.

[41] *Catalogue of the Law Library of the Late Hon. Rufus Choate* (Boston MA, 1859) 5.

continued to be strong and the iconic status of its author remained secure. How does one explain the longevity of a book one hundred years old, written thousands of miles away and intended for a very different audience than that which so eagerly cherished it in the post-bellum United States? Thomas M. Cooley, one of the giants of American jurisprudence of this period, Jay Professor of Law in the University of Michigan, author of the most important treatises on American Constitutional Law after Story,[42] and editor of a popular edition of the *Commentaries*, provides the beginning of an answer:

> Lapse of time does not seem to diminish their attractions, or to lessen materially their practical value. Large as is the proportion of the rules and usages here defined and described which have been modified by statute, or have become obsolete in the changes and habits and modes of thought among the people, the best book in which to take a comprehensive view of the rudiments of English and American law is still the work now before us of this eminent jurist.[43]

Cooley went on to explain that the advantages of Blackstone's *Commentaries* as the *first* book one opened to begin law study derived from two essential characteristics. (In this statement he sounds very much like St George Tucker, half a century before.)[44] The first was its comprehensiveness and 'scientific arrangement'. Cooley, like most of his contemporaries and predecessors, viewed the 'institutional' arrangement of Blackstone's work as the best way to give the beginning law student a view of the whole of the Anglo-American common law, unburdened by technical details.[45] He also believed that once the student had studied Blackstone, he could then move on to the 'American Blackstone', Chancellor James Kent's *Commentaries on American Law*. Only after having mastered these two overviews should one commence to study the specialised treatises on American law which had begun to appear in quantity during the antebellum period.[46]

Cooley's second justification for studying Blackstone's work in post-bellum America was the importance of a knowledge of legal history and the origins of modern legal doctrines to both the practising lawyer and the jurist:

[42] TM Cooley, *A Treatise on Constitutional Limitations* (Boston MA, 1868).

[43] W Blackstone, *Commentaries on the Laws of England*, ed TM Cooley (Chicago IL, 1871) v.

[44] See above, pp 173–4.

[45] Cooley speaks of the student who, reading the *Commentaries*, seeks to discover 'the sound reasons out of which rules apparently arbitrary have sprung': Blackstone ed Cooley (n 43) v.

[46] Blackstone ed Cooley (n 43) xv.

> Things which are abolished or obsolete may, nevertheless, have furnished the reasons for the things which remain: and to study rules while ignoring their reasons would be like studying the animal anatomy while ignoring the principle of life which animated it.[47]

In stressing the importance of the historical origins of modern legal doctrine, Cooley aligned himself with many of the greatest jurists of his age, including James Coolidge Carter, Oliver Wendell Holmes Jr and James Barr Ames.[48] And although much of the impetus for the growth of the historical school of jurisprudence came from Germany, it seems to have given new life to the century-old English work of Blackstone.

Certainly, the publishing history, the history of the sales of copies of Blackstone, and the continued appearance of the *Commentaries* in American law libraries confirms the sustained vitality of the book throughout the latter of half of the nineteenth century and well into the first half of the twentieth. It is also clear that the tradition of publishing 'Americanised' editions of Blackstone's *Commentaries* continued and gained strength during this period and, indeed, eclipsed both reprints of Blackstone's original texts and updated English editions.

The catalogues of law books for sale during the later nineteenth century continued to be filled with listings of Blackstone's *Commentaries*. In 1869 William Gould and Son of Albany, New York, offered three separate editions of the *Commentaries*, at least two of the Americanised versions, by Sharswood and Wendell, and a third, Chitty's edition.[49] The Chitty edition was the least expensive at $7.50; the Sharswood was $10 and the Wendell sold for $12. Gould also offered an illustrated copy of the *Comic Blackstone* at $2.50 for those of whimsical tastes.[50] In 1889 the FH Thomas Law Book Company of St Louis, Missouri, also offered three edition, by Sharswood, Cooley and an Americanised version of Chitty's edition.[51] They also advertised Chase's abridgement of the *Commentaries*, as well as a copy of the *Comic Blackstone*. The Cooley was $10; the Sharswood was $8, and the Chitty cost a mere $5.50. In 1892, Callaghan and Company of Chicago were selling the same three editions with one

[47] Blackstone ed Cooley (n 43) v.

[48] Blackstone ed Cooley (n 43). See on the historical school and its translation into American jurisprudence, M Reimann, *Historische Schule und Common Law. Die deutsche Rechstwissenschaft des 19 Jahrhderts. Im amerikanischen Rechtsdenken* (Berlin, 1993).

[49] *Catalogue of Law Books* (Albany NY, 1860) 15.

[50] GA à Beckett, *The Comic Blackstone* (London, 1846) , a highly popular satire on the *Commentaries* with illustrations by the noted caricaturist, George Cruickshank, was published in multiple editions both in England and the United States throughout the nineteenth century. In the United States it was even published in parts, bound in paper, much like Dickens's serial novels: see eg GA à Becket, *The Comic Blackstone* (Philadelphia PA, 1845), in parts.

[51] *Catalogue of Law Books* (St Louis MO, 1889) 9–10.

addition, that by William Gardiner Hammond.[52] The Sharswood, Cooley, and Hammond editions each cost $10 per set, while the Chitty was $7.50. The catalogue issued in 1884 by the Wait Publishing Company of Chicago devoted an entire section to the *Commentaries*, abridgements of the *Commentaries*, and books about the *Commentaries*, nineteen titles in all, including all of the editions previously mentioned.[53] The prices were exactly the same as those offered by Callaghan & Company two years earlier. Interestingly, Wait Publishing also had an engraved portrait of Blackstone for sale at $3.00.[54] Finally, in 1917 Bancroft-Whitney & Company of San Francisco issued a catalogue of law books for sale containing thirteen Blackstone items, including all the standard editions, the comic version, abridgements, and question and answer volumes, as well as deluxe editions with translations of all foreign words and phrases for the American lawyer without linguistic skills.[55]

There are several important facts to be gleaned from this litany of Blackstone editions and related works offered for sale by booksellers in the latter part of the nineteenth century. First and foremost, they attest to the continuing popularity of the *Commentaries* in the United States. Second, it is noticeable that after the Civil War the vast majority of editions for sale by booksellers were Americanised editions. This seems unsurprising. By the end of the Civil War, American jurisprudence had developed a large literature of its own. Law schools could be found throughout the nation. Treatises on American law were common. With the passage of a hundred years much of the original *Commentaries* was glaringly obsolete, as Cooley noted. Even in England, updated versions had captured the market. American lawyers wanted American—or at least Americanised—texts. Indeed, the prices of the various editions also indicate that lawyers would pay a premium for the latest editions and those by the best known American jurists: Cooley, Sharswood and Hammond.

In fact, the continuing market for and use of editions of Blackstone's *Commentaries* throughout the nineteenth century and well into the first half of the twentieth century is a testament to several important aspects of American legal education and the American bar in general. First, American legal education was–and continues to be–highly conservative and opposed to radical innovation. The continuing use of Blackstone's *Commentaries* more than a century after their initial publication illustrates the extent to which American lawyers cherish the traditions of the bar and its iconic figures. The very fact that portraits of Blackstone could be and still are found in so many law schools and law offices indicates the reverence in

[52] *Catalogue of Law Books* (Chicago IL, 1892) 22–3.
[53] *Law Books* (Chicago IL, 1894) 8–9.
[54] *Ibid* ix: 'Portrait in Photogravure. By Gainsborough, Folio.' See further below, ch 15.
[55] *Law Book Catalogue* (San Francisco CA, 1917).

which he has been and still is held. In many ways, Blackstone's *Commentaries* are a secular professional analogue of religious holy texts.

By the second half of the twentieth century, the publication and revision of Blackstone's *Commentaries* had come to an almost total halt. There may be many reasons for this, including the growing cult of the new, the inability of American law students to understand the linguistic usages of the text, and the changing style of American legal scholarship. In the past half century, the republication of the *Commentaries* has been almost exclusively for historical purposes. But interest in the book continues and Blackstone's iconic status certainly remains, even if most American lawyers have absolutely no idea of what he actually wrote.[56]

[56] Of course, this phenomenon is not limited to lawyers and jurists: see P Bayard, *How to Talk About Books You Haven't Read* (trans). J Mehlman (New York NY, 2007).

12

Did Blackstone get the Gallic Shrug?

JOHN EMERSON

BEFORE HE DIED Blackstone saw his *Commentaries* appear in two separate French translations. Yet notwithstanding his enormous success in England and in America, how was he received in France? Did he get the Gallic shrug, or has he had a larger impact than we might reasonably expect of any writer on the common law? What follows is an exploratory mission, seeking traces of any significant influence William Blackstone may have had in France since the publication of the *Commentaries*, especially after they became available in French.

I BEFORE THE REVOLUTION

French eighteenth-century thought was overwhelmingly dominated by French writers, notably Voltaire, Rousseau and Montesquieu. How could a primarily descriptive work on the English legal system compete with the conceptual passion of the French debates of the day? Moreover, France and England for much of the century were at war; their enmity only deepened with the Revolution, and Napoleon. To make things worse, in 1778 Jeremy Bentham was actively mailing off copies of his own anti-Blackstone *Fragment on Government* to key French writers, such as d'Alembert, his collaborator on the *Encyclopédie* André Morellet, and François Jean de Chastellux.[1] Yet of these three, only Chastellux seemed in agreement with the ambitious young Bentham. D'Alembert replied politely and Abbé Morellet not at all.[2] Morellet may well already have had his own copy of

[1] Bentham, *Correspondence* vol 2, pp 115–16, 118–19, 149–50.
[2] Letter to Chastellux, 4 August 1778: *ibid* 143.

Blackstone's *Commentaries*, the quarto edition of 1774 sent over to him by Lord Shelburne, and preferred to form his opinions without young Bentham's aid.[3]

Indexes to the standard collected works of Voltaire, Rousseau, Diderot and d'Alembert reveal an almost conspicuous absence of Blackstone's name. Nevertheless, Edouard Tillet did find a passing reference to Blackstone in Voltaire's *Prix de la justice et de l'humanité*, published in 1777; here Voltaire briefly acknowledged in Blackstone the merit of 'having made known the best and the worst of English criminal law'.[4] Elsewhere the Swiss jurist Jean-Louis de Lolme (1741–1806), an English resident since 1768, invoked Blackstone on several occasions to support his favourable views of the common law in *The Constitution of England,* published first in French in 1771, then in English from 1775.[5]

Blackstone was certainly not without supporters in pre-revolutionary France. Auguste-Pierre Damiens de Gomicourt (1723–1790) published in London a French language review from 1769 to 1772 entitled *L'Observateur français à Londres*, which included occasional extracts from the *Commentaries*.[6] Gomicourt's extracts 'spurred demand for the whole work' ('firent désirer l'ouvrage entier') . He accordingly undertook a complete translation of the fourth edition, published in Brussels over the course of the years 1774–76 in six quarto volumes.[7] Also in that last momentous year, Gabriel François Coyer published a translation of the fourth volume of Blackstone's *Commentaries*, 'Of Public Wrongs' or criminal law. In his preface, Coyer claimed that 'if ever there was a time ripe for reform of France's criminal law, it was now, yet for that to happen, to form public opinion, his book would have to be read by many'.[8]

Catherine the Great read Gomicourt's translation with great enthusiasm. Anthony Cross cites her praise in a letter written in August 1776 to her friend and confidant Baron von Grimm: 'his commentaries and I are inseparable; he is an endless source of topics and ideas'.[9] But Abbé Coyer,

[3] *Lettres de l'Abbé Morellet à Lord Shelburne* (Paris, 1898) 45–6. Morellet asked Lord Shelbourne to send him the *Commentaries* in a letter dated 20 October 1774; it is not known if he received them, and there is no further mention of the work in their correspondence.

[4] Voltaire, *Prix de la justice et de l'humanité* (Geneva, 1778), cited E Tillet, *La constitution anglaise, un modèle politique et institutionnel dans la France des lumières* (Aix-en-Provence, 2001) 446.

[5] Reprinted in 1821 in London by Wilks and Co.

[6] A-A Barbier, *Examen critique et complément des dictionnaires historiques les plus répandus* (Paris,1820) vol 1, p 235.

[7] *Cf* CS Eller, *The William Blackstone Collection in the Yale Law Library: A Bibliographical Catalogue* (New Haven CT, 1938). 72–3.

[8] G-F Coyer, *Commentaire sur le code criminel d'Angleterre* (Paris,1776) ix: 'Pour former l'opinion public, il faut qu'un ouvrage soit beaucoup lu'.

[9] Anthony Cross, *Catherine the Great and the British* (Nottingham, 2001) 79. Cited in the original French: 'ses commentaires et moi, nous sommes inséparables ; c'est un fournisseur de choses et d'idées inépuisable'.

who really had hoped to stir up some reform of French criminal law, was very disappointed. In 1779, three years after the publication of his selection of Blackstone, he lamented its failure to achieve that end :

> This simple man genuinely believed that the public would welcome the work with open arms; that without being asked lobbyists would take it in hand; that the legal profession, the judges in particular, would consider it and incorporate it into their criminal law, which is a blot on this nation . . . He flattered himself perhaps (as all authors do) with a revolution. Vain hope; he doubts even having been read; and his bookseller has sworn that he will no longer stock any book urging reform of law or morals.
>
> (Cet homme simple croyait bonnement que le public allait accueillir l'ouvrage; que les Prôneurs et les Prôneuses, sans en être priés, le prendraient sous leur protection; que les gens de Loi, que les premiers magistrats, principalement, le méditeraient, le comporterait avec leur code criminel, qui calomnie d'une nation douce... Il se flattait peut-être (comme tous les auteurs se flattent) d'une révolution. Vaine espérance; il se doute s'il a été lu; et son libraire a juré qu'il ne se chargeraient plus d'aucun ouvrage, qui tendrait à la reformation des lois ou des mœurs.)[10]

Both Gomicourt and Coyer would be later criticised for their efforts. In 1820 Gomicourt's translation was said to be 'not highly regarded; one hopes for a more accurate and elegant version'.[11] In 1854 the author of Coyer's entry in the *Biographie universelle*, while allowing that some of his observations were correct, accused him of 'devoting himself too much to praising the English'.[12]

Blackstone himself was aware of the shortcomings of one of these translations, though we will never be quite certain which. In a letter written in French from Oxford on 25 May 1775, perhaps to the Parisian advocate Jean-Baptiste-Élie de Beaumont, perhaps to one of the translators, he expressed his thanks

> for the details you provide about the translation of my work. I knew already that it was not faithful, truncated in more than one section, but there are protocols in every country to which it is necessary to conform. I am not complaining, therefore, about being subjected to the scissors. I won't conceal from you, however, that I am astonished you are not happy with it.

[10] G-F Coyer, *Nouvelles Observations sur l'Angleterre, par un voyageur* (Paris, 1779) 66–7.

[11] A-A Barbier, *Examen critique et complément des dictionnaires historiques le plus répandus* (Paris, 1820) vol 1, p 235: 'Cette traduction n'est pas estimée ; on en désire une plus exacte et plus élégante.'

[12] L-G Michaud (ed), *Biographie universelle* (Paris, 1854) vol 9, p 419: 'Quelques-unes de ces observations sont justes et bien présentées, mais cet auteur affecte trop de louer les Anglais.'

(Je vous remercie, Monsieur, des détails que vous me donnez au sujet de la traduction de mon ouvrage. Je savais déjà qu'elle était infidèle, tronquée en plus d'un endroit mais il y a des formes obligées dans tous les pays auxquelles il faut se conformer quand on veut y vivre. Je ne me plains donc pas des coups de ciseaux que j'ai reçus. Je ne vous dissimule pas néanmoins que je suis étonné que vous n'en soyez pas satisfait.)[13]

Blackstone almost certainly did not know perhaps the most appreciative of his readers in 1770s France. Honoré Gabriel Riqueti, comte de Mirabeau (1749–1791), had been several times incarcerated in the dungeons of the château of Vincennes by his autocratic father for running up debts, and became a critic of arbitrary imprisonment as a result. In 1776 Mirabeau published an *Essai sur le despotisme* condemning the practice, for which he was again locked up in Vincennes from 1777 to 1780. During this period he completed an exhaustive comparative study of various penal systems, in particular focusing on the relationship between crime and punishment.

Not having access to writing paper, Mirabeau tore out blank pages from the books he was allowed to borrow and read, wrote in tiny writing and sewed the resulting text into his clothing. These notes were only published during the 1830s, as part of his collected works. They always cite Blackstone in the original English, especially in volume 7, *Des lettres de cachet et des prisons d'état*, first published in 1835, which covered *habeas corpus*, jury selection, breach of the peace, civil liberties and feudal customs. Mirabeau's interest in Blackstone's jurisprudence was not motivated solely by his own plight; he was concerned for the French legal system overall, writing that 'The severity of laws, says Blackstone, is an almost certain symptom that the State is being attacked by some insidious disease, or at very least indicates the weakness of its constitution.' ('La sévérité des lois, dit Blackstone, est un symptôme presque certain que l'État est attaqué de quelque sourde maladie, ou tout au moins elle indique la faiblesse de sa constitution.')[14]

Mirabeau's conclusion, written a decade before the Revolution, shows a concern for one of the most precious of the English legal system's concepts, lack of which in France allowed people to be thrown into prison without reason shown, or recourse:

The scholarly and judicious Blackstone argues that the use of trial by one's peers or by juries, and upholding the law of *habeas corpus*, is sufficient to guarantee for ever the liberty of a nation ....But on Blackstone's own assumptions, British liberty is now seriously threatened or rather being damaged, since the English are

[13] *Letters* 152.

[14] Mirabeau, *Œuvres* (Paris, 1835), vol 7, p 407.

abandoning, bit by bit, trial by jury, and it is not obvious that they are sufficiently guaranteeing the security of *habeas corpus*, which is suspended at this moment that I am writing.[15]

(Le savant et judicieux Blackstone soutient que l'usage de l'examen par pairs ou par jurés, et le maintien de la loi d'habeas corpus, suffisent pour garantir à jamais la liberté d'une nation. … Mais dans la supposition même de Blackstone, la liberté britannique est très menacée ou plutôt entamée; car les Anglais abandonnent, petit à petit, l'examen par jurés, et l'on ne voit pas qu'ils aient une sûreté suffisante du maintien de la loi d'habeas corpus, suspendue au moment où l'auteur écrivait.)

The contemporary relevance of Blackstone's and Mirabeau's concerns for such fundamental rights as *habeas corpus* cannot be overlooked in the post-2001 world. But Mirabeau's letters, although written in the late 1770s, would not see the light of day for over 50 years. In the meantime there was the Revolution.

II FRENCH REACTIONS DURING AND AFTER THE REVOLUTION

One reliable sign of French sympathies regarding English thinkers after the Revolution is the honorary French citizenship awarded to Jeremy Bentham on 23 August 1792. Bentham's star had risen in Europe during the previous decade. When he sent his *Essay on Political Tactics* to Abbé Morellet in February 1789—11 years after the Abbé had ignored his *Fragment on Government*—the reception was quite different. Morellet replied, without delay, full of praise:

Light-minded and unreflecting persons cannot estimate the importance of the subject you have treated in your 'Parliamentary Tactics'. It is an instrument by which great victory will be won by reason and by freedom, over ignorance and the tyranny of bad laws and vicious constitutions.[16]

The previous year Bentham's *Defence of Usury* had brought him to the attention of d'Alembert, whom he met while in France. Bentham would become a valued supporter of the new republic.

Blackstone, on the other hand, almost disappeared from sight. The literature on the principal constitutional theorist of the Revolution, Sièyes, shows no sign of Blackstone's name. True, Blackstone was mentioned at least three times in the early republican parliamentary debates on matters relating to jury trial and other aspects of criminal law reform. In April

[15] *Ibid* 496; the final reference must be to the provisions of 17 Geo III c 9 (1777): see TE May, *Constitutional History of England since the Accession of George III 1760–1860* (London, 1865) vol 2, p 263.

[16] Letter from Abbé Morellet, undated, in response to Bentham's of February 1789: *The Works of Jeremy Bentham* ed J Bowring (Edinburgh, 1838–43) vol 1, p 199.

1790 the lawyer François Tronchet elaborated a long argument on the subject of a jury's sphere of competence. He compared the positions taken by Sièyes and another French writer, Adrien Duport, to the English system.[17] Duport was in favour of only asking juries to decide questions of fact, as in England, while Sièyes argued that they should be entrusted with matters both of fact and of law. Tronchet, however, believed that it was impossible to follow the English system because, unlike the French, it gave precedence to sworn oral testimony over written submissions:

> In England the jury's verdict must always focus on what they call the issue of the cause, or in other words, the point upon which the issue is joined. An example will allow you to see both the truth and the peculiarity of English case law. I take this example from Blackstone, book III, chapter XXIII, 'of the jury'.[18]
>
> (En Angleterre l'objet sur lequel doit porter le jugement du jury est toujours un point simple et unique, fixé par ce qu'on appelle l'issue de la cause, c'est-à-dire la question prise entre les parties. Un exemple va vous faire sentir tout à la fois cette vérité et la bizarrerie de la jurisprudence anglaise. Je prends cet exemple dans Blackstone, livre III, chap. XXIII, du jury.)

Tronchet later shifted to the question of jury selection, again turning to Blackstone, this time to defend the system's merits:

> If, Blackstone says, the administration of justice were entirely entrusted to a body of men, all chosen by the prince, made up of people who possess the highest State offices, whatever one supposes about their integrity, their decisions will unconsciously almost always lean towards those who are closest to them in rank and status.[19]
>
> (Si, dit Blackstone, l'administration de la justice était entièrement confiée à un corps d'hommes, tous choisis par le prince, composé de gens qui possèdent les plus grands offices de l'Etat, quelque intégrité qu'on leur suppose, leurs décisions pencheront presque toujours involontairement vers ceux qui les approchent en rang et en dignité.)

Next year, in July 1791, the Assembly's reporter recorded a speech by the Girondin leader Jacques-Pierre Brissot on the topical subject of whether a monarch could be put on trial by his subjects:

> Brissot then passes to England, and says that this country's famous commentators, Locke, Sidney, Milton, Macaulay, Blackstone, Jones, have unanimously taught that the prince can be judged, deposed by the nation, and that his legal inviolability does not extend to crimes against the nation.[20]

[17] François-Denis Tronchet (1723–1806) a politician and lawyer, was among those appointed by Napoleon in 1804 to draft the *Code Civil.*

[18] P-J-B Buchez and P-C Roux, *Histoire parlementaire de la Révolution française, ou Journal des assemblées nationales depuis 1789 jusqu'en 1815* (Paris, 1838) vol 5, p 263.

[19] *Ibid* vol 5, p 275

[20] *Ibid* vol 11, p 9.

(Brissot passe ensuite à l'Angleterre et dit que tous les publicistes fameux de cette contrée, Locke, Sidney, Milton, Macaulay, Blackstone, Jones, ont unanimement enseigné que le prince peut être jugé, déposé par la nation, et que son inviolabilité cesse en matière de crime national.)

Brissot then moved on to cite examples of the tyranny that results where the king can do no wrong and is not required to obey the law.

Three more partial translations of Blackstone appeared over the next decade or so. In 1792 the lawyer (or '*homme de loi*') Clement-François Blanc published *Du Jury en matière civile et criminelle traduit de Blackstone*, a work doubtless reflecting earlier interest in the topic but which seems to have attracted little notice in the deepening revolutionary crisis.[21] Ten years later, under Napoleon, Antoine Ludot '*membre du Tribunat*' brought out another volume on the administrative and criminal laws of England, translated (once again) from the fourth book of the *Commentaries*.[22] Signs of a slightly broader interest in Blackstone's work came in 1803, when one M Joguet published a French translation of the precursor to the *Commentaries*, Blackstone's *Analysis of the Laws of England*.[23] But if the availability of Blackstone in translation indicates some mild continuing professional interest, nineteenth-century French attitudes generally seem to have ranged from indifference to outright hostility.

This seems to hold true across the political spectrum. Thus Maurice Rubichon, the conservative French Catholic 'Christian economist', whose observations as a royalist *émigré* formed the basis of the account of England's government and economy which he published between 1815 and 1819, attacked Blackstone in the following terms:

> My reader must see already that it is rather interesting to travel in that country, holding in one's hands the writings of the likes of Montesquieu, de Lolme or any number of other foreign writers, and to compare what they say to what there is. But the philosopher Blackstone has been translated into French; browsing through him one finds commentary on law and custom; often he deplores what I permit myself to admire, and he admires what I permit myself to deplore; perhaps, however, he would be better appreciated by my reader; Blackstone is anyway one of the most fallacious talents ever produced by fertile England.[24]

[21] C-F Blanc, *Du jury en matière civile et criminelle* (Paris, 1792). The anonymous *Recherches sur les cours et les procédures criminelles d'Angleterre: extraits des Commentaires de Blackstone* (Paris, 1790) appears to be the translation 'inferior to the other two' (ie de Gomicourt and Coyer) listed by Ludot in 1801 (n 22 below, vii–viii: Eller (n 7) 73).

[22] AN Ludot, *Des lois de police et criminelles d'Angleterre; des divers modes d'y instruire les proces des prevenus; et specialement, de l'institution du jury en matiere criminelle; ouvrage tr de l'anglais de Blackstone, avec des notes* (Paris, 1801).

[23] AM Joguet, *Analyse de lois anglaises, précédé d'un discours préliminaire sur l'étude des lois, traduite de l'anglais de William Blackstone* (Paris, 1803).

[24] M Rubichon, *De l'Angleterre* (Paris, 1817) vol 2 , p 4; A Dign, *French Political Thought from Montesquieu to Tocqueville* (Cambridge, 2008) 55–6.

> (Mon lecteur doit voir déjà qu'il est curieux de voyager dans ce pays-là, tenant à la main les écrits des Montesquieu, des Delolme ou de tant d'autres romanciers étrangers, et de comparer ce qu'ils disent avec ce qui est. Mais le philosophe Blackstone a été traduit en français; en le parcourant, on y trouvera la loi et la coutume commentée; souvent il déplore ce que je me permets d'admirer, et il admire ce que je me permets de déplorer; peut-être n'en sera-t-il pas moins bien accueilli par mon lecteur; Blackstone est d'ailleurs un des esprits le plus faux qu'ait jamais produit la fertile Angleterre.)

Having satisfied his bloodlust, Rubichon then moves to another topic, making no further mention of Blackstone, whose vigorous defence of anti-catholic penal laws had embarrassed even the otherwise favourably disposed Coyer.

Despite a second full translation of the *Commentaries* by the Parisian lawyer Nicholas Maurice Chompré in the early 1820s, Blackstone retained only a marginal presence in France. He was occasionally criticised for undue complacency over the lack of any constitutional separation of powers in Britain. In 1850 the radical democrat Ledru Rollin (chief of the 'Red Republicans' according to his English translator) charged Blackstone, along with other British writers, of having ignored the manner in which the judiciary served as a tool of the aristocracy:

> 'The judges are the masters', cried Chancellor Bacon three centuries ago; for three centuries this dictum has vainly been repeated by the likes of Romilly, Bentham, Mackintosh, and Taylor. Even Blackstone, that great apologist of English law, cannot help but recognise that at every step these laws are blanketed in the deepest obscurity.[25]

> ('Les Juges sont les maîtres', s'écriait le chancelier Bacon, il y a trois siècles; et, depuis trois siècles, cette parole a été vainement répétée par les Romilly, les Bentham, les Mackintosh, les Taylor. Blackstone, ce grand apologiste des lois anglaises, ne peut s'empêcher de reconnaître, à chaque pas, qu'elles sont recouvertes de ténèbres épaisses.)

Considerably more moderate in his political views, the novelist Stendhal also vehemently denounced Blackstone's faith in the English system. Stendhal's sentiments were published posthumously in his *Mémoires d'un touriste* (1854). In an extraordinary outburst, he claimed that

> The parliamentary reforms in England are entirely due to Blackstone's lies. There have never been three powers in England: when the famous Blackstone published the work in which he argues that there are three powers—the King, the Lower House and the Upper House – he was regarded as a reckless innovator. There has never been in England, up to the moment of the parliamentary reforms carried out these days, but one single power, the aristocracy, or the House of Lords,

[25] A-A Ledru-Rollin, *De la décadence de l'Angleterre* (Paris, 1850) I 78; L Rollin, *The Decline of England* (London, 1850) vii.

> which nominated the House of Commons. The King and his ministers inevitably followed in the same direction as the two Houses. Blackstone's error was to claim that the people were represented by the House of Commons, and this has been repeated by Montesquieu and de Lolme. Soon this lie was accepted everywhere as the truth.[26]
>
> (La réforme parlementaire en Angleterre est due entièrement aux mensonges de Blackstone. Il n'y eut jamais trois pouvoirs en Angleterre : lorsque le célèbre Blackstone publia l'ouvrage où il avance qu'il y a trois pouvoirs : le roi, la chambre basse et la chambre haute, il fut regardé comme un novateur téméraire. Il n'y a jamais eu un Angleterre, jusqu'au moment de la réforme parlementaire opérée de nos jours, qu'un seul pouvoir, l'aristocratie ou la chambre des pairs, laquelle nommait la chambre des communes. Le roi et ses ministres marchaient forcément dans le sens des deux chambres. L'erreur de Blackstone, qui prétendait que le peuple était représenté par la chambre des communes, fut répétée à l'étranger par Montesquieu et Delolme. Bientôt ce mensonge fut admis généralement comme une vérité.)

Stendhal concluded his rant with the suggestion that a humourless and dogmatic person might make a nice book out of the history of Blackstone's lie.[27]

On 2 July 1853, the celebrated French liberal commentator Alexis de Tocqueville wrote to the English political economist NW Senior in terms revealing that he was far from overawed by the *Commentaries*:

> I have followed your advice, my dear Senior, and I have read, or rather re-read, Blackstone. I studied him twenty years ago. Each time it has made upon me the same impression. Now, as then, I have ventured to consider him (if one may say so without blaspheming) an inferior writer, without liberality of mind or depth of judgment; in short, a commentator and a lawyer.[28]

Tocqueville's reaction provides a clue to Blackstone's lukewarm reception in France. The French held a very narrow view of what constitutes a writer. Tocqueville sought to squeeze Blackstone into the French notion of a *jurisconsulte* or *publiciste*, rather than allowing for the fact that he came from a very different philosophical and intellectual tradition. The very title *Commentaries* sufficiently indicated the nature of Blackstone's aims. Tocqueville dismissed Blackstone as nothing more than a 'commentator'; yet, had he taken any notice of this title, he might have recognised that that was exactly what Blackstone aimed to be.

In contrast to the usual negative remarks of the time, we may notice one positive, if brief, treatment of Blackstone. In 1842 Léon Galibert and Clément Pellé mentioned Blackstone's famous comparison of the English

[26] Stendhal, *Mémoires d'un touriste* (Paris,1854), 1150. Since Montesquieu died in 1755, he could hardly have repeated anything originating from Blackstone.

[27] *Ibid* 1151–2.

[28] A de Tocqueville, *Memoirs, Letter and Remains* (London, 1861) vol 2, p 223.

legal system to an old Gothic castle, adding a substantial footnote which demonstrates an awareness for the English point of view that Ledru-Rollin, Stendhal and Tocqueville seemingly lacked. They cite Lord Mansfield's response when asked about the best introductory work for young lawyers:

> 'till of late I could never, with any satisfaction to myself, answer that question; but since the publication of Mr Blackstone's *Commentaries*, I can never be at a loss. In that work you will find analytical reasoning displayed a pleasing and perspicuous style. The student will find in it with no trouble the first principles on which our excellent laws rest!'[29]

> ('Ce n'est que dans ces derniers temps et depuis la publication des Commentaires de M. Blackstone, disait Lord Mansfield, que j'ai pu répondre à cette question. Dans cet ouvrage, vous trouverez un raisonnement analytique fait dans un style clair et agréable. L'élève y reconnaîtra sans peine les premiers principes sur lesquels reposent nos excellentes lois!')

Galibert and Pellé then mention Jeremy Bentham's heated attack ('beaucoup de chaleur') on the *Commentaries* and his concession that Blackstone was nevertheless the first jurist to write clearly about the English legal system.

In short, isolated mentions of Blackstone occur in a number of works published in France over the course of the nineteenth century. It is obvious that Blackstone was largely perceived as peripheral to the French legal and political system.

III A CHANGE IN THE TWENTIETH CENTURY

In 1907 we witness a startling challenge to French thought regarding William Blackstone, with the posthumous publication of a volume of essays by the Anglophile comparative lawyer, educationist and political writer Émile Boutmy (1835–1906).[30] Here Boutmy examined the origins of the Declaration of the Rights of Man (1789), with special attention to Article 2, which outlines the fundamental rights of liberty, property, security and resistance to oppression. He argued that, despite the accepted wisdom that the French were directly influenced by the Americans in drafting this clause, its wording is significantly different from the American constitutional guarantee of 'life, liberty and the pursuit of happiness'. The source must be elsewhere, and Boutmy cites Blackstone's elevation of precisely these rights to absolute:

[29] L Galibert and C Pellé, *Angleterre* (Paris, 1842–44) vol 4, pp 173–4, paraphrasing J Holliday, *The Life of William, late Earl of Mansfield* (London, 1797) 89–90.

[30] *ODNB*.

> If Blackstone really used this language from 1754 on, if he repeats it in his celebrated *Commentaries* which appear in 1765, why would we not suppose as much that our Declaration, promulgated in 1789, no less than the American Bill of Rights, published between 1776 and 1786, directly borrowed its formula from the English jurist? Is there a logical necessity, a proof of fact, that France borrowed directly from the United States?[31]

> (Si Blackstone a véritablement tenu ce langage dès 1754, s'il le répète dans ses célèbres Commentaries qui parurent en 1765, pourquoi ne supposerait-on pas qu'autant notre Déclaration, promulguée en 1789, que les Bills of rights américains, publiés de 1776 à 1786, ont emprunté directement sa formule au légiste anglais? Y a-t-il une nécessité logique, y a-t-il une preuve de fait, que la France ait fait directement cet emprunt aux Etats-Unis?)

Boutmy proceeds to challenge what he sees as the astounding assumption that France would choose to borrow from the Americans rather than the English:

> If it is almost certain that Blackstone's maxims were known by the Anglo-Saxons of the new continent, what reason do we have to believe that the draftsmen of the French Constitution, having in front of them a highly authoritive text, already old, a text which had had the time to act on the minds of the eighteenth century and win them over to its ideas, had deliberately neglected it to go in search of a model beyond the Atlantic, from some colonies who then hardly figured in the world, and whose acts had had little impact? Blackstone no doubt had no need of an intermediary to inspire either people.[32]

> (S'il est à peu près certain que les maximes de Blackstone ont été connues des Anglo-Saxons du nouveau continent, quelle raison a-t-on de croire que nos constituants français, ayant tout près d'eux un texte d'une grande autorité, déjà ancien, un texte qui avait eu le temps d'agir sur les esprits du XVIII siècle et de les gagner à ses idées, l'aient de propos délibéré négligé, pour aller demander un modèle, au-delà de l'Atlantique, à des colonies qui faisaient alors bien peu de figure dans le monde, et dont les actes avaient peu de retentissement? Blackstone n'a sans doute pas eu besoin d'intermédiaire pour inspirer l'un et l'autre peuple.)

This is quite a jump from the peremptory passing mentions of Blackstone in the preceding one hundred and twenty years or so. Boutmy does not mention Blackstone again in this essay, and he died just before his book was published. Has his work been followed up by more detailed studies of the French Constitution and Blackstone's *Commentaries*? It appears that his hypothesis may have been left aside and taken no further.

Twenty years later, another startling assertion was published by Henri-Lévy Ullmann, in his study of the *English Legal Tradition*, translated into

[31] É Boutmy, *Études politiques* (Paris, 1907) 145.
[32] *Ibid* 145–6.

English in 1935.[33] Blackstone is mentioned in discussion of various topics during the course of this volume, but at one point Lévy-Ullmann follows Holdsworth in stressing Blackstone's proven authority over the fullness of time, notwithstanding Bentham's damaging assaults:

> 'the Blackstonian synthesis, far from suffering from the [triumph of Benthamism], found in the test a proof of its good quality. Like Littleton's work, which we have seen, came out on the eve of the expansion of Equity, Blackstone's *Commentaries* had to encounter the itch for legislation which marked the 19th century in England—an encounter favourable in every respect both to the new legislation and to the Common law. The sound framework provided for the latter enabled it to receive, without breaking, the rush of new law, and, at the same time, helped jurists to get their bearings and open up a way through 'the labyrinth of statutes which have changed the face of English law'. To these highly suggestive views of Sir William Holdsworth, may a Continental jurist add, on the basis of French experience, that Blackstone's books may have served in the defence of unwritten law as the impassable trenches which shattered all Bentham's assaults in the cause of codification? *Who will venture to assert that our ancient Common Lawyers, authors of the Civil Code, such as Tronchet, would not have deemed their task devoid of purpose had their guide and master, Pothier—the French Blackstone—endowed our country with a full Commentary on the 'Loix' of ancient France?*'[34]

Thus Lévy-Ullmann dared to suggest that the French *Code civil* had only been necessary because no French author—by implication Montesquieu as well as Pothier—had managed to emulate Blackstone's achievement.

The year before he first published these views, Lévy-Ullmann supervised the appearance of the first extended study of Blackstone by a French scholar, Dunoyer's *Blackstone et Pothier*; familiarity with that work is likely to have inspired his speculation. Yet Dunoyer's conclusion was, curiously, quite different from Lévy-Ullmann's, arguing that Pothier's success was greater in France than Blackstone's in England, for the very reason that he prompted the *Code civil*. But Dunoyer's work is rather negative overall, concluding that neither of the two authors he studied had any enduring relevance:

> Whatever the legal system of each country, there comes a time when the legal scholars lose their influence on the destiny of their national law. In England, where the law has not been codified, Blackstone's works, on the surface, still inspire a few modern works, although in reality one no longer finds a trace of Blackstone in them. In France, the *Code civil* has borrowed the substance of

[33] H Lévy-Ullmann, *The English Legal Tradition*, tr M Mitchell (London, 1935); first publ as *Éléments d'introduction générale à l'étude des sciences juridiques, tome II, Le système juridique de l'Angleterre* (Paris, 1928).

[34] *Ibid* 157 (emphasis added).

> Pothier's arguments, but today, our *Code* lives its own existence, and the author on whom it was modelled has lost credibility.[35]
>
> (Quel que soit le système juridique du pays auquel ils appartiennent, il vient un moment où les juristes perdent toute influence sur les destinées de leur droit national. En Angleterre, où le droit n'a pas été codifié, les œuvres de Blackstone peuvent, en apparence, inspirer encore certains ouvrages modernes, en réalité, l'esprit de notre auteur en est éliminé. En France, le Code civil a emprunté la substance des traités de Pothier, mais aujourd'hui, notre Code vit d'une existence propre, et l'auteur qui fut son modèle a perdu tout crédit.)

These two speculative passages by Émile Boutmy and Henri Lévy-Ullmann nevertheless represent a transformation in French opinion on the impact of William Blackstone. They point to a petty nationalist jealousy among French writers since the Revolution, who tended to criticise Blackstone for incidental and trivial reasons—such as being an 'inferior writer'—missing the point of what Blackstone had set out to do. Sylvester Douglas came across this attitude when talking to Madame de Staël just after the battle of Waterloo: 'She was surprised when I mentioned to her that I thought Blackstone perhaps the best prose-writer in England of our days, and she begged Mr Schlegel to attend to this.'[36] Blackstone had not set out to compete with Montesquieu or Voltaire; he was concerned to make sense of hundreds of years of piecemeal case law in England, to synthesise it into a coherent intellectual construct. Lévy-Ullmann believed that if Blackstone had not published his *Commentaries*, English law would have been doomed 'after a majestic course, [to] vanish in a waste of sandbanks'[37]—exactly what happened to pre-revolutionary French law.

IV IN GUISE OF A CONCLUSION

Two larger questions seem to beg the resolution of a more extensive survey of Blackstone's impact in France:

1 How well translated was Blackstone by Gomicourt, Coyer and Chompré and others? Were specific concepts and terms (eg 'writ') dealt with accurately? If not, what effect did this have on the French reception of Blackstone? (Of course, even if read in the original, French readers' comprehension of English customs and practices may have been insufficient for full understanding.)

[35] LH Dunoyer, *Blackstone et Pothier* (Paris, 1927) 159.

[36] *The Diaries of Sylvester Douglas*, ed F Bickley (London, 1928) vol 2, p 162.

[37] Lévy-Ullman (n 35) 158; see also F Lessay, 'Blackstone et les libertés anglaises : l'individu entre mythe et histoire' in GM Cazzaniga and YC Zarka (ed), *L'individu dans la pensée moderne* (Pisa, 1995) 577–94.

2 Did Blackstone indeed directly influence the making of the 1789 French Constitution? What do the records of its drafting show? Has anyone gone further than Boutmy?

Blackstone's role in the making of modern France remain largely unmapped. It looks likely that his influence was more considerable than generally accepted, and though the modern French legal system differs largely from the English one, at their constitutional core the difference may not be so great as it is customary to believe. It is also likely that Dunoyer's conclusions were unnecessarily gloomy, and perhaps even miss the point. Blackstone, like Pothier and the *Code civil*, might not now figure in the day-to-day workings of the common law. But if the *Commentaries* helped draft the original French bill of rights, then Blackstone was virtually responsible for their modern soul, regardless of whether his name is known now, then, or ever. Hence a thorough assessment of Blackstone's French reception and impact is undoubtedly well worth pursuing.

POSTSCRIPT

After this chapter was completed and in the publication process, I discovered that Mirabeau actually presided over the drafting of the original *Déclaration des Droits de l'Homme et du Citoyen*, ratified by King Louis XVI in August 1789. Articles 7 and 8 claiming rights in criminal law to be charged and to receive appropriate punishment suggest influence from Blackstone through Mirabeau. But with intense debates among competing authors and six drafts, this would need verification.

JE, May 2009.

13

Blackstone in Germany

HORST DIPPEL

'BLACKSTONE IN GERMANY' is a challenging topic which may tell us more about the legal and political impact of Britain on Germany from the late eighteenth through the nineteenth centuries than the paucity of German translations of Blackstone's works would suggest. Any check of the library catalogues will reveal that just three titles were published under his name in Germany between 1767 and 1823. The first booklet of some seventy pages is a German translation of the preface and the introductory 'Discourse on the Study of Law' prefixed to his *Analysis of the Laws of England*, taken from the fourth edition (Oxford, 1759). The second item, published in Bremen in 1779, is a translation of the introductions to the four volumes of Blackstone's *Commentaries on the Laws of England*, whereas the third publication is a two-volume abridgement of the *Commentaries*, published in Schleswig in 1822–23. No established publishing houses for one of the foremost European legal authors, no obvious printing places, with the one exception of Göttingen, and no complete edition of his *opus magnum* for which the world knew and continues to know him, or of his other major writings.

A faint excuse may have been that some of his works were available in French. Several complete and partial translations of Blackstone's *Commentaries* were published between 1774 and 1845. His *Analysis of the Laws of England* was published in French in 1803. Though his book on *The Great Charter and Charter of the Forest*, his *Law Tracts*, and other publications were not translated, Blackstone appears to have been much more accessible in French than in German, and for most educated Germans, at least in the late eighteenth and early nineteenth centuries, French made all the difference as compared to English. The reviewer of the first two volumes of the French translation of Blackstone's *Commentaries* exclaimed in the *Leipziger Gelehrte Zeitungen* in late 1774: 'a translation of this work, so well received in England, has long been desired and only the many difficulties of such a task have prevented it'. ('Man hat schon lange eine Uebersetzung dieses in England so wohl aufgenommenen Werks gewünscht, und nichts als die vielen Schwürigkeiten einer solchen Arbeit haben sie zurükgehalten').[1] Obviously, French or German did not matter, as long as it was not English. However, even in this period there existed scholars and others able to read English, though it appears that they may have been less numerous in the south of Germany than in the north, which had manifold political, commercial, and other relations with Britain. Still today the Göttingen University Library holds what may be the most important collection of Blackstone's English publications in Germany, including several complete sets of the *Commentaries* starting with the first edition

With these restrictions in mind, why were Germans interested in Blackstone? What may an inquiry into the topic 'Blackstone in Germany' really tell us? My hypothesis is that investigating the impact of Blackstone on Germany will help to correct the assumption that it was due to Montesquieu and de Lolme that the English Constitution was considered as a model for Germany from the second half of the eighteenth through the nineteenth centuries.[2] A study of Blackstone's impact on Germany demonstrates that this appraisal was, instead, closely connected with his name and basically restricted to the period between the Congress of Vienna and the revolutions of 1848.

In order to verify my hypothesis, I shall proceed chronologically and first deal with the second half of the eighteenth century up to around 1815. A second part will be devoted to the 1820s and the decades up to 1848, while a third will analyse the second half of the nineteenth century, to be followed by some very brief remarks on the twentieth century. More than highlighting the role the British Constitution played in that time in Germany, analysing Blackstone's impact will also give us major insights into German legal scholarship of the epoch and its approach to English common law. Thus, the subdivision of my topic will demonstrate the transition in the appreciation of Blackstone: it begins with his evaluation as a scholar of English law. This develops into the liberal interpretation that assesses him as the interpreter of the English constitutional model. Finally, as a consequence of the widespread rejection of a political system considered meaningless for modern Germany, his role diminishes into that of a standard source for English legal and constitutional questions.

During the final decades of the eighteenth century, including the French Revolution and the Napoleonic era, Blackstone presented himself to a

[1] *Neue Zeitungen von Gelehrten Sachen auf das Jahr 1774* (Leipzig, 26 December 1774) 837.

[2] *Cf* eg H-C Kraus, 'Die deutsche Rezeption und Darstellung der englischen Verfassung im neunzehnten Jahrhundert' in R Muhs (ed), *Aneignung und Abwehr. Interkultureller Transfer zwischen Deutschland und Großbritannien im 19. Jahrhundert* (Bodenheim, 1998) 89–126; W Pöggeler, *Die deutsche Wissenschaft vom englischen Staatsrecht. Ein Beitrag zur Rezeptions- und Wissenschaftsgeschichte, 1748–1914* (Berlin, 1995).

German audience as the author of the system of the common law and English legal institutions. Germans could learn from Blackstone 'how the English study jurisprudence, what they think about Roman law, and what has been its fate there' ('wie die Engländer die Rechtsgelehrsamkeit erlernen, wie sie von dem römischen Rechte denken, und was selbiges vor Schicksale dort gehabt').[3] Justus Claproth was a Göttingen law professor, lecturing on criminal law and criminal procedure. Enlightenment ideas had influenced his approach to law reform, among others Montesquieu and Beccaria,[4] which made him thoroughly aware of the substantial differences between his own Roman law-based jurisprudence and common-law-based England. Blackstone might provide a highly welcome introduction to these distinct legal approaches.

The same appears to be true for the reviewer of volume three of Blackstone's *Commentaries* in the *Göttingische Gelehrte Anzeigen*, Philipp Heinrich Seyberth. He was fascinated by Blackstone's arrangement of the common law, dealing in his first two volumes with the rights of persons and the rights of things. But he had difficulties in explaining to a German audience Blackstone's 'Private Wrongs' and 'Public Wrongs', awkwardly paraphrasing instead his further procedure as 'so he arrives rather naturally at those undertakings which run contrary to these authorisations' ('so kommt er itzt ganz natürlich auf die Unternehmungen, so diesen Befugnissen zuwider laufen').[5]

Both statements reveal the widespread ignorance, even among German academics, of the English legal system. Though this deficiency was realised by contemporaries and some of them articulated it in clear terms, no comprehensive translation of the *Commentaries* was produced to redress it. One reason for this inconsistency may have been that in spite of public statements to the contrary, interest in English law was all but superficial and feigned. Another explanation may be that this interest was scholarly and restricted to quite a small number of experts who had sufficient command of the French or English languages to read Blackstone in one or the other. This certainly applied to Georg Forster, who persuasively summarised English legal writing with the comment 'Lyttleton (*sic*), Coke and Blackstone are still the most outstanding commentators (of English

[3] W Blackstone, *Der neueste Zustand der Rechtsgelehrsamkeit in Engelland* (Göttingen, 1767) v (introductory remarks by the translator, Justus Claproth).

[4] Cf F Schaffstein, 'Anfänge der Strafrechtswissenschaft in Göttingen: Meister Vater und Sohn Justus Claproth, JD Michaelis', and W Henckel, 'Justus Claproth (1728–1805), Göttinger Lehrer des Konkursrechts im 18. Jahrhundert', both in F Loos (ed), *Rechtswissenschaft in Göttingen. Göttinger Juristen aus 250 Jahren* (Göttingen, 1987) 26–8, 100–122.

[5] *Göttingische Anzeigen von gelehrten Sachen* (23 January 1769) I 89. For the complete review, *cf* 89–104. The authorship of the review is revealed in the copy held by the Göttingen University Library. For a review of Claproth's translation two years earlier, *cf ibid* (1767) vol 2, pp 705–8.

law' ('Lyttleton, Coke und Blackstone, sind noch immer die vorzüglichsten Commentatoren').[6] A few years earlier, Ernst Brandes had written similarly about the *Commentaries*: 'An indispensable work for the understanding of English civil law' ('Ein unentbehrliches Werk zur Kenntnis der Englischen bürgerlichen Rechts'),[7] while Gebhard Friedrich August Wendeborn had assessed its author as 'one of the most distinguished English legal scholars' ('einer der vornehmsten englischen Rechtsgelehrten').[8]

Göttingen professors also made use of Blackstone, among them Gottfried Achenwall whose *Staatsverfassung der heutigen vornehmsten Europäischen Reiche* [*Constitution of the present foremost European realms*] listed in his chapter on England among its works of reference, from 1762, Blackstone's *Analysis of the Laws of England*, only adding the *Commentaries* as late as 1790.[9] A Göttingen colleague, Ludwig Timotheus Spittler, had earlier made use of Blackstone's *The Great Charter and Charter of the Forest* for his analysis of the origins of the English Parliament.[10] In Hamburg, August Hennings, even mentioning Blackstone in his title, had used his *Commentaries* as a source on the evolution of English law in the Middle Ages,[11] while Heinrich Christoph Albrecht referred to the *Commentaries* only in passing, assuming that Blackstone was no interpreter of the actual Constitution, but would rather have preferred to change it.[12]

No doubt there were German authors in the late eighteenth and early nineteenth centuries sufficiently qualified to speak of Blackstone as 'einer

[6] G Forster, 'Geschichte der Englischen Litteratur, vom Jahr 1788' in *Georg Forsters Werke. Sämtliche Schriften, Tagebücher, Briefe*, vol 7 ed G Steiner 2nd edn (Berlin, 1990) 78.

[7] [E Brandes] 'Ueber den politischen Geist Englands' (1786) 7 *Berlinische Monatsschrift* 111. Brandes inserted this brief comment while writing on the British Constitution and referring extensively to de Lolme and, afterwards, to Hume, a context from which he deliberately excluded Blackstone. The article was sent anonymously to the journal by Christian Gottlob Heyne, Georg Forster's father-in-law.

[8] GFA Wendeborn, *Der Zustand des Staats, der Religion, der Gelehrsamkeit und der Kunst in Grosbritannien gegen das Ende des achtzehnten Jahrhunderts* (Berlin, 1785–88) vol 1, p 4.

[9] G Achenwall, *Staatsverfassung der heutigen vornehmsten Europäischen Reiche im Grundriße* (Göttingen, 1762) 251; *ibid* 5th edn (1768) 279; *ibid* 6th edn (1781), vol 1, p 298; *ibid* 7th edn (1790), vol 1, pp 278, 295. No references to Blackstone had been included in the 3rd edn of 1756.

[10] [LT Spittler], 'Summarische Entwicklung der Entstehungs-Geschichte des Englischen Parlaments' in (1789) 5 *Göttingisches Historisches Magazin* 629.

[11] A Hennings, *Philosophische und statistische Geschichte des Ursprungs und des Fortgangs der Freyheit in England, Nach Hume, Blackstone und andern bewährten Quellen ausgearbeitet* (Copenhagen, 1783) 22, 32, 38, 40, 41 and passim (to 245, together more than 30 references). See also G Phillips, *Englische Reichs- und Rechtsgeschichte seit der Ankunft der Normannen im Jahre 1066 nach Christi Geburt* (Berlin, 1827–28) vol 2, pp 93, 95, 102, 126, 308, 328.

[12] HC Albrecht, *Untersuchungen über die englische Staats-Verfassung. Nach den neuesten Veranlassungen der Geschichte des Landes* (Lübeck and Leipzig, 1794) vol 2, pp 31–2.

der berühmtesten Rechtsgelehrten' (one of the most famous legal scholars)'.[13] But the debate on German legal reform at this time had taken a different turn,[14] as codification had become the magic word of the age. In spite of Blackstone's name having become more familiar, and in spite of his civilian sympathies,[15] he failed to have any significant impact, when after the defeat of Napoleon, Carl Friedrich von Savigny won the internal debate in Germany and his historical law school became the ruling legal force for the subsequent decades.[16] There may not have been many more German authors during this period beyond those mentioned above who found Blackstone in any way inspiring or even useful. Among those who did was Ludwig von Vincke who still in 1815 regretted,

> that English jurisprudence was so little known in Germany; much of singular usefulness, such as the common origin, might have made it interesting, and a translation of Blackstone's *Commentaries on the Laws of England* would have been worth as much as a fair number of English novels and presumably also some of the countless translations and revisions of another foreign law code with which we have been swamped since last year.
>
> (daß die englische Rechtslehre in Deutschland so wenig bekannt war; viel einzeln Zweckmäßiges, so wie der gemeinschaftliche Ursprung, würde sie interessant gemacht haben, und eine Uebersetzung von Blackstones Commentaries on the Laws of England wohl eine ganze Anzahl englischer Romane, vielleicht auch einige der unzähligen Uebersetzungen und Ueberarbeitungen eines andern fremden Gesetzeswerks, womit wir seit einem Jahr überschwemmt werden, aufgewogen haben.)[17]

[13] W Blackstone, *Vermischte Abhandlungen über verschiedene Rechtsmaterien* (Bremen, 1779) [v] . For Christian Garve, Blackstone was 'der Ausleger' (the interpreter), and mostly also 'der Bewundrer' (the admirer) of English laws (W Paley, *M. Payley's Grundsätze der Moral und Politik, Aus dem Englischen übersezt. Mit einigen Anmerkungen und Zusätzen von C. Garve* (Frankfurt and Leipzig, 1788) vol 2, p 520. H-C Kraus, *Englische Verfassung und politisches Denken im Ancien Régime, 1689 bis 1789* (Munich, 2006) 542–631.

[14] *Cf* H Schlosser, 'Strafrecht und Strafrechtsreformen im Europa des ausgehenden 18. Jahrhunderts' in (2000) *5 Georg-Forster-Studien* 35–59; R Vierhaus, 'Das Allgemeine Landrecht für die Preußischen Staaten als Verfassungsersatz?' in *200 Jahre Allgemeines Landrecht für die preußischen Staaten. Wirkungsgeschichte und internationaler Kontext* ed B Dölemeyer and H Mohnhaupt (Frankfurt am Main, 1995) 1–21.

[15] *Cf* P Stein, 'England and Continental Legal Literature' in *Englische und kontinentale Rechtsgeschichte: ein Forschungsprojekt*, ed H Coing and KW Nörr (Berlin, 1985), 80; M Reimann, *Historische Schule und Common Law. Die deutsche Rechtswissenschaft des 19. Jahrhunderts im amerikanischen Rechtsdenken* (Berlin, 1993), esp 27–9.

[16] Cf. H-U Stühler, *Die Diskussion um die Erneuerung der Rechtswissenschaft von 1780–1815* (Berlin, 1978), in which Blackstone and the common law play no role.

[17] L von Vincke, *Darstellung der innern Verwaltung Großbritanniens* ed BG Niebuhr (Berlin, 1815) 5 (this book had been written in 1808). Cf also, Pöggeler (n 2) 39–42.

Juxtaposing Blackstone's *Commentaries* to the *Code Napoleon* may sound bizarre, but it reflected conflicting foreign influences in Germany at the beginning of the century, with Vincke unmistakably leaning toward the English side.

He was an admirer of British institutions, even if he definitely did not believe in copying constitutions. But the masterpiece he understood the British Constitution to be could provide invaluable insights, 'in the separation and mixing of powers and in the agreement of all for the common good' ('in der Sonderung und Mischung der Gewalten, und der Einigung aller zum gemeinen Besten'). These lessons would result in good laws of one's own making without having to adopt actual British institutions.[18] For these purposes, according to Vincke, reading Blackstone might be useful.

Vincke's appreciation of Blackstone was still echoed in the editions of the *Brockhaus* encyclopedia of the early 1820s. Blackstone continued to be 'the famous legal scholar', due to his *Commentaries*. 'For he did not restrict himself to collecting the laws, to ascending to their origin, and to explaining them clearly and firmly; he penetrates into the principles of legislation, into the spirit of the laws, and he analyses their effects and treats jurisprudence like a philosopher' ('die Gesetze zu sammeln, zu ihrem Ursprung hinaufzusteigen, und sie klar und bestimmt zu erklären; er dringt in die Principien der Gesetzgebung, in den Geist der Gesetze ein, er untersucht ihre Wirkungen, und behandelt die Rechtswissenschaft als Philosoph').[19]

In these years, however, a further reason for applauding Blackstone was already gaining ground. By the end of the decade, Carl von Rotteck would speak of the 'era of constitutions' into which Germany had entered.[20] It was a time that called not for general legal scholars, but for constitution makers and constitutionalists. Nikolaus Falck, law professor at the University of Kiel, readily acknowledged the merits of the 'großen englischen Rechtsgelehrten' ('great English legal scholar'). 'Blackstone's presentation of English law has received the unanimous approval of educated Europe, and maintains, unchallenged by later works, its honourable rank among Britain's classic writings' ('Blackstone's Darstellung des englischen Rechts hat sich die einstimmige Anerkennung des gebildeten Europa's erworben, und behauptet, von spätern Arbeiten nicht verdrängt, einen ehrenvollen

[18] Vincke (n 17) 6–8.

[19] 'Blackstone (William)' in *Allgemeine deutsche Real-Encyclopädie für die gebildeten Stände (Conversations-Lexicon)* 5th edn (Leipzig, 1820) vol 1, pp 795–6. Identical in 6th edn (1824) vol 1, pp 793–4, and with only one insignificant correction in 7th edn (1827) vol 1 , p 915.

[20] C von Rotteck, *Lehrbuch des Vernunftrechts und der Staatswissenschaften* (Stuttgart, 1829–35) vol 2, p 172.

Platz unter Brittaniens classischen Schriften').[21] Without hesitation Falck then moved from Blackstone to the current German situation

> The more recent movements in Germany, the striving for free constitutions in all states, the incessantly continuing investigations of the essence and meaning of those constitutions have in a particular degree directed the view towards England, which has long since enjoyed and continuously maintains a firmly rooted legal liberty.
>
> (Die neuern Bewegungen in Deutschland, das Streben nach freien Verfassungen in allen Staaten, die über das Wesen und die Bedeutung solcher Verfassungen ununterbrochen fortgehenden Untersuchungen haben in einem besondern Grade den Blick auf England, welches eine festgewurzelte gesetzliche Freiheit lange genossen hat und fortwährend behauptet, von neuem hingeleitet.)[22]

For Falck, as for a number of other German liberals, Blackstone thus took centre stage.

> Finally, Blackstone's arrangement deserves praise for his political genius or the manner in which he traces all legal determinations back to civil liberty and the character of the English constitution and tries to explain and elucidate legal norms with political perspectives.
>
> (Endlich ist in Blackstones Bearbeitung der politische Geist zu loben, oder die Art, wie er alle Rechtsbestimmungen auf bürgerliche Freiheit und auf das Wesen der englischen Verfassung bezieht, und die gesetzliche Normen durch politische Blicke zu erläutern und aufzuklären sucht.)[23]

Though Falck was not entirely uncritical of Blackstone, accusing him of not meeting the scholarly standards of the legal profession in Germany,[24] he placed Blackstone right in the centre of the liberal debate, which extended from the 1820s through the decades of the *Vormärz* to the March Revolution of 1848, on the British Constitution as a model for constitutional reform in Germany. Such renowned liberals as Friedrich Christoph Dahlmann or Friedrich Murhard, to name just two, referred to Blackstone approvingly whenever they dealt with details of the British Constitution,[25]

[21] W Blackstone, *Handbuch des Englischen Rechts, im Auszuge und mit Hinzufügung der neueren Gesetze und Entscheidungen von John Gifford* (Schleswig, 1822–23) vol 1, p iii (from Falck's preface). *Cf* also KW Nörr, 'The European Side of the English Law: A Few Comments from a Continental Historian' in Coing and Nörr (eds) (n 15) 25.

[22] Blackstone (n 21) vol 1, pp iv–v.

[23] *Ibid*, p lii.

[24] *Ibid*, pp lii–liii.

[25] *Cf* FC Dahlmann, *Die Politik auf den Grund und das Maß der gegebenen Zustände zurückgeführt*, ed O Westphal (Berlin, 1924) 119; F Murhard, 'Englands Staatsverfassung' in *Das Staats-Lexikon. Encyklopädie der sämmtlichen Staatswissenschaften für alle Stände*, ed C von Rotteck and C Welcker, 2nd edn (Altona, 1845–48) vol 4, pp 360, 386, 390, 402, 403. For the background and with further details, T Wilhelm, *Die Englische Verfassung und der vormärzliche deutsche Liberalismus. Eine Darstellung und Kritik des Verfassungsbildes der liberalen Führer* (Stuttgart, 1928) esp 15–21.

whereas Johann Christoph von Aretin felt obliged to praise his 'vortrefflicher Kommentar' ('superb commentary'),[26] but was basically too ignorant of its contents to make further use of it.[27]

A decade later, the first edition of the *Staats-Lexikon* (1834–43), the 'bible' of German *Vormärz* liberalism,[28] contained a whole article on Blackstone, written by Johannes Weitzel. He presented the *Commentaries* as a monument:

> The author demonstrates in it so profound a knowledge of the public and private law and its historical shape and evolution and judges so impartially and correctly its purpose and merit in its various stipulations that it is still considered as classic and indispensable for all who deal with the subject and want to be profoundly instructed.
>
> (Der Verfasser zeigt in demselben eine so gründliche Kenntniß des öffentlichen und Privatrechts und seiner geschichtlichen Gestaltung und Entwicklung, und ein so unbefangenes, richtiges Urtheil über dessen Zweck und Werth in seinen einzelnen Bestimmungen, daß es auch jetzt noch für classisch gilt und Allen, die sich mit diesem Gegenstand beschäftigen und in demselben gründlich unterrichten wollen, unentbehrlich ist.)

Weitzel concluded with two statements of particular interest in the present context:

> He is hardly less known abroad than in England as, due to the general striving for improvements and reforms, in recent times the Constitution and laws of this state have become an object of research and review of all legal writers and scholars.
>
> (Das Ausland kennt ihn kaum weniger als England selbst, da in der neuern Zeit die Verfassung und die Gesetze dieses Staates, bei dem allgemeinen Streben nach Verbesserungen und Reformen, ein Gegenstand der Forschung und Beurtheilung aller Publicisten und Rechtsgelehrten geworden ist.)[29]

Weitzel not only confirms our reading of Dahlmann, Murhard and others who had referred to Blackstone as a household name, so familiar to

[26] JC von Aretin, *Staatsrecht der konstitutionellen Monarchie. Ein Handbuch für Geschäftsmänner, studirende Jünglinge, und gebildete Bürger* (Altenburg, 1824–28) vol 1, p 52.

[27] 'Blackstone's superb commentary on the English laws became known abroad only much later. For us Germans a constitutional extract of this work would be a welcome gift.' ('Blackstone's vortrefflicher Kommentar über die englischen Gesetze wurde im Auslande erst viel später bekannt. Für uns Deutsche wäre ein staatsrechtlicher Auszug aus diesem Werk ein willkommenes Geschenk.'): *ibid*. The Munich-based Aretin was obviously less well informed about Blackstone than his colleagues further north had been for almost half a century and was, evidently, unaware of the recent Schleswig edition.

[28] Cf H Brandt, 'Das Rotteck-Welckersche Staats-Lexikon. Einleitung zum Neudruck' in Rotteck and Welcker (ed) (n 25) vol 1, p 20, and generally 5–62 (with list of contributors, both parts with separate pagination from the facsimile reprint).

[29] J Weitzel 'Blackstone (William)' in Rotteck and Welcker (ed) (n 25) vol 2 , p 540.

their readers that no specific introduction was needed. He also presented Blackstone as the very personification of the English political system. Blackstone's rise to high judicial rank and status—exemplary for a German bourgeoisie demanding equal access to political offices—demonstrated in his view the secret of the system: 'that it integrates the most influential elements, which might become dangerous if among its enemies, for its own preservation' ('daß sie sich der einflußreichsten Elemente, die in der Reihe ihrer Feinde ihr verderblich werden könnten, zu ihrer Erhaltung bemächtigt').[30]

Weitzel's article marked the zenith of Blackstone's appreciation in Germany, presenting him as the embodiment and interpreter of the British Constitution so highly esteemed by German liberals on the eve of the revolution of 1848. In fact, the high estimation in which he was held seems rather odd for an author reputedly a staunch conservative, whose conception of the British Constitution was even more outdated in 1848 than it had already been in 1765.

German liberals and the Tory Blackstone made seemingly strange bedfellows indeed; but no German conservatives lined up with Blackstone. While vocally rejecting the British Constitution they preferred to ignore Blackstone altogether.[31] A distinctively ambiguous assessment of Blackstone's thought came, however, from a rather unexpected quarter. The eighth edition of the standard *Brockhaus* encyclopedia of 1833, included the following evaluation of Blackstone and his *Commentaries*:

> In his [Blackstone's] work he did not restrict himself to a mere explanation of the laws but tried to solve the task of their profound interpretation, and his achievement was all the more commendable as he had no predecessors; and not only did he only supply a philosophical discussion of the principles of English civil and public law, but also a clear portrayal and defence of the existing system; and apart from some liberal statements, he was on the whole a keen advocate of the prerogatives of the Crown and not liberal in his opinions about religious toleration.
>
> (Er begnügte sich in diesem Werke nicht mit einer bloßen Erklärung der Gesetze, sondern suchte die Aufgabe einer gründlichen Auslegung derselben zu lösen, und seine Leistung war um so verdienstlicher, da er keine Vorgänger hatte; doch lieferte er nicht sowol eine philosophische Erörterung der Grundsätze des engl. Civil- und Staatsrechts, als eine klare Darstellung und Vertheidigung des bestehenden Systems; und einzelne freisinnige Behauptungen abgerechnet, ist er im

[30] *Ibid*.

[31] *Cf* JG Beschorner, *Prüfung der englischen Staatsverfassung und Vergleichung derselben mit der deutschen* (Leipzig, 1821), vol 2, p 35, vol 3, pt 2, p 101. Beschorner obviously knew Blackstone but he never crossed swords with him directly and excluded him from his list of authorities: *ibid* vol 1, pp xiv–xx.

Ganzen ein eifriger Verfechter der Vorrechte der Krone und nicht liberal in seinen Ansichten über religiöse Duldung.)[32]

So, at last, one is inclined to say, we can recognise the influence of Bentham's criticism of Blackstone first developed in *A Fragment on Government* (1776), reprinted in 1823 and then again in 1838, in volume one of the collected *Works* of Jeremy Bentham. Bentham had meticulously documented the static character of Blackstone's approach, which took for granted the common law and the existing political institutions with all their inconsistencies and fallacies and viewed them as an expression of reason, where Bentham only saw the need for radical reform.[33] Why this criticism did not reach the *Brockhaus* before 1833, more than half a century after it had appeared in England, remains a mystery, as does the name of the author of this article.

Bentham's critique of Blackstone never seems to have become popular in Germany. That Blackstone's reputation was declining in the second half of the nineteenth century from the lofty heights achieved during the *Vormärz* had less to do with Bentham than with the failure of the revolutions of 1848 and the diminishing importance of the British Constitution as a model or inspiration for Germany. As early as the 1850s, substantial criticism of Blackstone was voiced by a number of authors.

Particularly damaging to his reputation were the verdicts of leading German legal and constitutional scholars. Robert von Mohl in his highly influential *Geschichte und Literatur der Staatswissenschaften* fired three broadsides at Blackstone. According to Mohl, great damage was caused by Blackstone's division of the common law into four parts, as the whole field of public law thus became part of Blackstone's 'Rights of Persons'—a sheer horror for a Roman lawyer. This could only result in an incomplete, deficient and erroneous presentation of the British institutions. Secondly, he lacked systematic scholarly training. Finally 'he adheres to the above described doctrine of Montesquieu. Even while admitting that it is not as dominant here, it does constitute his fundamental philosophy which has a great impact on his factual presentation.' ('hängt er der oben bezeichneten Lehre von Montesquieu an. Muss auch zugegeben werden, dass sie bei ihm der Form nach weniger hervortritt, so ist sie doch seine Grundanschauung,

[32] 'Blackstone (William)' in *Allgemeine deutsche Real-Encyclopädie für die gebildeten Stände (Conversations-Lexicon)*, 8th edn (Leipzig, 1833) vol 1, p 919; with only a few minor corrections again in 9th to 12th edns (1843–75). The 12th edition also contained a more neutral evaluation of Blackstone, which was to continue through the decades of the German Empire and the Weimar Republic..

[33] *Cf* J Bentham, *A Comment on the Commentaries and A Fragment on Government*, ed JH Burns and HLA Hart, *The Collected Works of Jeremy Bentham* (London, 1977).

welche auf die sachliche Darstellung grossen Einfluss hat.')[34] For Montesquieu's thesis of a separation of powers in England was mistaken, as Mohl had already demonstrated.[35]

Blackstone's indebtedness to Montesquieu had already been discussed in the review of the *Leipziger Gelehrte Zeitungen* of 1774, though it judged that claim to be exaggerated.[36] In the first half of the nineteenth century, with liberals tending to accept Montesquieu's doctrine, the issue had no impact on their appreciation of Blackstone. After 1850, however, things had changed, and whereas liberals such as Mohl would go no further than to argue that Montesquieu was in error as far as England was concerned, conservatives totally rejected any idea of a separation of powers.

Heinrich von Marquardsen, another legal authority in the second half of the nineteenth century readily acknowledged Blackstone's fame for 'having provided for the first time in a modern language an instructive legal reference work available for all educated persons' ('zum ersten Mal in einer modernen Sprache eine lehrreiches, allen Gebildeten zugängliches Handbuch des Rechts geliefert zu haben'.). He thoroughly denounced Blackstone, however, for having taken up Montesquieu's ideas and thus misleading foreign readers about the British Constitution:

> Only for non-Englishmen seeking to acquaint themselves with the public law of England, Blackstone has always been a dangerous heretic, as, apart from the errors in his fundamental philosophy adopted from Montesquieu, he only describes the letter of the constitution, rather than the animated workings of the national spirit.
>
> (Nur für den Nichtengländer, der das Staatsrecht von England kennen lernen wollte, ist Blackstone stets ein gefährlicher Irrlehrer gewesen, weil er abgesehen von den Irrthümern der Grundanschauung, die er von Montesquieu hat, nur den Buchstaben der Verfassung und nicht das lebendige Walten des Nationalgeistes darin schilderte.)[37]

A third major authority in the field was Rudolph von Gneist. In the first volume of his *Das heutige englische Verfassungs- und Verwaltungsrecht*, published in 1857, he made entirely clear that, in his view, Montesquieu knew nothing about English constitutional history and that French constitutional ideas were generally worthless. Though restrained in his verdict on Blackstone, the negative tendency of his argument was evident: 'due to the

[34] R von Mohl, *Die Geschichte und Literatur der Staatswissenschaften. In Monographien dargestellt* (Erlangen, 1856) vol 2, p 42.

[35] *Ibid* 38–9.

[36] Neue *Zeitungen von Gelehrten Sachen Auf das Jahr 1774* (Leipzig, 26 December 1774) 837.

[37] H von Marquardsen, 'Blackstone' in *Deutsches Staats-Wörterbuch*, ed JC Bluntschli and K Brater (Stuttgart und Leipzig, 1857) vol 2, p 160.

interpolation of Blackstone's *Commentaries* no modern English constitutional law can come into being. Where the complete correlation with the past is missing, it will also be missing for the future' ('weil durch die Interpolation von Blackstone's Commentaries kein heutiges englisches Staatsrecht entstehen kann. Wo die vollständigen Zusammenhänge mit der Vergangenheit fehlen, fehlen sie auch für die Zukunft.')[38]

The reply to Gneist's attack on Blackstone came instantly and in one of those rare articles of the third edition of the *Staats-Lexikon* still breathing the revolutionary spirit of *Vormärz* liberalism, which had generally faded from the new edition.[39] Remarkably enough, Karl Welcker, the surviving editor of the third edition, not only reprinted Weitzel's original article on Blackstone but had considerably enlarged it under his own name, without either toning down Weitzel's eulogy or distancing himself from it. Though he acknowledged Blackstone's conservatism, he added:

> His thought could be censured by some modern German scholars under the malign influence of that most recent philosophical tendency which—before the complete refutation of its bankrupt system—was known as the natural philosophy of Hegel. Now as this intoxication must evaporate, they will gradually get acquainted again with the practical views of all free peoples.

> (Tadel konnte es nur finden bei einzelnen modernen deutschen Gelehrten, welche verleitet wurden durch die neueste Schulphilosophie, die bis zum bereits erfolgten Umsturz aller Grundlagen ihres bankbrüchigen Systems die naturphilosophische Hegel'sche war. Nun, wo dieser Rausch verfliegen muß, werden auch sie sich allmälig wieder mit der praktischen Ansicht aller freien Völker befreunden.)[40]

In addition to this broadside against Hegel and his disciples, Welcker targeted a second one directly at Gneist:

> Rather one might reproach Blackstone for insufficiently emphasizing and exemplifying the living free development of civil society in the liberal form of public consensus, which is the living renewal of contract and identical with a living free constitution. This is what he experienced and practiced on a daily basis as an Englishman and which was evident and self-explanatory to his countrymen. That is why his work cannot adequately explain the English constitution to a non-British person, as little as can the work of any other Englishman, or any other book in the world.'

> (Eher könnte man B. verwerfen, daß er die lebendige freie Fortentwicklung der staatsgesellschaftlichen Verhältnisse in der Freiheitsform des öffentlichen Consenses, welche eben die stets lebendige Vertragserneuerung begründet und mit

[38] R Gneist, *Das heutige englische Verfassungs- und Verwaltungsrecht* (Berlin, 1857) vol 1, pp iii, 258, 704, 720.

[39] On the transition towards the third edition, *cf* Brandt (n 28) p 25.

[40] J Weitzel and K Welcker, 'Blackstone (William)' in *Das Staats-Lexikon. Encyklopädie der sämmtlichen Staatswissenschaften für alle Stände* ed K Welcker (Leipzig, 1858) vol 2, p 748.

der lebendigen freien Verfassung zusammenfällt, oftmals zu wenig hervorhebt und veranschaulicht, weil er das, was er als Engländer täglich miterlebte und mitbetrieb, als sich von selbst verstehend und Allen bekannt voraussetzte. Deshalb kann auch sein Werk nicht genügen, einem Nichtbriten eine befriedigende Erkenntniß von der englischen Verfassung zu geben, ebenso wenig als das Werk irgendeines andern Engländers, ebenso wenig als irgendein Buch in der Welt.)

—written by Gneist, one is tempted to add.[41]

Welcker was fighting an honourable but lost cause. The epoch belonged to Gneist, and his interpretation of British constitutional law and development. Gneist's attitude towards Blackstone remained ambiguous throughout his life. On the one hand, he felt bound to pay tribute to Blackstone's *Commentaries* as 'the world-famous work' ('die weltberühmte Schrift').[42] On the other hand, he let it be known that it lacked deep insight into the historical origins of the English Constitution and, referring approvingly to Mohl's view that Blackstone was excessively committed to Montesquieu and his mistaken idea of a separation of powers and lacked 'a clear insight into the manner of the origin and connection (of parliamentary evolution) with society' ('eine klare Einsicht in die Weise der Entstehung und in den Zusammenhang mit der Gesellschaft').[43] What matters even more than these scattered statements is the fact that Gneist did not give the impression that the *Commentaries* deserved any major attention, as the British Constitution due to its development over recent decades had lost its importance for Germany. While Gneist does not refer to him directly, one is reminded of Friedrich Julius von Stahl and his rejection of the British parliamentary system, as he called it. Having fallen victim to selfish political parties it represented the exact opposite of the German monarchical system, where government was headed by a wise monarch ruling for the benefit of the whole.[44]

At the turn of the century, Josef Redlich brilliantly analysed Blackstone's role and impact, while at the same time heavily criticising Gneist for having been blind to the evolution of the British Constitution and administration

[41] *Ibid* 749.

[42] R von Gneist, *Englische Verfassungsgeschichte* (Berlin, 1882) 629, 704; *Das Englische Parlament in tausendjährigen Wandlungen vom 9. bis zum Ende des 19. Jahrhunderts* (Berlin, 1886) 341.

[43] R von Gneist, *Die heutige englische Communalverfassung und Communalverwaltung oder das System des Selfgovernment in seiner heutigen Gestalt* (Berlin, 1860), 918. *Cf* Gneist, *Verfassung geschichte* (n 42) 629, 704, 711 Gneist, *Parlament* (n 42) 341.

[44] *Cf* FJ Stahl, *Das Monarchische Princip. Eine staatsrechtlich-politische Abhandlung* (Heidelberg, 1845), 2, 36, and passim; also Gneist, *Die heutige englische Communalverfassung* (n 43) 920–64.

under the impact of nineteenth-century reform ideas nourished by liberalism, democracy and socialism.[45] In Redlich's view the *Commentaries* had become the 'Katechismus des englischen Rechts' ('catechism of English law)',[46] a role they were easily able to assume thanks to Blackstone's luminous style and their great utility in the controversies of the 1760s and 1770s as argumentative ammunition not only for the Whigs but indeed for all sides. Blackstone's presentation of King in Parliament took up Montesquieu and gave credence to his interpretation bolstering it with sophisticated legal argument. Redlich concluded that, through sanctifying Montesquieu's errors, Blackstone proved the singular excellence of the British Constitution while at the same time obscuring its actual mechanisms, of which he himself was ignorant.

> In this way England's academic Gaius became the author of that myth of the English constitution which, founded on the theory of Montesquieu, became the productive source of that continental liberalism of the nineteenth century which firmly believed it understood and was reproducing the English institutions, thus securing true liberty, as long as it could call on Blackstone and Montesquieu as witnesses for the accuracy of its principles.
>
> (Auf solche Weise ist der akademische Gaius Englands zum Urheber jener Legende von der englischen Verfassung geworden, die, auf dem Unterbau der Montesquieuschen Theorie beruhend, zur produktiven Quelle jenes festländischen Liberalimus des XIX. Jahrhunderts geworden ist, der fest daran glaubte, die englischen Institutionen zu verstehen, nachzubilden und durch sie die wahre Freiheit zu sichern, wenn er Blackstone und Montesquieu als Zeugen anrufen konnte für die Richtigkeit seiner Grundsätze.)[47]

With this prevailing liberal misunderstanding having lost its magic in the second half of the nineteenth century, Blackstone's impact diminished, though he remained relevant for different reasons. Blackstone continued to be regarded as 'der grosse Commentator des englischen Rechtes' ('the great commentator of English law'), as Eduard Fischel described him.[48] Throughout the decades of the German Empire and the Weimar Republic, the *Brockhaus* encyclopedia classified the *Commentaries* as an ideologically neutral reference work, 'which still are considered as authoritative in all constitutional questions and were distributed in numerous editions' ('welche noch jetzt als Autorität in allen constitutionellen Fragen gelten und in zahlreichen Ausgaben verbreitet worden sind').[49]

[45] J Redlich, *Englische Lokalverwaltung. Darstellung der inneren Verwaltung Englands in ihrer geschichtlichen Entwicklung und in ihrer gegenwärtigen Gestalt* (Leipzig, 1901) xvi–xvii.

[46] *Ibid* 89.

[47] *Ibid* 90–1.

[48] E Fischel, *Die Verfassung Englands* (Berlin, 1862) 277.

[49] 'Blackstone' in *Brockhaus Konversations-Lexikon*, 12th edn (Leipzig, 1875) vol 3, p 486; with minor purely stylistic variations again in 13th edn (1882), 14th edn (1896) and

The preceding 150 years had demonstrated that Blackstone could serve many purposes in Germany, from providing an introduction to English law, to proving the excellence of the British Constitution, to finally serving as a mere reference work in random questions of law.[50] Throughout this time, he had been considered more of an authority on law than a major figure within British legal discourse. As Heinrich Brunner concluded: 'Yet one may boldly claim that no modern law can boast such a well-rounded and comprehensive presentation as the English with Blackstone. Abroad he is virtually the representative of English jurisprudence.' ('Dennoch kann man dreist behaupten, daß keines der modernen Rechte eine derartig abgerundete Gesamtdarstellung aufzuweisen hat, wie sie das englische in Blackstone besitzt. Für das Ausland ist dieser geradezu Repräsentant der englischen Jurisprudenz geworden.')[51]

Due to this perception, Blackstone's English critics and opponents were hardly noticed and the evolution of the British Constitution was largely ignored, as were the nineteenth-century authors writing about it. Bagehot's *The English Constitution* was first published as a book in a German translation as late as 1971.[52] Dicey's *Introduction to the Study of the Law of the Constitution* fared even worse, for a German translation did not appear before 2001. Julius Hatschek, who in 1905–6 published two thick volumes on *Das Englische Staatsrecht* [*English Constitutional Law*] was ignorant of Dicey, despite the six editions already published up to that time in England, even though Hatschek was very critical of Blackstone and devoted much space to Bentham, Austin, Maine and other of his critics.[53]

A few years later, Hatschek was less polemical about Blackstone. In his constitutional history of England he all but ignored him, except when dealing with the role of the monarch in the later eighteenth century.[54] He concluded that Blackstone, having wrong-headedly adopted Montesquieu,

15th edn (1929). On the German image of England in these decades, *cf* generally WJ Mommsen, 'Zur Entwicklung des Englandbildes der Deutschen seit dem Ende des 18. Jahrhunderts' in *Studien zur Geschichte Englands und der deutsch-britischen Beziehungen. Festschrift für Paul Kluke*, ed L Kettenacker et al (Munich, 1981) esp 379–91.

[50] *Cf* O Koellreutter, *Verwaltungsrecht und Verwaltungsrechtssprechung im modernen England. Eine rechtsvergleichende Studie* (Tübingen, 1912) 12–13, 14, 21; G Jellinek, *Allgemeine Staatslehre* 3rd edn (Berlin, 1922) 167, 211, 308, 359, 372, 384, 413–14, 463, 465–6, 498, 563–4, 574, 576, 593, 703.

[51] H Brunner, *Geschichte der englischen Rechtsquellen im Grundriss. Mit einem Anhang über die normannischen Rechtsquellen* (Leipzig, 1909) 58.

[52] *Cf* however, Pöggeler (n 2) 91–4.

[53] J Hatschek, *Englisches Staatsrecht mit Berücksichtigung der für Schottland und Irland geltenden Sonderheiten* (Tübingen, 1905–06) vol 1, pp 18–19, 28–35.

[54] This had already been done by G Kaufmann, 'Die englische Verfassung in Deutschland' in *Hansische Geschichtsblätter* 28 (1900) 3–22, who had referred to Montesquieu and Burke, among others, and particularly to de Lolme, while never mentioning Blackstone, only to conclude with a Gneistian perspective.

was ignorant and mistaken about the developments of his own time and thus obsolete from the perspective of the early twentieth century.[55]

It was a harsh verdict by the rather dogmatic Hatschek, and it reflected the decline of Blackstone's reputation during the preceding decades. Hatschek's own view failed to evaluate accurately legal and constitutional discourse in contemporary Britain, just then emerging from a deep constitutional crisis, it also further obfuscated the view of Britain from Germany, which had already struggled to gain a real understanding of the changing British Constitution since 1832, in spite of, or, more properly perhaps, because of Gneist.

Far from actually becoming obsolete, Blackstone resurfaced time and again in twentieth-century Germany. Even in 1938 a book could be published about *Die Systematik des Privatrechts in Blackstone's 'Commentaries on the Laws of England'. Ein Beitrag zur Geschichte des Rechtssystems [The system of private law in Blackstone's* Commentaries on the Laws of England. *A contribution to the history of the legal system].*[56] Immediately after the Second World War, Gustav Radbruch remembered Blackstone and his ideas about the relationship between law and reason, rejected by Bentham.[57] A few years later, a doctoral dissertation was written in Göttingen on Blackstone's natural law ideas.[58] Towards the end of the century, the Blackstone renaissance sparked by the University of Chicago Press facsimile reprint of the first edition of the *Commentaries* reached Germany, together with a new level of cooperation between different legal systems as a result of the European unification process. In this context. Hans-Christof Kraus's *Habilitationsschrift* on the *Englische Verfassung*, largely focusing on Blackstone,[59] may only mark the beginning of what could become a more intensified debate in the future.

[55] J Hatschek, *Englische Verfassungsgeschichte bis zum Regierungsantritt der Königin Victoria* (Munich and Berlin, 1913), 604–21. Among others, in F Tönnies, *Der englische Staat und der deutsche Staat. Eine Studie* (Berlin, 1917) there is no mention at all of Blackstone.

[56] R Benser, *Die Systematik des Privatrechts in Blackstone's 'Commentaries on the Laws of England'*, ed K Michaelis, *Abhandlungen aus dem Kieler Seminar für deutsches Gemeinrecht*, no 3 (Heide in Holstein, 1938). *Cf* also H W Goldschmidt, *English Law from the Foreign Standpoint* (London, 1937), 8–9.

[57] *Cf* G Radbruch, *Der Geist des englischen Rechts* (Göttingen, 1958) 44–6 (the first edition had appeared in 1946).

[58] H-J Rinck, 'Das Naturrecht bei Blackstone' MS LLD diss. University of Göttingen, 1952. An extended resumé appeared in (1959) 2 *Ratio* 50–66.

[59] Kraus (n 13) esp 178–85. *Cf.* also his 'Montesquieu, Blackstone, De Lolme und die englische Verfassung des 18. Jahrhunderts' (1995) 1 *Jahrbuch des Historischen Kolleg*, 113–53.

IV Sources

THE TWO FOLLOWING (and final) chapters both address topics of some importance for students of Blackstone. His prolific output as an author, and the subsequent multiplication of editions, translations and other versions of his writings, constitute a considerable challenge for bibliographers and other scholars. Morris Cohen here recounts the history of previous attempts to capture Blackstone, bibliographically speaking, and outlines the resources, available now or anticipated in the near future, which identify, describe and reproduce his published and unpublished works.

Besides their intrinsic aesthetic and biographical interest, portraits, engravings, statuary and other iconographic representations can help us better appreciate how Blackstone has been visualised, not only by artists, but also by their patrons and viewers, over the past two and a half centuries. In his contribution Sir John Baker considers the surviving likenesses of Blackstone executed during the subject's lifetime, and documents the remarkable proliferation of engravings and other works on paper derived from these portraits before and after 1780. The editor then describes how some prominent memorial representations of Blackstone by sculptors and stained-glass artists have come to occupy their present sites in England, the USA and Australia.

14

Bibliography

MORRIS COHEN

IN PREPARING THIS chapter I considered the criteria which determine whether the work of a particular author merits serious bibliographic treatment. The volume of that author's work; the variety and complexity of his or her total output; and the importance of that work in its subject field seem like reasonable standards. Judging by all of these criteria, it is hard to imagine a legal figure whose works are more deserving of bibliographic coverage than William Blackstone. Blackstone's varied career, his extensive body of publications, and his contribution to legal thinking fully justify a published bibliography. The frequent reprinting of his *Commentaries*, both in England and America, their translation into several foreign languages, and the many works based on Blackstone's *Commentaries*, make such a project a challenging undertaking.

Fortunately, we have already been blessed with a good Blackstone bibliography—that prepared by Catherine Spicer Eller and published by the Yale Law Library in 1938.[1] The original core of the Blackstone collection in the Yale Law School Library was donated in 1907 by Magrane Coxe, a Yale College graduate, and has been added to over the years. In fact it is still being augmented—during every one of the twenty-seven years that I've been at Yale, additions have been made to those holdings. The collection, as it was constituted approximately fifteen years ago, is also available on microfiche from the Law Library Microform Consortium. In due course, the fiche collection will undoubtedly be digitized as part of LLMC's programme to convert all of their fiche collections to an electronic format. Later in this chapter, I shall describe those online sources which *are* now available for full-text electronic searching of Blackstone's published works.

I should mention that, while Eller's bibliography went out of print some years ago, it was reprinted without change in 1993 by the Lawbook

[1] CS Eller, *The William Blackstone Collection in the Yale Law Library: A Bibliographical Catalogue* (New Haven CT, 1938).

Exchange Ltd, an American reprint publisher and antiquarian lawbook dealer. Despite continuing additions, Yale's holdings are not a complete collection of Blackstone imprints, so Eller is not a definitive bibliography of Blackstone's published works. A revision and expansion of Eller's bibliography is now in preparation by Ann Laeuchli, formerly Deputy Librarian of the Yale Law Library; I will describe that project below.

Any discussion of Blackstone bibliography must begin with his life and work, leading us inevitably to the available biographies. David A Lockmiller, an American legal historian, published a biography, *Sir William Blackstone*, in 1938,[2] which is now out of date and not really adequate by modern scholarly standards. Lewis C Warden's *The Life of Blackstone* (also published in 1938)[3] is even more disappointing. Blackstone's brother-in-law and executor, James Clitherow, wrote a biographical sketch which appeared in the Preface to Blackstone's *Reports*.[4] A contemporary work, published anonymously, is *The Biographical History of William Blackstone, late one of the Justices of Both Benches . . . And a Catalogue of all Sir William Blackstone's Works, Manuscript, as Well as Printed*.[5] Neither the biographical history nor the catalogue are of much use to the modern scholar.

For a more recent and much more useful outline of Blackstone's life and publications one could well peruse Ian Doolittle's *William Blackstone, a Biography*,[6] which has a remarkably good bibliography for so brief a study. The Blackstone entries in the *Dictionary of National Biography* and the *Oxford Dictionary of National Biography* offer useful but even shorter biographies and surveys of the publications. Finally, we note the recent publication of Wilfrid Prest's *William Blackstone: Law and Letters in the Eighteenth Century*,[7] which discusses the publication history of Blackstone's legal and non-legal writings. Professor Prest also includes an extensive bibliography.

We can begin our study of Blackstone bibliography with Catherine Eller's catalogue of the Yale Law Library collection. Eller's work is divided into nine sections, which itself indicates the thoroughness and complexity of her project:

[2] DA Lockmiller, *Sir William Blackstone* (Chapel Hill NC, 1938).

[3] LC Warden, *The Life of Blackstone* (Charlottesville VA, 1938).

[4] *Reports* reprinted Dublin, 1781, 1789 and 1828: Eller 225–8. Clitherow's Preface was also reprinted separately, probably in Dublin, in 1789 (see Eller 227a).

[5] *The Biographical History of William Blackstone, late one of the Justices of Both Benches* (London, 1782). Eller 252 attributes it to one 'D. Douglas', but also notes another attribution to 'Sylvester Douglas, afterwards Lord Glenbervie'. Lockmiller ((n 2) 285) attributes the work to 'D Douglas'; and I Doolittle, *William Blackstone, a Biography* (Haslemere, Surrey, UK, 2001) 110 fn 139 to 'W. Douglas'.

[6] Doolittle, *Blackstone* (n 5).

[7] Prest, *Blackstone*.

The Commentaries: English and Irish Editions
The Commentaries: English Abridgments and Extracts
The Commentaries: American Editions
The Commentaries: American Abridgments and Extracts
The Commentaries: Foreign Editions, Abridgments, and Extracts
The Commentaries: The Comic Blackstone
Works Founded on the Commentaries
Blackstone's Miscellaneous Works
Blackstone's Biography and Criticism

Her individual entries include title page transcription (without line breaks), a simple collation, indication of folded tables or other unusual physical features, and dimensions in centimetres. She provides a brief description of each listed work, its sources, and its relation to other listed editions. Eller's descriptions are based on her own physical examination of the actual volumes. In a few instances where she has not seen a volume but knew of its existence, she notes it, but without a full entry. Her work is carefully done and, although undoubtedly supervised by the Yale Law Librarian, Frederick C Hicks, constitutes an amazing achievement for a single individual simultaneously working at a full-time job. The little we know about Catherine Eller comes from her obituary published in 1974 on her death at the age of seventy-one, in Norwalk, Connecticut.[8] According to that obituary, Ms Eller graduated from the University of Oklahoma, was a member of Phi Beta Kappa, and received a master's degree from Columbia University. She retired from the Yale Law Library in 1964, after having served for over thirty years under Hicks and his successor as Library Director, the distinguished legal historian Samuel E Thorne.

Eller's introduction to her *Catalogue* shows a sense of humour, considerable knowledge of bibliographic traditions, and a good background in English literature. What was the state of historical legal bibliography at the time Eller was preparing her Blackstone work and what influences might have helped shape her project? In 1847, James G Marvin, a lawyer, published his annotated bibliography of English, Irish, Scottish and American law books which included several pages on Blackstone. As he often did, Marvin included critical comments on the listed works by other authors and reviewers. These are often lively and even irreverent on occasion. Examples include the following comments on Blackstone's *Commentaries*: 'A good gentlemen's book, clear but not deep'; 'Blackstone is a feeble reasoner and a confused thinker' and 'Blackstone's opinions on the criminal law . . . are to be regarded as an offspring of eager rather than a

[8] *New Canaan Advertiser* (New Canaan CT, 22 August 1974).

well informed mind.'[9] While undoubtedly familiar with Marvin's bibliography, Eller does not seem to have been influenced by its unbuttoned brashness.

Eller notes a few earlier attempts at Blackstone bibliography. William G Hammond, one of the late nineteenth-century American editors of the *Commentaries*, included a bibliography of the early editions of the *Commentaries* in volume one of his 1890 edition.[10] Charles Soule, the Boston bookseller and bibliographer, contributed a Blackstone bibliography to the periodical, *Legal Bibliography*.[11] But neither of these are comparable in scope or detail to Eller's work.

Although not a bibliography, it does seem appropriate to note here *Bibliotheca Blackstoneiana*, a catalogue of an 1845 sale of books and personal effects from the libraries of William Blackstone and his son James who also became Vinerian professor at Oxford, arranged by his grandson, WS Blackstone.[12] An earlier sale in 1803 had joined 'the Reserved Part of the Library of the Late Justice Blackstone' with the law books of one Philip Stanhope.[13]

In 1921, before becoming Law Librarian at Yale, Frederick Hicks had published *Men and Books Famous in the Law*, which devotes a long chapter to Blackstone.[14] A few years later Percy Winfield published his *Chief Sources of English Legal History*. This work of reference, based on lectures delivered at the Harvard Law School, gave extensive bibliographic attention to Blackstone's writings.[15] In 1926, Joseph Beale of the Harvard Law School published his *Bibliography of Early English Law Books*,[16] which, although not reaching Blackstone, helped shape historical English legal bibliography. Eller was undoubtedly acquainted with each of these books. An example of a contemporary single-author bibliography which also might have influenced her was Thomas Holmes's magnificent work on Increase Mather, published in 1930.[17] That two-volume bibliography was followed by the same author's three-volume bibliography of Cotton Mather[18] and his single volume, *The Minor Mathers*, both in 1940.[19]

[9] JG Marvin, *Legal Bibliography, or a Thesaurus of American, English, Irish, and Scotch Law Books* (Philadelphia PA, 1847; reprinted Buffalo NY, 1953) 122–8.

[10] W Blackstone, *Commentaries*, ed WG Hammond (San Francisco CA, 1890): Eller 130.

[11] C Soule (1903) ns 1 *Legal Bibliography* 8–9.

[12] *Bibliotheca Blackstoneiana: a Catalogue of a Library of 4500 Volumes . . . Which Will Be Sold at Auction* (London, 1845).

[13] *A Catalogue of the Law Library of Philip Stanhope . . . To which is added the Reserved Part of the Library of the Late Justice Blackstone. . . Leigh, Sotheby & Son* (London, 1803).

[14] F Hicks, *Men and Books Famous in Law* (Rochester NY, 1921). See ch 5, 'Blackstone and His *Commentaries*'.

[15] P Winfield, *Chief Sources of English Legal History* (Cambridge MA, 1925).

[16] J Beale, *Bibliography of Early English Law Books* (Cambridge MA, 1926).

[17] T Holmes, *Increase Mather, a Bibliography of His Works* (Cleveland OH, 1931).

[18] T Holmes, *Cotton Mather, a Bibliography of his Works* (Cambridge MA, 1940) .

[19] T Holmes, *The Minor Mathers, a List of Their Works* (Cambridge MA, 1940).

What can we say about the variety of Blackstone publications covered by Eller? There are, of course, the many editions of his *Commentaries*, including the pirated Irish editions, four French editions, the German, Italian, and more than sixty American editions. The first American edition, printed by Robert Bell in Philadelphia in 1771–72, has been researched by Whitney Bagnall, formerly of the Columbia University Law School Library. The publication of that edition on a subscription basis will be treated in detail in a study now in preparation by Michael Hoeflich of the University of Kansas.

There are many Blackstone publications besides the *Commentaries*: political pamphlets and tracts; briefs; poems; versions of the *Commentaries* designed for teaching purposes, and as schoolbooks and even catechisms for children. There were the inevitable spoofs of Blackstone, the most popular being the *Comic Blackstone* which appeared in at least fourteen editions in England and America.[20]

As already noted, Catherine Eller was unable fully to describe a number of Blackstone publications which were not at that time in the Yale collection. For that reason, and since standards of bibliographic description have changed since her work, Ann Laeuchli, formerly of the Yale Law School Library, has undertaken an expansion and revision of Eller's work. Eller, at the end of her Introduction, stated that information about other editions, other Blackstone items, and any corrections to her entries, would be gratefully received. She had no idea of the amount of material which remained unrecorded. While Eller listed 266 entries, Laeuchli has so far identified and will be listing over 500 items.

Laeuchli will also be adding a tenth section to the bibliography, listing published catalogues of exhibits devoted to Blackstone and his work. To illustrate other differences between the two bibliographies, the Appendix to this chapter reproduces two Eller entries (for the 1857 London edition of the *Commentaries* and the 1887 London edition of *The Comic Blackstone*) followed by Laeuchli's descriptions of those same imprints. Among the differences are the inclusion of line-breaks in the title transcription by Lauechli, and her more detailed collation based on Fredson Bower's modern descriptive bibliographic standards.[21] Laeuchli also includes biographical information about the editors and annotators and references to post-Eller bibliographies.

If the purposes of an author bibliography are to list the work of the subject author in its totality, to describe each individual publication accurately, and to provide basic information about the specific titles within

[20] See Eller, ch VI, entries 185–97.

[21] F Bowers, *Principles of Bibliographic Description* (Princeton NJ, 1949).

the context of the author's work, I think Eller has served us well and I expect that Laeuchli will do even better.

Where else can one find post-Eller bibliographic treatment of Blackstone's works? Of course, from the pre-electronic age the (US) *National Union Catalog* has many pages of Blackstone listings.[22] Extensive coverage of printed books and pamplets for that period, as well the full text of the actual works searchable electronically, is provided by the database *Eighteenth Century Collections Online*.[23] That is bibliography plus, and may become the gold standard for evaluating bibliographic works in the future—does this lead me to a searchable full-text copy of the work listed ? American editions up through 1819 are listed and are similarly searchable electronically via *Early American Imprints Online*.[24] Many (but not all) English and American editions of Blackstone's works published between 1800 and 1926 are likewise available online through the database *Making of Modern Law*.[25]

All pre-1861 American printings of Blackstone's works are included in my own six-volume *Bibliography of Early American Law*.[26] Then there is *A Bibliography of Eighteenth-Century Legal Literature*, by J N Adams and G Averley.[27] Providing access to its author file via a pack of accompanying microfiches, that work lists many Blackstone entries, but with a very confusing structure and a number of errors and omissions .

I have not attempted here to deal with bibliographic treatment of Blackstone manuscripts. Neither Eller nor Laeuchli list non-printed material, but there is a significant corpus of Blackstone's writings in manuscript, much of it known and recorded. However, I know of no single, substantial bibliographic source which focuses on just that material. One can, of course, search through Sir John Baker's superb attempts to record law manuscripts and their migration, both as occasional lists published in the *Journal of Legal History*, and in his catalogue of *English Legal Manuscripts in the United States of America* (1985, 1990). Beyond that, the standard general searching tools for manuscripts, like *ArchiveGrid*,[28] *Archives Finder*,[29] and OCLC *First Search*,[30] and similar sources outside

[22] *National Union Catalog, Pre-1956 Imprints* (London, 1968–81).

[23] *Eighteenth Century Collections Online* (Farmington Hills MI: Gale Cengage Learning) www.gale.cengage.com/DigitalCollections/products/ecco/index/htm.

[24] *Early American Imprints Online* (Naples FL: Readex) www.readex.com/readex/index.cfm.

[25] *Making of Modern Law* (Farmington Hills MI: Gale Cengage Learning) www.gale.cengage.com/about/Makingofmodernlaw

[26] M Cohen, *Bibliography of Early American Law* (Buffalo NY, 1998; supplement 2003).

[27] JN Adams and G Averley, *A Bibliography of Eighteenth-Century Legal Literature* (Newcastle upon Tyne, 1982).

[28] *ArchiveGrid* (Dublin OH: Online Computer Library Center) www.archivegrid.org.

[29] *Archives Finder* (Ann Arbor MI: ProQuest Learning and Information Company) www.archives.chadwyck.com/home.do.

the USA, such as the UK's *Access to Archives* (*A2A*) yield considerable Blackstone documentation. Wilfrid Prest's collection of Blackstone letters,[31] both in its contents and its apparatus, serves a major bibliographic function with regard to that important segment of Blackstone writings. The bibliography in Ian Doolittle's biography has an interesting section on manuscripts which offers a nice survey of the types of material available for those with a lot of free time and generous travel budgets. The recently published *Catalogue of the Legal Manuscripts of Anthony Taussig* contains entries for a number of Blackstone letters and other documents in that collection.[32]

Before closing, I must note the contributions to Blackstone bibliography made by the late Professor Roy M Mersky of the University of Texas at Austin Law School, both during his scholarly career and at the University of Adelaide Blackstone Symposium in December 2007. Since I was unable to attend the Symposium, Professor Mersky very kindly read my paper to the conference. He also contributed his own introduction on Blackstone's life and work to accompany a bibliography focusing on 'Blackstone, the man'.[33] That work reflected Professor Mersky's long interest in the subject, beginning with his earlier bibliography of articles on Blackstone.[34] It was a great loss to legal scholarship and to his many friends and colleagues when Professor Mersky died in Austin, Texas, on 6 May 2008, following a brief illness.

After his admission to the Middle Temple in 1741, Blackstone wrote a poem which celebrates his decision to give up verse (a field in which his talents were at best doubtful) in favour of dedication to the law. I close with a quotation from this poem revealing a side of Blackstone very different from the stodginess which Bentham mocked:

> Then welcome business, welcome strife,
> Welcome the cares, the thorns of life;
> The visage wan, the pore-blind sight,
> The toil by day, the lamp by night,
> The tedious forms, the solemn prate,
> The pert dispute, the dull debate,
> The drowsy bench, the babbling Hall,
> For thee, fair Justice, welcome all!

[30] OCLC *First Search* (Dublin OH: Online Computer Library Center).

[31] *Letters.*

[32] *A Catalogue of the Legal Manuscripts of Anthony Taussig* (ed) JH Baker and A Taussig (London, 2007).

[33] RM Mersky,'The Man Behind the Commentaries: a Bibliography of Sir William Blackstone' (unpublished typescript, 2008).

[34] 'A Bibliography of Articles on Blackstone', (1959) 3 *American Journal of Legal History* 78–87.

APPENDIX

Eller

Commentaries . . . A new ed., adapted to the present state of the law, by Robert Malcolm Kerr . . . London, John Murray, 1857.

[43]

4 v. 3 folded tables. 23 ½ x 15 ½ cm.
Collation: Vol. 1. xxxvi, 547, [1] p. Vol. 2. xviii, 603, [i] p. Vol. 3. xiii, 576 p. Vol. 4. xix, 561, [I] p. (Blackstone's paging retained in margin.)

This edition by 'Robert Malcolm Kerr, LL.D., barrister-at-law' is his first edition of the *Commentaries.* According to his preface in vol. I dated March 1857, Kerr's alterations and additions to Blackstone's text are indicated by inverted commas, the only exceptions being changes in the original text from the present to the past tense. Portions of Blackstone's text which are entirely obsolete are converted into notes, and marked with inverted commas. The notes of Blackstone are distinguished from those of the editor by the latter's use of the modern method of quotation. Appendixes in vol. 2–4 have been altered and forms in contemporary use included. Vol. 1–3 contain indexes to individual volumes, vol. 4 a general index. A 'Table of consanguinity' and two different 'Table[s] of descents' are in vol. 2.

Laeuchli

COMMENTARIES | ON THE |LAWS OF ENGLAND:| ***In four Books.*** **|By SIR WILLIAM BLACKSTONE, KNT.| ONE OF THE JUSTICES OF THE COURT OF COMMON PLEAS.| A** ***New Edition,*** **| ADAPTED TO THE PRESENT STATE OF THE LAW, | BY | ROBERT MALCOLM KERR, LL.D. | BARRISTER-AT-LAW.| VOL. I. [II, III, IV] | OF THE RIGHTS OF PERSONS. [OF THE RIGHTS OF THINGS, OF PRIVATE WRONGS, OF PUBLIC WRONGS] I LONDON: JOHN MURRAY, ALBEMARLE STREET. I 1857.**
4Vols. [E43] [49]
Collation: (22.2 x 14 cm.)
Vol. 1: a^2 b–c^9 B–2M^8 2N^2 [$2 (–2N2) signed]; 292 leaves;
pp.[i–v] vi [vii] viii–ix [x–xi] xii–xxxvi [1] 2–107 [108–109] 11–537 [538] 539–547 [548]
[Blackstone's paging in the margins in all volumes].
Vol. 2: a2 b^8 c1 B–2M^8 2N^4 2O^2 2P–2R^8 [$2 (–2N2, 2O2; +b3) signed];
311 leaves; pp. [i–v]vi-xviii[1]2–603 [604].

Vol. 3: a^2 b^4 cl B-20^8 [$2 (–b2) signed]; 295 leaves; pp.[i–v]vi–xiii[xiv][1]2–535[536]537–576.
Vol. 4: a^2 b^8 B–2N^8 201 [$2 signed]; 291 leaves; pp. [i–v] vi–xix[xx][112–52715281529–561[562].

Contents

Vol. 1:
Half title: COMMENTARIES ON THE LAWS OF ENGLAND. VOL. I. OF THE RIGHTS OF PERSONS., p. [1].
Printer's imprint, p. [ii].
Title, p. [iii], p. [iv] blank.
Blackstone's preface, pp. [v]–vi.
Postscript, p. vi.
Editor's preface, pp. [vii]–ix, p. [x] blank.
Contents, pp. [xi]–xxxvi.
Text, pp. [1]–537, p. [538]blank.
Index, p. 539–547.
Printer's imprint, p. [548].

Vol. 2:
Half title: COMMENTARIES ON THE LAWS OF ENGLAND. VOL. II. OF THE RIGHTS OF THINGS., p. [1]. Printer's imprint, p. [ii].
Title, p. [iii], p. [iv] blank.
Contents, pp. [v]-xviii.
Text, p. [1]-556.
Appendix, pp. 557-593, p. [594] blank.
Index, pp. 595-603.
Printer's imprint, p. [604].

Vol. 3:
Half title: COMMENTARIES ON THE LAWS OF ENGLAND. VOL. III. OF PRIVATE WRONGS., P. [i].
Printer's imprint, p. [ii].
Title, p. [iii],p. [iv] blank.
Contents, pp. [v]–xiii, p. [xiv] blank.
Text, pp. [1]–535, p. [536] blank.
Appendix, pp. 537–564.
Index, pp. 565–576.
Printer's imprint, p. 576.

Vol. 4:
Half title: COMMENTARIES ON THE LAWS OF ENGLAND.
VOL. IV. OF PUBLIC WRONGS., p. [i]
Printer's imprint, p. [ii].
Title, p. [iii], p. [iv] blank.
Contents, pp. [v]–xix, p. [xx] blank. Text, pp. [1]–516.
Appendix, pp. 517–527, p. [528] blank.
Index, pp. 529–561.
Printer's imprint, p. [562].

Notes This is the first of four editions of the *Commentaries* by Robert Malcolm Kerr. The printers' imprint reads: Printed by W[illiam]. Clowes and Sons, Stamford Street and Charing Cross.

According to his preface in vol. 1 dated March 1857, Kerr's alterations and additions to Blackstone's text are indicated by inverted commas, the only exceptions being changes in the original text from the present to the past tense. Portions of Blackstone's text which are entirely obsolete are converted into notes, and marked with inverted commas. Blackstone's notes are distinguished from those of the editor by the latter's use of the modern method of quotation. Appendixes in vol. 2–4 have been altered and forms in contemporary use included. Vol. 1–3 contain indexes to individual volumes, vol. 4 a general index. Vol. 1 has a 32 page publisher's advertisement, 'Mr. Murray's General List of Works', bound in following the index. Vol. 2 has 3 folded tables: one 'Table of descents' after p. 196, a second 'Table of descents' after p. 230, and a 'Table of consanguinity' after p. 536.

Robert Malcolm Kerr (1821–1902), a barrister of the Middle Temple, was a judge of the City of London Court and a Commissioner of the Central Criminal Court. According to a review of this edition, cited in Kerr's *The Student Blackstone* (1858), the *Guardian* said, 'Mr. R. M. Kerr's edition of *Blackstone's Commentaries* is not only the newest, but, as far as we can judge, the best.'

Copy seen CtY-L. 19th C.L.T., fiche 3582–3607 MOML (MH–L)

Eller

The comic Blackstone, by Gilbert Abbott a' Beckett, metropolitan police magistrate, of Gray's Inn, barristerr-at-law . . . Revised and extended by Arthur Wm. a' Beckett . . . With ten full-page coloured illustrations & others by Harry Furniss. New and revised ed. London, Bradbury, Agnew & co., 1887.

[196]

xxviii, 324 p. 10 plates incl. frontispiece, illustrations.
22 ½ x 15 cm. 'List of illustrations': p. [xxvii]–xxviii.

According to the preface dated 20th July, 1887, *The Comic Blackstone,* the 'earliest' work of the author, was in this edition revised and brought up to date by his son, Arthur William à Beckett 'of Gray's Inn, barrister-at-law.' This is the first *revision* of the text to be published; it is a parody of the *Commentaries,* the introduction and parts I–IV corresponding to Blackstone's introduction and four books. The artist, Harry Furniss, was an English caricaturist, author, and lecturer.

Laeuchli

THE | COMIC BLACKSTONE | BY | GILBERT ABBOTT À BECKETT,| METROPOLITAN POLICE MAGISTRATE, OF GRAY'S INN, BARRISTER-AT-LAW. | AUTHOR OF THE COMIC HISTORIES OF ENGLAND AND ROME, ETC.| REVISED AND EXTENDED | BY ARTHUR WM. À BECKETT, | OF GRAY'S INN, BARRISTER-AT-LAW. | WITH TEN FULL-PAGE COLOURED ILLUSTRATIONS & OTHERS | BY HARRY FURNISS. | [RULE] | NEW AND REVISED EDITION. [RULE] | LONDON: | BRADBURY, AGNEW, & CO., 8, 9, 10, BOUVERIE STREET. | 1887.

[E196] [443]

Collation [22 x 13.3 cm.]
[a]^8 b^6 B–C^8 D^2 E–F^8 G^2 H–T^8 K^2 L–M^8 N^2 0–P^8 Q^2 R–S^8 T^2 U–X° Y^2 Z–2A^8 2B^2 2C–2D^8 2E^2 [$2 (–D2, G2, K2, N2, Q2, T2, Y2, 2B2, 2E2) signed; 176 leaves; pp. [i–vii] viii [ix] x–xxvi [xxvii] xxviii [1] 2–324[pages beginning chapters are unnumbered].

Contents Half title: THE COMIC BLACKSTONE, p. [i], p. [ii] blank.
Title, p. [iii].
Printer's imprint, p. [iv].
Dedication, p. [v], p. [vi] blank.
Preface, pp. [vii]-viii. Contents, pp. [ix]-xxvi.
List of illustrations, pp. [xxvii]–xxviii. Introduction, pp. [1]–22.
Section title: OF THE RIGHTS OF PERSONS, p. [23], p. [24] blank.
Part I, pp. [25]–108.
Section title: PART II. REAL PROPERTY, p. [109], p. [102] blank.
Part II, pp. [111]–178.
Section title: PART III. PRIVATE WRONGS AND THEIR REMEDIES, p. [179]. p. [180] blank.

Part III, pp. [181]–244.
Section title: PART IV. OF PUBLIC WRONGS AND THEIR REMEDIES, p. [245], p. [246] blank.
Part IV, pp. [247]–324.

Notes For the first partial revision of *The Comic Blackstone* by Gilbert À Becketts's son, Arthur Wm. À Beckett, *see* no. 442. The printers' imprint reads: London: Bradbury, Agnew, & Co., Printers, Whitefriars. The dedication is 'To the Successors in the folly of the Commissioners of the Courts of Request, to whom (before they were happily abolished) for extracting merriment from a dry subject by rendering law a burlesque and justice a farce, the original edition of the "Comic Blackstone" was inscribed by the late Gilbert Abbott à Beckett, this new and revised edition of the same work is dedicated by the author's son, the compiler of the present version.'

The preface is signed Arthur William À Beckett, of Gray's Inn, Barrister-at-law, and dated 2, Temple Gardens, E.C., 20th July, 1887. The editor notes that his father 'had a nobler object in view in producing . . . (his) works than merely to create a laugh'; he had wished to combine 'instruction with amusement.'

There are ten plates of illustrations including the frontispiece, signed by Harry Furniss and etched by Swain: 'A Study of the Law--Step by Step.' Other illustrations are: The Survival of the Fittest, after p. xxviii; The Supreme Court of Appeal, after p. [44]; Husband and Wife, facing p. 93; A Real Advantage, facing p. (111); The Fate of Knight Service, facing p. 119; The Policy of the Law, facing p. (157); The Seat of Justice, facing p. 223; All the Fun of the Law, facing p. 229; The End of Law, facing p. 317.The library of the Yale Center for British Art has a set of the ten hand painted water-colored proofs of the Furniss illustrations, perhaps originally used as a guide for the printer.

Arthur Wm. À Beckett (1844-1909), a student of Gray's Inn called to the bar in 1882, was on the staff of *Punch*.

Harry Furniss (1854–1925), born in Ireland, contributed to *Punch,* was a lecturer, and wrote an autobiographical *Confessions of a Caricaturist.* The British Museum *Catalogue of Political and Personal Satires* notes that 'Furniss's swift and economical style stands out from that of most other illustrators of his period.'

Copy seen CtY-L. 19th C.L.T., fiche 3147-3150 MOML (MH–L)

15

Iconography

I Likenesses: Portraits and Engravings

JH BAKER

THE PAUCITY OF contemporary likenesses of Sir William Blackstone provides a striking contrast with the iconography of some of the other great legal figures of the eighteenth century, such as Lord Mansfield[1] and Lord Camden.[2] There are, it is true, numerous Blackstone engravings, the earlier ones mostly from successive editions of the *Commentaries*, the later and larger ones produced for the adornment of lawyers' offices. But all the prints derive from two contemporary images, and only one other independent portrait is known for certain. There were no caricatures, and no large mezzotints published (for framing) in the eighteenth century. This dearth of images is at first puzzling. Blackstone was widely known and respected in learned society, though admittedly he did not hold the highest office or have the popular appeal of a Mansfield or a Camden. Perhaps the real reason was not so much the low demand as the sitter's own reticence about his appearance. By all accounts he took little or no exercise and became extremely corpulent, a condition which is reflected in the two principal portraits which we have. Evidently he did not often sit for painters.

An idea of what the younger Blackstone might have looked like can be gained from two portraits which seem to play down his obesity.[3] A miniature by Charles Dixon (*fl* 1748–1798), in a jewelled frame, now at the Harvard Law School, shows a rather featureless face. It is, however, not altogether certain that it represents Blackstone. The sitter is wearing a bag-wig with a plain neckerchief rather than the bands of an academic or a

[1] Over 30 different portraits are known, including paintings by Van Loo (three), Martin (two or three), Copley, Reynolds and Hoppner.

[2] Over 20 different portraits are known, including paintings by Wilson, Hudson, Reynolds, Hoare and Gainsborough.

[3] Further details of all portraits mentioned will be found in the appendix to this chapter.

barrister, and in neither the eyes nor the mouth does his face resemble that in the other portraits. But it is possible that it was commissioned at the time of Blackstone's marriage in 1761, and that it is the companion of the enamelled miniature (now lost) of Lady Blackstone on her husband's tortoiseshell snuffbox.[4]

Much more striking is the fine three-quarter length painting in the Bodleian Library which bears the signature of Tilly Kettle (1735–1786). This can be dated to the second half of the 1760s, when Blackstone was in his early 40s, and represents a rather handsome figure in academic finery and a bag-wig. He is stout, certainly, but the artist has placed him in an elegant pose and caught his intelligence. The subject is standing in the scarlet cloth gown of an Oxford Doctor of Civil Law, with rose-pink silk facings, worn over black velvet court dress, with lace bands and sleeve-ruffles. His right hand points to a folio volume resting on a table, lettered 'The Great-Charter'; this was the edition of Magna Carta which Blackstone published in 1759. The contemporary painted inscription at the top describes him as 'Vinerian Professor of the Laws of England, Solicitor-General to the Queen, & Member for Hindon, Wilts', which indicates a date of 1763/66. If the two other volumes standing on the table represent his *Commentaries*, then the date must be 1766. Kettle was working in Oxford at that time, and it has been suggested that the portrait was commissioned for Blackstone himself through the agency of a mutual acquaintance, Richard Kaye BCL of Brasenose College.[5] Full court dress seems rather grand for Oxford purposes and may indicate Blackstone's 1763 appointment by Queen Charlotte (the dedicatee of his *Commentaries*), which would have required presentation at court, though he would hardly have worn his scarlet gown on such an occasion. The painting was acquired by Blackstone's successor in the Vinerian chair, Dr Richard Wooddeson, and presented to Oxford University by him and other former Vinerian scholars 'in respect and gratitude' in 1781, the year after Blackstone's death.[6] The portrait seems never to have been engraved, though it has recently been reproduced as a colour plate.[7]

A better known portrait, which has been dated as early as *circa* 1755, when Blackstone was only 32, shows a seriously overweight person who looks older than his years and whose character is quite obscured by the weight of flesh on his face and slightly gaping mouth. If indeed this is Blackstone, as is generally accepted, it may be a more realistic likeness; and it would certainly have been reason enough for retaining Kettle to paint

[4] See Prest, *Blackstone* 278.

[5] JD Milner, *Tilly Kettle (1735–1786)* (1927) 15 *Walpole Society* 57–8.

[6] RL Poole, *Catalogue of Portraits in the Possession of the University, Colleges, City, and County of Oxford* (Oxford, 1912) vol 1, p 107, no 265; Milner (n 5) 83.

[7] *Ibid* pl xvi(a); *Letters* (frontispiece).

more sympathetically. Yet there is no apparent reason to place it as early as 1755, and it is not clear that it predates Kettle's painting. The subject is seated in the same scarlet festal gown of a Doctor of Civil Law, over a velvet court suit, but instead of the lace bands are plain lawn bands, and instead of the bag-wig he wears a full-bottomed wig. This is reminiscent of the full dress of an advocate in the Court of Arches, which Blackstone was not; but the costume may possibly allude to his judicial position as chancellor's assessor at Oxford (1753–60) or it may simply be a representation of academical full dress. The identification as Blackstone is probably safe, though the earliest evidence for its attribution is the engraving by Scriven for the 1826 edition of the *Commentaries*. Scriven's engraving attributed the painting to Sir Joshua Reynolds (1723–1792), and this was also generally accepted until recently. Only one painted version is known. The first known reference to its ownership is in 1858, in the will of a London solicitor, Philip Goode (1782–1860), who bequeathed it to his wife as an 'original portrait of Sir William Blackstone by Sir Joshua Reynolds'. Goode practised in Howland Street (between Goodge Street and Fitzroy Square, near Tottenham Court Road). How he came by the painting can only be a matter of conjecture. He was not even born in Blackstone's lifetime, though his senior partner Benjamin Goode (1772–1851) was admitted as a solicitor in 1796, fifteen years after Blackstone's death. Philip Goode's estate was litigious,[8] and the painting was eventually sold in 1874 by order of the Court of Chancery. It was acquired by the National Portrait Gallery soon after the sale, through one 'Graves', presumably Henry Graves (1806–1892), the print publisher, or possibly his son Algernon Graves (1845–1922), the cataloguer of paintings.[9] As doubts grew in the twentieth century, it was latterly described in the gallery catalogues as 'attributed to Reynolds', but in the most recent catalogue Dr John Ingamells rules positively that the attribution is untenable on stylistic grounds.[10] It is nevertheless a very well-known image, not least by reason of the four large mezzotint versions published between 1874 and 1930 for display in lawyers' offices. Restrikes of the 1927 mezzotint are still on sale; and the image has been reproduced more recently on a medal struck in 1973 by the American Judicature Society.

The best known image of Blackstone is not, however, the orphaned 'Reynolds' but the quarter-length portrait which Thomas Gainsborough

[8] *Fanny Joseph* [daughter] *v Mary Ann Goode and others, Re Goode's Estate* (1860–84) 1860 J. 64 (now TNA, C30/1729); other papers in TNA, J91/18; J Ingamells, *Mid-Georgian Portraits 1760–1790* (London, 2004) 57.

[9] The picture is listed in A Graves & WV Cronin, *History of the Works of Sir Joshua Reynolds* (London, 1899–1901) vol 1, p 87. Henry Graves & Co published a mezzotint version of the Gainsborough portrait of Blackstone in 1874.

[10] Ingamells (n 7) 57 ('the figure sits uncomfortably and the composition overall is inelegant').

(1727–1788) painted in 1774.[11] It is the only contemporary portrait which shows him in judicial costume, the scarlet robes faced with miniver of a justice of the Common Pleas. In his right hand he holds a folded document with pendent seal of King John, evidently intended as an original Magna Carta. The sitter's bulk is an unmistakable inference from the massive double chin, and the eyebrows are especially impressive. Indeed, it has been supposed that Gainsborough may have exaggerated the features.[12] Yet it is implicit in a letter from Blackstone, quoted below, that the sitter and his family were satisfied with it. At any rate, this one was used—presumably with Blackstone's permission—in successive editions of the *Commentaries* from 1775; and no further portraits, so far as we know, were commissioned in Blackstone's lifetime.

The first engraving, dated 30 March 1775, was made by John Hall, doubtless for the 1775 Oxford edition of the *Commentaries*, though examples are sometimes found bound into earlier editions.[13] The portrait is reversed and slightly cut down, omitting the seal and the fur edging of the hood, and is set in an oval within an architectural frame. It is not well done, and does not reproduce at all skilfully the features in the painting. Its shortcomings no doubt account for the new plate which Hall engraved for the next (1778) edition of the *Commentaries*. This is dated for publication 1 January 1778, but 'Engraved by Jno. Hall 1777'. It is the right way round and shows the full extent of the painting, which is now attributed to to 'T. Gainsborough 1774'. The seal is now shown and has a seated figure of a king holding a sword and a sceptre, with a legend around the circumference reading 'IOHANNES . . . HIBERNIE'—a tolerably accurate representation of King John's great seal as used on Magna Carta. Beneath the rectangular frame is a shield with the arms of Blackstone (*Argent, two bars and in chief three cockerels gules*) supported by two putti, flanked in the lower corners by classical medallions, one with a figure of Justice inscribed AEQUITAS AUGUSTI and the other depicting a seated female figure inscribed RHEDYCINA (a poetical Latin name for Oxford). The portrait itself is much more faithful to Gainsborough's painting than was Hall's previous effort, and Blackstone himself effectively approved it in a letter to the publisher William Strahan on 11 January 1778:

> I have received a Proof of Mr Hall's Print and think it extremely well executed. I am no Judge of my own Likeness. But Lady Blackstone thinks the Contraction of

[11] The date is given on the 1775 engraving by John Hall.

[12] See CF Bell, introduction to CRL Fletcher & E Walker, *Historical Portraits 1700–1850* (Oxford, 1919) vol 1, p xii.

[13] See Eller 5, where it is noted that the Hampton L Carson collection at the Free Library of Philadelphia has a version printed on a quarto leaf in the London quarto edition of 1774.

> the Brows and consequent Sternness of Look, a little too strongly marked. I hope Mr Gainsborough has seen a Proof of it; and if he approves the Engraving, I am sure I can make no Objection.[14]

The '1777' engraving exists in a number of different states, as a result of reworking the copper plate for different impressions and editions,[15] and these vary considerably in the treatment of the eyebrows and the shape of the mouth. The best of them, however, is superior to any of the subsequent line engravings. It is superior, indeed, to Hall's own new plate dated 1 March 1793, which we can only suppose was executed without recourse to the original painting.

The Gainsborough portrait was to be engraved more than 30 times in all, chiefly as frontispieces to the *Commentaries* or as illustrations to successive editions of the *Letters of Junius*, some of the versions being crude to the point of caricature, others (such as the later mezzotints) being improvements upon Hall. The very latest examples may have benefited from access to the original painting, though it is probable that all the line and stipple engravings before 1850 were derived from Hall. The portrait was also copied several times in oils, at least six versions being known to us. But the original painting itself has a clear pedigree, not least because—like the 'Reynolds'—it eventually came into national ownership. It hung for some 70 years in Blackstone's home, Priory Place (Castle Priory), Wallingford, until his grandson, William Seymour Blackstone MP (1809–1881) fell heavily into debt after building a new house. In 1845 the grandson was obliged to sell the Blackstone library and some other contents of Castle Priory, including the Gainsborough portrait, at an auction in Chancery Lane. It was bought by Sir Robert Peel, Bt, for 90 guineas,[16] and exhibited in Peel's picture gallery at Drayton Manor. Peel died in 1850; the third baronet squandered the family fortunes, and the fourth became bankrupt, thereby necessitating sale of the portrait in 1900. The painting was acquired by George Salting, who bequeathed it to the nation in 1910. It was housed in the National Gallery of British Art, known informally as the Tate Gallery, which was a dependency of the National Gallery until 1954.[17]

[14] *Letters* 158. It will be noted that Gainsborough's consent was not required. Although published engravings were by this date protected by copyright law, the same protection was not given to paintings until 1862.

[15] A copper plate engraving required retouching after a few thousand impressions had been taken, since the pressure of the printing press tended to flatten out the incised lines. Over 10,000 copies of the *Commentaries* were sold between 1775 and 1787 alone: TA Baloch, 'Law Booksellers and Printers as Agents of Unchange' (2007) 66 *Cambridge Law Journal* 405 fn 85.

[16] *Bibliotheca Blackstoneiana. A Catalogue of a Library of 4,500 Volumes . . .* (London, 1845) lot 524.

[17] This explains the statements in some earlier works that the painting was in the National Gallery. This did not mean the main National Gallery in Trafalgar Square.

As befits the work of a master, it is an intriguing portrait, into which the beholder may read many alternative interpretations[18]—dullness or intelligence, pomposity or a suppressed twinkle, smirking self-satisfaction or diffident affability. In the end, though, we must judge Blackstone by his works rather than his eyebrows.

APPENDIX[19]
LIST OF PORTRAITS

1 Painting formerly attributed to Joshua Reynolds [?*c*1755], 49 × 40 in; three-quarter length seated in Oxford DCL robes over black velvet court dress, with lawn bands and full-bottomed wig. National Portrait Gallery, London, no 388. Provenance: Philip Goode (1782–1860) of Lampton House, near Hounslow; his son; Christie's, 31 January 1874, lot 300, to Graves; bought by the National Portrait Gallery, March 1874. Only one painted version known.

Engravings

(i) steel engr by E[dward] Scriven [1826]. From *Commentaries*, ed Chitty (1826). BM 10; HLC 22; HLS.
(ii) mezzo by George Saunders (*fl* 1860); described as a three-quarter length in robes, seated full face. The Hon James T Mitchell (d 1915) owned two proof impressions which were sold in 1908 (nos 57–58 in his catalogue) for $23 and $18.
(iii) mezzo by R[obert] B[owyer] Parkes, 8vo, publ H Graves & Co, 1874. HLS (proof).
(iv) steel engr by F[rank] Raubicheck, with arms in bottom left margin, publ Charles Barmore, 1897. Very inaccurate. HLS.
(v) large coloured mezzo by George P James, publ JFE Grundy, 1927. HLC 21; HLS; JHB. Still on sale (coloured restrike).
(vi) coloured mezzo, cut to half length, by T Hamilton Crawford, publ by Frost & Reed [Bristol, USA], 1930. HLS.

[18] For an extreme example of imaginative speculation see B Tarkington, 'Gainsborough's Blackstone' in *Some Old Portraits* (London 1939) 148, where it is suggested that Blackstone was 'laughing inwardly' at ribald stories told to him by the artist.

[19] Abbreviations: BM = British Museum (Department of Prints & Drawings); *Commentaries* = W Blackstone, *Commentaries on the Laws of England* (various editions; the portrait, when present, was a frontispiece to vol 1); engr = engraving; HLC = Hampton L Carson Collection, Free Library of Philadelphia; HLS = Harvard Law School; JHB = Sir John Baker; mezzo = mezzotint; publ = published by.

Medallic copy

Mirror-proof bronze medal by WS, bust, with legend 'SIR WLLIAM BLACK-STONE 1723–1973'. Struck by the American Judicature Society 1973. JHB.

2 Painting by Tilly Kettle (signed) [*c*1766], 49½ × 39 in; three-quarter length standing in DCL gown of scarlet cloth with rose pink silk facings, and black velvet court dress, with lace bands and ruffles. Bodleian Library, Oxford. Provenance: presented by Dr Richard Wooddeson and others, 1781. Exhibited: Exhibition of the Royal House of Guelph, New Gallery, Regent Street (1891), no 118; Oxford Historical Portraits (1906), no 103.

3 Painting by Thomas Gainsborough [1774], 30 × 25 in; half-length in judicial robes of scarlet cloth faced with white miniver, holding before him in his right-hand a folded copy of Magna Carta. Tate Gallery, London, no 2637. Provenance: Blackstone family, Castle Priory; sold by William Seymour Blackstone MP at an auction in Chancery Lane, London, 1845, lot 524, to Sir Robert Peel, Bt (d. 1850); Peel Heirlooms sale, Robinson & Fisher, 11 May 1900, lot 250; bought by George Salter (d 1910); bequeathed by him to the National Gallery of British Art, now the Tate Gallery.

Copies in oils

(a) copy in Wallingford Town Hall, 33½ × 27½ in, attributed to Gainsborough Dupont (d 1797) but perhaps later. Provenance: presented to Wallingford corporation by William Seymour Blackstone MP on 22 September 1841.
(b) copy by John Rising, probably after Hall's engraving, 1808. Bodleian Library, Oxford. Exhibited: National Portrait Exhibition (1867), no 744; Oxford (1906), no 102.
(c) anonymous copy, 29½ × 24¼ in, Bodleian Library, Oxford.
(d) copy by John Bridges, 1835. Middle Temple, London.
(e) copy attributed to Sir George Hayter (1792–1871). All Souls College, Oxford.
(f) anonymous copy sold at Christie's, 24 February 1933, lot 75, to Charlesworth; with FT Sabin, the picture dealer, in 1933.

Engravings

(i) engr by John Hall, reversed, in an oval, publ W Strahan, T Cadell and D Prince, 30 March 1775. This was probably engraved for the 1775 edn of the *Commentaries*, printed at the Clarendon Press, Oxford, for William Strahan, Thomas Cadell and David Prince, though HLC has a copy of the 6th edn (London, 1774) which contains this portrait printed on a 4to leaf, perhaps inserted later. BM 5; HLC 6; HLS; JHB.

(ii) line engr by John Hall after T Gainsborough (1774), with arms and medallions below, 'Engraved by Jno. Hall 1777', publ W Strahan, T Cadell and D Prince, 1 January 1778. HLC 6a; HLS; JHB (three states, one without date). This was the frontispiece to the 8th edn of the *Commentaries* (1778), and was also used as the frontispiece to [Douglas?], *The Biographical History of Sir William Blackstone* (1782). There is a reproduction in W G Hammond's San Francisco edn of the *Commentaries* (1890).

(iii) line engr by S[amuel] Hill [1790], a close copy of (ii). This was the frontispiece to the edn of the *Commentaries* printed in Worcester MA, in 1790; it was reused in the Boston edn of 1799. Eller 83–4.

(iv) line engr by John Hall, publ W Strahan, T Cadell and D Prince, 1 March 1793. A less accurate copy of (ii). BM 3; HLC 7; JHB. This was the frontispiece to the 1793 edn of the *Commentaries*; reused in subsequent edns until 1809.

(v) line engr by [Philipp] Audinet after Gainsborough, reversed, in an oval, publ Harrison & Co, 1 January 1795. From the *Biographical Magazine*, with letterpress memoir of Blackstone. BM 7; HLC 15; JHB.

(vi) stipple engr by W[illiam] Ridley, reversed, in an oval, publ Vernor & Hood, 1 April 1798. From *Letters of Junius*. BM 9; HLC 13; HLS; JHB.

(vii) stipple engr by J Chapman (reversed), in an oval, with a figure of Justice, 24 May 1800. BM 8; HLC 16; JHB. Some versions are printed in colours. Reprinted in facsimile (coloured version) by Wildy & Sons, Lincoln's Inn Archway, London.

(viii) stipple engr by J[ames] Hopwood, in an oval, publ Vernor & Hood, 1 October 1805. From *Letters of Junius* BM 10; HLC 11; JHB.

(ix) anonymous engr by Ridley & Holl, 1805. HLC 12.

(x) line engr by David Edwin, publ T B Wait & Co., Portland ME [1807]. Frontispiece to the Portland edn of the *Commentaries* (1807); reused 1818. Eller, 43–4.

(xi) stipple engr. by E[dward] Bocquet, publ Sherwood, Nely & Jones [1812]. From *Letters of Junius*. BM 1; HLC 3; HLS.

(xii) stipple engr by [James] Godby, reversed, in an oval, 'Printed for J. Bell's edition of Blackstone, 1813'. From *Commentaries* (publ Bell, 1813); reused in the 1814 edn (with the error 'Blackstones') and the 1823 edn. According to an advertisement, this edn was originally issued in 28 parts, the first (price 1s. 6d.) containing the new portrait. BM 2 (says 1827?); HLC 9; JHB.

(xiii) stipple engr by R[obert] Hicks, bust in an oval [1814]. HLC 17; JHB (bound copy). Frontispiece to the 3rd edn of *Complete English Lawyer* (1814); reissued in the '3rd' edn by Giffard (1819) and in the 1822 edn. One version in a rectangle: HLC 18.

(xiv) engr by Holl, 1819. From the *Biographical Magazine*, vol 1, p 6, with a letterpress memoir of Blackstone. HLC 19.

(xv) engr (reversed), publ Thomas Kelly, 1 September 1820. HLC 20; JHB.

(xvi) stipple engr by [John] Scoles, in an oval; 'Judge Blackstone' in print [1822]. HLC 10; HLS. Frontispiece to a Philadelphia edn of the *Commentaries* (1822). There is a careful copy of this engraving in pen and ink by 'J.B.', probably a law student, in HLS MS. 4237.

(xvii) stipple engr by E[dward] Finden, publ T Cadell, 25 March 1825. Frontispiece to the 1825 edn of the *Commentaries*. BM 12; HLC 5; JHB.

(xviii) engr by C Phillips [1829]. Frontispiece to the 1829 edn of the *Commentaries*; reused in the 1836 and 1844 edns. HLC 8.

(xix) anonymous engr (undated), 3½ × 3¼ in., bust in a rectangle. BM 13; JHB.

(xx) anonymous engr (undated), 2¼ × 1¾ in., bust in an oval; 'Judge Blackstone' in script. BM 14; JHB.

(xxi) anonymous stipple engr (undated), bust and top of charter. JHB.

(xxii) anonymous stipple engr (undated), small 8vo, vignette in a rectangle, surmounted by a helmeted Greek head flanked by putti writing and spinning. JHB.

(xxiii) steel engr by R. Whitechurch 'at J. M. Butler's establishment 252 Chestnut St Philadelphia'. Frontispiece to G Sharswood's edn of the *Commentaries* (1859); reused in numerous edns until 1893 (NYU copy). HLC 23.

(xxiv) woodcut, half-length, holding charter. Somewhat crude. *From The Popular History of England*, publ Charles Knight, 1862.

(xxv) small engr, reversed, in an oval, by Samuel Hollyer, New York, incorporated in the bookplate of John V[an Schaick] L[ansing] Pruyn [1811–77; member of US Congress]. HLC 24; JHB.

(xxvi) mezzo by G[eorge] E[dward] Perine (after Holl), in oval, publ Moore & Co, New York. HLC 2; HLS. This was first engr for the 1872–73 Chicago edn of the *Commentaries* ('Engraved Expressly for this Work'), publ 'Callaghan & Cockcroft, Chicago'; reused in the 1876, 1884 (publ Callaghan & Co), & 1885 edns.

(xxvii) mezzo, 5 × 4 in, by A[rthur] N Sanders after the Gainsborough portrait belonging to Sir Robert Peel, Bt, publ H Graves & Co, 1873. BM 6; HLC 14; HLS.

(xxviii) mezzo by Samuel Bellin [1799–1893]. BM 16; HLS.

(xxix) steel mezzo by John Sartain [d 1897], publ William J Campbell, New York. HLS (proof); HLC 4; JHB (advertisement only).

(xxx) mezzo engr by William Sartain prefixed to a Philadelphia edition of the Commentaries by W D Lewis (publ Rees Welsh & Co, 1897); reissued 1898, 1902.

(xxxi) mezzo by S Arlent Edwards, in an oval, publ William Clausen & Co (New York), 1896. HLS (two signed proofs).
(xxxii) etching by Schneider, publ Albert Roullier (Chicago) [before 1925]. HLS (proof without letters, signed in pencil; acquired 1925).
(xxxiii) mezzo by Parker, 8vo. BM 15.
(xxxiv) anonymous engr after Holl, publ Moore & Goodspeed, New York. HLC 1.

Uncertain

1 Miniature on ivory by C[harles] D[ixon] (*fl* 1748–1798), oval, 1½ × 1 in, in private dress [*c* 1760]; in a gold frame set with pearls and turquoise. HLS, no 11 (acquired 14 November 1928 from James Sefitue).
2 Painting by Daniel Gardner (d 1805), 21 × 17 in, in judicial robes. It is not clear whether this was an independent portrait or a copy of the Gainsborough; the latter seems more likely. Provenance: Heathcote family, Bighton Wood, Hants; Heathcote Heirlooms sale (by order of the Ven Sir Francis Heathcote, Bt), Christie's, 27 May 1938, lot 26. Present location unknown.
3 Portrait by ____ Walker of Berwick Street, London, *c*1782. *Cf* James Walker (d 1808), who published mezzo portraits in the early 1780s from other addresses. As a posthumous portrait, this was perhaps based on the Gainsborough. Exhibited: Society of Artists (1782), no 256. Present location unknown.
4 Coloured miniature wax portrait by Samuel Percy (d 1820), in judicial robes. Victoria & Albert Museum, London, no A 40–1940. This is at present in store and unavailable for inspection, but it may be supposed to have been based on one of the paintings. Another portrait in wax was sold at Christie's, 18 March 1975, lot 38; present location unknown.

II Images: Statues and Stained Glass

WILFRID PREST

On 8 December 1780 the fellows of All Souls College accepted a recommendation from Warden Tracy and the college officers 'that a Statue be erected to the memory of Sr W Blackstone deceased'.[20] Since Blackstone had died nearly 10 months before, this might seem a somewhat belated decision. But Oxford colleges were not accustomed to memorialise their distinguished former members with statues, as distinct from funerary brasses, slabs or tablets. At All Souls even the college's medieval founder rated only a marble bust in the library ante-room. This had been commissioned from the sculptor Roubiliac by Blackstone himself, who likewise treated with Roubiliac's teacher Henry Cheere for the 'Bustoes' of 25 fellows of more recent vintage still adorning the gallery bookshelves of the Codrington Library.[21] Some years before Cheere had provided the college's sole statue of a former fellow, Christopher Codrington, whose large bequest built the library which bears his name and where his effigy now stands. Since Blackstone was no such munificent benefactor, and indeed became a divisive figure in the latter days of his fellowship, it would not be surprising if some members of the college had questioned any proposed outlay of funds on his statue.

In the event Tracy's personal contribution of £100 doubtless helped to counter opposition, especially on the understanding that the total cost would 'not much exceed four hundred guineas'. Given the right to choose the sculptor, Tracy nominated John Bacon, a recently elected Royal Academician whose career (like Blackstone's) had blossomed under the personal patronage of George III, hence making him a peculiarly appropriate choice for this commission. But even with the assistance of a further £50 bequeathed by Blackstone's close friend Benjamin Buckler, plus £25 from another fellow, the college was still eventually obliged to find £364 from its Benefactors fund to cover the sculptor's fee and other costs. For this substantial sum they received in October 1784 what the college historian Thomas Wenman eulogised as 'a magnificent statue of white marble . . . placed at the upper end of the Hall, in memory of Sir W Blackstone. He is sitting, dress'd in his Judge's Robes, holding in one Hand, a Book of his *Commentaries*; in the other, a scroll, being intended to represent Magna Carta, of which he publish'd the correctest Edition'.[22] In the early nineteenth century Blackstone's statue was moved from its lonely eminence in the dining hall to the ante-chapel, and again relocated in 1872 to the east end of the Codrington Library, where it still surveys the interior which Blackstone himself was largely responsible for completing. Bacon placed his image on a marble pedestal, inscribed with the single word 'Blackstone', so elevating the strong-featured if undeniably chubby face

[20] P Neill, 'Blackstone, Oxford, and the Law', in SJD Green and P Horden (ed), *All Souls under the Ancien Régime* (Oxford, 2007) 296–7.

[21] See above, p 38.

[22] All Souls College, Warden's MS 22/4, fo 414v [I have restored the word 'magnificent', struck out in the ms]. See Plate 5.

well above the viewer's eyelevel. The composition and realistic modelling are both highly accomplished, with the sculptor making'very subtle use of full-bottom wig and the robes of a Common Pleas judge to tent the corporal mass'.[23] His formidable subject gazes impassively ahead, his right arm draped over (rather than holding) a massive elephant folio representing the *Commentaries*; the extended index finger shows clear signs of its vulnerability to damage over the years. Although Blackstone seems comfortably seated, his right shoe extends slightly over the forward edge of the pedestal, as though its wearer were about to raise himself from his chair and step forth again on yet another project.

In its origins and siting the All Souls statue was essentially a tribute from colleagues and friends to an outstanding former member of an Oxford collegiate community. Subsequent sculpted representations of Blackstone have had a more public and symbolic character. The largest and most striking example is a monumental full-length bronze originally commissioned by the American Bar Association for presentation to their British counterparts in July 1924, when the ABA held its annual meeting in London. The sculptor was Paul Wayland Bartlett, then nearing the end of a distinguished trans-Atlantic artistic career in France and America. Bartlett had executed numerous public commissions in New York and Washington, which helps explain the present location of his statue in the Federal Triangle of the national capital, on the south-east corner of the E Barrett Prettyman US Federal Courthouse.[24] For what was ceremonially unveiled in London in 1924 was merely a plaster cast or model, as both the ultimate site for and medium of the American gift were then still undecided. Bartlett died in September 1925, but three years later a marble effigy of Blackstone, completed in France under the direction of Bartlett's widow, was installed in the Great Hall of the Royal Courts of Justice in the Strand. Although standing just over two metres high, this figure seems dwarfed by its Victorian Gothic surroundings and the outsize book it bears.[25] The original much larger bronze (which Bartlett designed to be 'about 8 feet, 6 inches in height' with a 'low pedestal' adding a further three feet), apparently rejected as too massive for that site, was presented to the US government and installed in front of the Federal Court of Appeals on Constitution Avenue before being moved to its present location. Blackstone also appears in another public Washington setting, among a large series of 'Lawgivers'

[23] TG Barnes, 'Notes from the Editors' in *Commentaries on the Laws of England Book the First William Blackstone, Esq* (Birmingham AL, 1983) 4.

[24] www/anb.org.rp.nla.gov.au.2048/articles/17/17–00051; www.dcmemoirals.com/indexindiv00000340.htm

[25] (1924) 10 *American Bar Association Journal* 323, 397, 571–3; (1928) 14 *American Bar Association Journal* 643; TNA WORK 20/170 is a file concerning the dimensions and placement of this statue.

whose heads were rendered by Thomas Hudson Jones in stylised modernist profile on marble plaques for the House of Representatives Chamber on Capitol Hill.[26]

Just a few years later, in 1954, a marble bust of Blackstone was created for the College of William and Mary in Williamsburg, Virginia, by the Austrian-born American sculptor Felix de Weldon, best known for his depiction of the raising of the flag at Iwo Jima towards the end of World War II. Weldon had an edition of 250 bronzes cast from the same model, presumably in hopes of tapping a market among professional attorneys, whose offices (according to Erle Stanley Gardner, the creator of Perry Mason) were typically adorned with images of Blackstone.[27] The College of William and Mary, where the first American chair of law was established in 1779, subsequently received as a bicentennial gift from All Souls College another full-length depiction of Blackstone, this time in the form of a stained-glass window, one of a small series created in 1891 by the long-established London firm of James Powell & Sons (also known as Whitefriars Glass) for the college hall. In keeping with Nicholas Hawksmoor's high-windowed, light-filled interior, the whole composition is framed by a wide border of clear glass. Blackstone himself is also depicted against a clear background, clad in full red judicial robes, holding a symbolic copy of his *Commentaries* and standing within an ornate classical arch. Despite its different pose, the detailed treatment of head and hands closely follow Bacon's statue. Removed for safe-keeping on the eve of the Second World War, and subsequently left in the cellar underneath the Codrington Library, this neo-classical window (together with one representing Christopher Wren, who provided sketches for the first college building erected at Williamsburg) was installed in the lobby of the new Marshall-Wythe School of Law building for its opening in 1980.[28]

An earlier depiction of Blackstone in a more familiar Victorian blue and red stained glass genre was commissioned for the first university established in another continent, then most decidedly a part of the second British Empire. Edward Thomas Blacket's 'Tudor perpendicular Gothic' Great Hall at the University of Sydney, which was opened in 1859, contains 33 individual stained-glass windows set in elaborate sandstone frames, representing notable British churchmen, philosophers, scientists and men of letters, together with larger composite groups of kings and queens of England and founders of Oxford and Cambridge colleges. This

[26] (1924) 10 *American Bar Association Journal* 397 <http://www.aoc.gov/cc/art/lawgivers/blackstone.cfm.>

[27] www.felixdeweldon.com/mess-blackstone.html. *Cf* ES Gardner, *The Case of the Sleepwalker's Niece* (New York, 1936) 209. The Blackstone building in Cleveland, Ohio, largely occupied by lawyers when it opened in 1882, featured a bust of Sir William Blackstone over the entrance: WG Rose, *Cleveland, The Making of a City* (Kent OH, 1990; 1950) 455.

[28] See Plate 7; ex inf Dr Roger Hood.

whole ambitious project, a colonial manifestation of the mid nineteenth-century stained-glass revival, was executed by the rising London firm of Clayton and Bell, 'being the first great work they had undertaken' under the supervision of Charles Nicholson.[29] The Blackstone window, one of a triptych on the south wall, presents its subject in judge's robes, holding not a symbolic book but a small scroll with pendent seal, possibly intended for his judicial commission or patent. Blackstone is the central figure, flanked by images of two near-contemporaries, the Scottish chemist Joseph Black, representing science, or the exploration of nature, and the explorer Captain James Cook, who first claimed the east coast of Australia for the British Crown. This placement was plainly not accidental or merely alphabetical (thus the adjacent group of 'late Augustan writers' presents Gray, Johnson and Burke in that order), but rather represented local aspirations to erase the convict stain and celebrate the rule of English law (as systematised and made accessible by Blackstone) following the granting of responsible government. In common with what has recently become its American counterpart, the Sydney window demonstrates that Blackstone's posthumous influence and reputation were no less and indeed significantly greater beyond than within the British Isles.

[29] B McKenzie, *Stained Glass and Stone: the Gothic Buildings of the University of Sydney* (Sydney, 1989) 12, 46. See Plate 8.

1. William Blackstone by Tilly Kettle (*c* 1766)

2. William Blackstone(?) by Charles Dixon (*c* 1760)

3. Sir William Blackstone by Thomas Gainsborough (1774)

1775

1777

'1793' (later state)

1809

4. Engravings by John Hall after Gainsborough showing their degeneration in later editions of the *Commentaries*

5. Sir William Blackstone by John Bacon (1784)

6. Sir William Blackstone, above, bronze statue by Paul W Bartlett, 1924–5, Constitution Ave and 3rd St NW, Washington DC. Photograph by Terry J Adams, National Park Service; below, marble statue after Paul W Bartlett (1928), Royal Courts of Justice, London

7. Stained-glass window, James Powell and Sons (1891)

8. Stained-glass window, Clayton and Bell (1857–8).
Photograph by Raymond de Berguelle

Index

Note

Facsimiles are shown by page numbers in italics
WB=William Blackstone